Tragedy, Tradition, Transformism

Tragedy, Tradition, Transformism

The Ethics of Paul Ramsey

D. Stephen Long

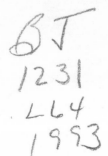

Westview Press

BOULDER • SAN FRANCISCO • OXFORD

Copyright © 1993 by Westview Press, Inc.

Published in 1993 in the United States of America by Westview Press, Inc., 5500 Central Avenue, Boulder, Colorado 80301-2877, and in the United Kingdom by Westview Press, 36 Lonsdale Road, Summertown, Oxford OX2 7EW

Library of Congress Cataloging-in-Publication Data
Long, D. Stephen, 1960–
    Tragedy, tradition, transformism : the ethics of Paul Ramsey / by
D. Stephen Long.
        p.   cm.
    Includes bibliographical references and index.
    ISBN 0-8133-8747-7
    1. Ramsey, Paul.   2. Christian ethics—History—20th century.
I. Title.
BJ1231.L64   1993
241'.092—dc20
                                                                93-29459
                                                                CIP

Printed and bound in the United States of America

    The paper used in this publication meets the requirements
(∞) of the American National Standard for Permanence of Paper
    for Printed Library Materials Z39.48-1984.

10   9   8   7   6   5   4   3   2   1

In thanksgiving for the work of
Paul Ramsey and Stanley Hauerwas

Contents

Acknowledgments

No manuscript is the work of a single author. Criticisms and comments suggested by friends, acquaintances and colleagues do as much to shape a work as do the author's intentions. This work is no exception. Nevertheless, in writing a *critical appreciation* of the work of such an important figure in the tradition of moral theology as Paul Ramsey, I do need to take responsibility for the following work before mentioning all of those who either made this work possible, or attempted to make it better. For their assistance through conversations, comments, or a critical reading of the text, I owe a debt of gratitude to David Atwater, Fritz Bauerschmidt, John Berkman, Dennis Campbell, Scott Davis, Michael Gillespie, Stanley Hauerwas, Willie Jennings, Thomas Langford, David Matzko, Ken Surin and William Werpehowski. I also need to thank all of the staff in the Special Collections Library of Duke University for their assistance with the Ramsey Papers, especially for the kindnesses shown to me by Pat Webb, who helped make reading through the forty some volumes of material much more delightful. This manuscript could not have been prepared without the help of Mollie Keel and John Bell as well as Marykay Scott of Westview Press. Of course this manuscript would not have been possible without Paul Ramsey's keen intellect, wit and work. All of us who work in the field of Christian ethics have benefited from his considerable gifts to our shared tradition of Christian moral reflection and owe him a deep sense of appreciation for keeping that tradition alive.

D. Stephen Long

Introduction

What follows is both an interpretation and criticism of Paul Ramsey's work. It begins by placing him within the context of Protestant liberalism that he endorsed as a student and teacher at Millsaps College. From 1935 to roughly 1943, Paul Ramsey was a theological idealist who essentialized the Christian Gospel into *agape*, and then sought to apply that essence for the complete transformation of society. He was a pacifist, a socialist, an inter-racialist, and as he himself states, even opposed to "organized intercollegiate football as a brutal sport." Such was the early Paul Ramsey who would later become the Niebuhrian realist and Protestant herald of the necessary place for the just war doctrine in the Christian life.

Ramsey did not leave his theological liberalism behind him without struggle. As a student under H. Richard Niebuhr, he was critical of Reinhold Niebuhr's work, particularly Niebuhr's early support of the allied cause in World War II. Yet under the tutelage of H. Richard Niebuhr, Ramsey developed a sophisticated idealistic anthropology that incorporated Reinhold's realistic criticism of Protestant liberalism. By 1950, Ramsey came to endorse war for the sake of one's neighbor "by the most effective means possible." If the cause is right, and it works, it must be done. Everything that *agape* requires is permitted. However, in the late fifties and beyond, Ramsey realized this unqualified pragmatist approach to the moral life actually diminished the space necessary to live as Christian. As a consequence of this insight, he developed a principled casuistry that stands as an alternative to the dominant pragmatist approach defining much of 20th century Christian ethics.

Although Ramsey left his pacifist commitments behind, his idealism did not remain behind with them. From his dissertation to *Nine Modern Moralists,* he worked with a version of philosophical idealism, incorporating it with his Niebuhrian realism. He sought to combine a transcendentally grounded anthropology that assumed a certain harmony and completeness to human existence, with a realism that considered earnestly the agonistic element present in all our actions. The result was a principled casuistry that sought to secure some space for the practice of the Christian moral life in a modern era that Ramsey equated with a large and vast concentration camp. But the result was also a metaphysics of democracy that grounded politics in an ontology of tragedy. The "Real" existed within a dialectic of freedom and necessity that resulted in tragedy both explicitly and implicitly defining political possibilities. This real-ism is what I mean by Ramsey's "ontology of tragedy." The space Ramsey's well-honed casuistry secures for the practice of the Christian moral life is always limited by the constraints of political responsibility within a structure that assumed tragedy. In telling the story of Paul Ramsey's reflections on Christian ethics, I hope to separate the casuistry from the tragedy.

Ramsey's reclamation of casuistry for Protestant social ethics represents an alternative movement with the dominant traditon of 20th century thought. It marks a decisive break with Reinhold Niebuhr's realism and the historical relativism of H. Richard Niebuhr's responsible self, while it maintains continuity with Reinhold's analysis of power, and H. Richard's conversionism. To these influences Ramsey added the neo-orthodoxy of Karl Barth and the integralism of Jacques Maritain. Also, lurking in the background was Nietzche's dark realism, reminding Ramsey that being "human, all too human" was not always a lovely sight. The result of these, and the many other, influences on Paul Ramsey is a theology that cannot be systematized but will remain somewhat elusive, only coming to the fore when he uses it to render intelligible particular issues in the use of violence, boycotts, property rights, the practice of medicine, and speaking to and for the church.

Any analysis of Paul Ramsey's work faces this obstacle; his work is inextricably connected with such a vast number of other people's work, particular historical movements, and complex ethical issues, that the story of his work cannot be told without reference to those people, movements, and issues. His resources were too broad and his mind too penetrating for anyone to give a complete systematic presentation of his work. Because it is that complex, the danger exists that it might be lost. That would be tragic because not only does Ramsey's ethical analysis offer us insight into the moral life, but he also lived in an age when, unfortunately, such an insight was sorely needed. One book could never contain the whole story, narrating adequately all the theological and philosophical connections, the particular historical movements and troubling moral issues that received his attention. The following book does not seek to be a complete and exhaustive account. It does seek to tell a story of his work, both favorably and unfavorably, in light of the philosophy, theology, and moral issues of the 20th century.

Man has called for anarchy, God lets him have it.
> −C. S. Lewis

Man's capacity for justice makes democracy possible; but man's inclination to injustice makes democracy necessary.
> − Reinhold Niebuhr

Creation is the external basis of the covenant, and the covenant is the internal basis of creation.
> −Karl Barth

. . . the human being is caught between two poles −a material pole, which, in reality, does not concern the true person but rather the shadow of personality . . . ; and a spiritual pole which does concern true personality.
> −Jacques Maritain

You can only act in a world you can see, and you can only see a world you can say.
> −Stanley Hauerwas

1

Theological Idealism

Paul Ramsey's first published work appeared in 1935, his last in 1989. The fifty-four intervening years were filled with startling moral predicaments -- obliteration bombing, attempted genocide, nuclear holocausts, civil rights struggles, counter-insurgency warfare, nuclear deterrence, in-vitro fertilization, abortion clinics, neo-natal infanticide. At the risk of sounding macabre, the twentieth century provided ample material to keep a moral theologian busy. In response to these predicaments, Ramsey did not seek to create new ethical paradigms; he only sought to illumine "what is going on" utilizing a well-crafted casuistry formed within Christian tradition.

Ramsey was not a systematic thinker (which does not imply he lacked careful thought). He was a theological commentator, drawing upon Christian theology to comment on puzzling events. But his theology was not monolithic; he underwent decisive theological shifts. Sometimes these shifts effected his moral commentary; sometimes they did not. Sometimes his moral commentary effected his theology; sometimes it did not. Ramsey's moral commentary on specific issues cannot be explained fully as a result of his prior theoretical constructions. Such an over-determined theoretically causative agency is unpalatable; it simplifies the complexity of moral judgments that always occur in the middle of inescapably historical human activity (Ramsey would disagree!). Rather than resulting from appropriately applied theoretical models, moral responses are the product of a formed-instinct and the habituation of virtues or vices. Nevertheless, theory does provide a discursive structure used to legitimate or falsify moral judgments. In so doing, theory becomes a component of the habituation both of virtues and vices.

Paul Ramsey did not need a theory to know that the exclusion of Blacks from the Jackson, Mississippi, public library in 1938 was morally illegitimate; he only needed to be a decent human being. However, his theoretical constructions, i.e., an idealistic anthropological commitment to self-transcendence, a "metaphysics of democracy," a political philosophy grounded on tragedy, and his commitment to a tradition-bound epistemology did constitute, and give credence to, specific practical responses to civil rights, law, property rights, warfare, and medicine.

Ramsey's early work can appropriately be called "idealist" though the term "idealist" has a variety of connotations. For Ramsey, it connotes an anthropology, i.e., the finite-infinite nature of human being, grounding human nature outside history in an "Absolute." It also connotes the location of moral judgment in the primacy of the intellectual virtues. Theologically, it is akin to "liberalism" in that it essentializes Christianity and understands the practical task of the faith to be the application of its essence to society for its transformation into the Kingdom of God. Politically, it views western civilization as the harbinger of a superior moral life because its "metaphysics of democracy" provides the individual with a hedge against totalitarianism. These are the "idealistic" commitments of the early Ramsey. After 1945, because of the tutelage of the Niebuhrs, Ramsey will qualify his idealistic commitments. Only the transcendent anthropology and the "metaphysics of democracy" will remain consistent throughout Ramsey's work as he develops it from theological idealism through realism to a Protestant casuistry.

Millsaps Liberalism:
"Christianity and War" (1935)

Paul Ramsey began his work as a theologian with the idealism that characterized the Christian Church in America during the first part of the twentieth century. During his undergraduate days, Paul Ramsey's theology was typical for his times. He was a theological liberal who believed the United States could be transformed to accord more fully with the Kingdom of God if people were simply not so stubborn by their willful opposition to a policy of goodwill to all.

Ramsey's early theological liberalism placed him in accord with mainline, liberal theology. This is not surprising; he was a member of the then powerful mainline Methodist Church, the son of a Methodist pastor, seeking to become a Methodist pastor himself, attending Millsaps College, a Methodist institution.

As the president of Millsaps' student body, Ramsey gave an armistice day speech entitled "The Futility of War." It appeared in the "Christian Advocate" February 15, 1935, titled "Christianity and War." Dr. D. M. Key, president of the college, sent the address to the Christian Advocate as "an example of what present-day students are thinking about peace."

In this essay, Ramsey reveals himself as a typical liberal Methodist; Social Gospel themes are evident in his concern to Christianize the munitions industry and usher in the Kingdom of God through public policy; Personalist themes are evident in his essentializing Christianity into the sacredness of personality.

The essay begins with the claim that the "entire [munitions] industry is but an outgrowth of Christianity's failure to apply itself in society."[1] The key concept involved in the application of Christianity is "love." We are to love as Jesus loved, and this means non-resistance of evil so that "personality" is not "injured."

> Any examination of the teachings of Jesus must reveal that he would not fight in a war today. The burden of his entire message to us was that the best way to better the status of human beings to reform society, to usher in the kingdom of God on earth, that the best way to accomplish good is by a policy of good will to all, love and kind treatment of enemies, non-resistance of evil, and active peace . . . . To love peace enough to fight for it is useless; to love peace enough to be willing to die for its preservation against the forces which tend to create war is Jesus' method of projecting his ideal into reality. Have we the courage to follow Jesus completely? Upon the answer we give to this hangs the destiny of our civilization.[2]

Several things are striking about this essay; the first of which is the irony that Paul Ramsey ever wrote, "Any examination of the teachings of Jesus must reveal that he would not fight in a war today." This theological commentary on the use of force between World War I and II would change decisively after World War II, similar to the theological shift that occurred in the mainline churches. The desire for a public policy that will control, and eventually eliminate, the munitions industry points to another idealistic theme: the best way to accomplish good is through the application of an appropriate policy; the moral life is primarily right intellectual virtues. The central question he addresses is which policy will best preserve the individual through doing no harm to "personality." The task of the Christian is to assist in the transformation of society by applying the essence of the Gospel -- love -- to public institutions. And the "destiny" of western civilization depends upon the actualization of the ideal. Given this idealistic theology, Ramsey argues for pacifism and the elimination of the munitions industry.

This early essay is more a commentary on the times than it is a position which has lasting impact on Ramsey. Interestingly, this essay does reveal something about theology which has been decisively lost. Theology actually mattered to an undergraduate student, and appears to have mattered to people outside the academic community. Ramsey even received his early theological training from institutions other than the academy. Because he was an English major, and spent most of his undergraduate course work studying poetry, the only theological courses he took at Millsaps were on the life of Paul and the life of Jesus. He did take a summer course in religion from the YMCA. Despite little formal theological training, Ramsey was able to articulate well the essence of liberal mainline theology in this 1935 essay. For a Methodist, in 1935, theological liberalism was the premier discursive structure available, and I think it safe to surmise that the Church formed its youth by the use of that discursive structure. Ramsey was an enthusiastic and active undergraduate espousing the mainline thought of his ecclesial background.

Upon completing his undergraduate degree in 1935, Ramsey went to Yale Divinity School to pursue his Bachelor of Divinity. This pursuit was interrupted in 1937 when he returned to Millsaps to be an instructor in History and Social Sciences. He spent two years teaching at Millsaps before returning to Yale to complete his B.D. in 1939.

Ramsey found himself in trouble the two years he was working as an instructor at Millsaps. Many assumed he had developed "liberal" views while attending school "up north." These "liberal" views included his concern for African Americans and his attitude toward war. While working at the public library Ramsey found out that African Americans were not allowed to receive services. He fired off a letter of protest to the mayor who responded to Ramsey writing that he "would be more happy in Moscow, Berlin, or Rome." The mayor wrote, " . . . don't express to me further your socialistic or social equality views."[3]

Mayor Walter Scott assumed Ramsey developed these liberal ideas while attending school "up north." But he was quite wrong. As the essay "The Futility of War" shows, they were very much with him throughout his undergraduate years at Millsaps, and a direct result of his theological commitments. While a student at Millsaps, Ramsey also gave a speech for the "peace movement." His notes from that speech say "No one has yet dressed Christ up in a uniform. [The] nation which has come closest to it is the United States -- not neglecting to [the] turning of our church into arsenals and our preachers into propagandists as happened in [the] World War."[4] He supports his point by speaking of the "insignia worn on all uniforms: crossed bayonets and underneath 'Follow Me.'" This greatly alarmed him. He concluded that "not Christianity, but the government has declared Christianity and the U.S. Army incompatible."

Ramsey's views on social equality and his pacifism were not limited to an undergraduate audience, or to his undergraduate days. On April 7, 1939, Ramsey was asked to give the commencement speech at his high school *alma mater*, Harrisville High School. In his commencement address he spoke of the popular mood in the country to join in the war movement and "put Herr Hitler in his place."[5] He said, "It is not the solution we need, and yet under Mr. Roosevelt's dubious leadership we seem preparing to take this bloody path." He then went on to speak of the more urgent need of pressing social issues close to home. He spoke of how our complicity in evil structures involves us in the evil itself, even when our intentions are good and sincere. "Mississippians," he said, "who for generations have been so concerned with holding the negro down in the ditch that they neglected to notice that in order to do so they have to stay there with them, are good folks. Goodness and sincerity linked with error is the cause of most our ills."[6] Once again moral failure is located in "error," making moral failure dependent on intellectual failure.

The dependence of moral problems on intellectual errors is readily seen in a speech Ramsey gave on war. In discussing the two apparently contradictory claims "preparedness [for war] always leads to war" and "non-preparedness always leads to war also," Ramsey stated:

> But the difficulty is that the peaceful moves have always been half-hearted, and we never actually get out of the traditional rut of preparedness for war and power politics. This war [WW II] is not proof of the failure of appeasement (taken in the right sense of reconciliation) but of the failure to appease. Domestically, it is the failure of the people really to be open-minded, and to learn fast from new movements and put programs into effect rapidly and efficiently. [Thus, the] necessity of radicalism -- going to the root of our problems, for [the] world cannot move too fast, since starving men will not wait.[7]

If people were more "open-minded" and capable of learning from "new movements," war would be unnecessary.

Ramsey also preached his liberal views. He concluded a sermon "Faith Is the Substance of Things Hoped For" with these words:

> In a word: we long for that day when the Kingdom or the Family of God shall be fully come, when God is father of all, and all men indeed brothers, when all our present personal, and world problems have been solved; and when new ones are progressively, orderly, and rapidly settled without injury to any living being. That is indeed *now* an impossibility!! But, also quite possible an impossible possibility. Let us really believe in this Family of God, adopt the attitude of true brothers and sisters, to [all] colors, and races, and nations — be willing to act as if the Kingdom of God were already come: by so doing we add faith -- the very substance itself of these hoped for things, and they are in a degree brought into being by a veritable act of creation.[8]

Such public claims were not popular and they earned Ramsey a reputation for being a "liberal." In 1942, when he was looking for work, he very much wanted to return to Millsaps. This was denied him. A friend wrote and told him he was rejected because of his "liberal, pacifist approach."[9] So instead of returning to Millsaps, Ramsey accepted a position at Garrett Biblical Institute.

Few conclusions can be drawn from Ramsey's early theological formation other than that he was thoroughly immersed in mainline liberal theology. Calling him a "theological idealist," at this point, is not particularly helpful. His "idealism" will soon become much more sophisticated and qualify his commitment to the utopianism of mainline liberal theology, as well as to his pacifism. Still, if "idealism" is understood as a general theoretical orientation that understands Christianity as an "ideal" to be actualized, the term adequately describes his early theology. The task of the Christian is to actualize the ideal in economic practices, military practices, and racial practices. This assists the building of the Kingdom of God, which is a present possibility, capable of encompassing the entirety of social existence. The church's role is to be one instrument among many for the application of the ideal so that society can be transformed. Given this understanding of theology, Ramsey's attraction toward the discipline of ethics is unsurprising. He was preoccupied with the ethical events of his time -- race relations, business practices, and particularly war. In 1939 he returned to Yale. In 1940 he completed his B.D. He then entered the Graduate School of Yale University where he pursued a degree in the field of ethics.

"The Use of Destructive Force Is Never Justifiable" (1940?)

Somewhere between late 1939 and early 1942 Ramsey delivered a paper to the Yale University Philosophy Club. It is entitled "Destructive Force Is Never Justifiable." An early date is suggested in this essay by a reference to Hitler's recent invasion of Poland and Czecholslovakia. Yet the essay also conveys a seasoned account of H. Richard Niebuhr's lectures on Protestant ethics which suggests a date after Ramsey entered the doctoral program (post 1940).[10]

In this essay, Ramsey explains the methodological assumptions behind his ethical commitments.

> The view which I hold concerning the use of force is frankly that of a theological or Christian ethic, although it is not, in the bad sense of the word, a dogma, nor is it a pacifism founded upon a scriptural literalism. But, it is a theological as distinct from what attempts to be a philosophical ethic. By this I mean that it is grounded in an initial assumption which you may call a "faith" and does not attempt to proceed all the way by reason. It may be, as Mannheim and the Sociology of

Knowledge School assert, that genetically one's beginning assumption is mediated to one through the community in which one is born -- in my case the Christian Church, in John Dewey's case, the society of a pioneer American capitalism (which two communities have of course interacted and had mutual influence on one another). [Every person has] an *ultimate principle* of some sort in terms of which everything else is judged, but which itself is never subjected to the same scrutiny of universal doubting save by the *sheer adoption* of another implicit ultimate principle.

Ramsey argues (to the Yale Philosophy Club!) that his method is distinctly theological rather than philosophical. Thus he begins with an initial assumption of faith mediated to him by the Church. He does not ground this assumption in something more logical than communal mediation; instead he claims all ethical judgments begin with a communally mediated ultimate principle. His community happens to be the "Christian Church."

This methodology reveals Ramsey's early indebtedness to H. Richard Niebuhr's relativism. In Niebuhr's course "Protestant Ethics," which Ramsey must have taken by the time of this essay, Niebuhr offered a lecture entitled "The Relationship between Theological and Philosophical Ethics." According to Ramsey's notes, H. Richard stated:

Christian ethics has a first principle which in a sense is beyond ethics, and not concerned with our duties toward fellow finites; where philosophical ethics assumes that problems of conduct can be approached, in disinterested fashion without any assumptions. There is a question here as to whether or not philosophical ethics succeeds in approaching its problems without any assumptions or loyalties; or is it not true that where ethics is not monotheistic it is polytheistic in its loyalties. There are many theories of philosophical ethics; there is no one ethics for all time: remembering this we will not be so prone to get out of our system to a so-called "disinterested" point of view. . . . [Philosophical ethicists] also make certain assumptions, they do have their dogmas. We Christians can say to philosophical ethics that they should confess their faith, and so no longer disguise it and so become aware of their own assumptions. There are things which each system has which it can only affirm or state and no longer defend.[11]

Ramsey's argument for a theological pacifism based on an ultimate principle, communally mediated, and acquired through "sheer adoption" is identical to Niebuhr's first principle which is "beyond ethics." Niebuhr's lecture provides Ramsey's epistemology.

After this epistemological discussion, Ramsey moves to his "constructive case" for a theological pacifism. He begins with a "first principle," "God is good and all the beings whom He has created are good" (p. 5). This first principle is his "definition of value" from which "two principles of Christian obligation or duty" are "deducible:" first -- ""Thou shalt love the Lord thy God with all thy heart." This is the supreme obligation to the supreme value." Second -- the "subordinate principle of obligation" is ""Thou shalt love thy neighbor whom God has created and given thee" (p. 5). This "subordinate principle" forms the basis for Ramsey's discussion of pacifism. Because this subordinate principle of "God's creation in one's fellow beings" would be violated, the United States would be wrong to enter World War II, even though Hitler invaded Poland.

Although H. Richard Niebuhr was not a pacifist, the similarity between Ramsey's defense of theological pacifism and H. Richard Niebuhr's lecture is obvious. In both cases you begin with a first principle which cannot be defended for it is "beyond ethics." For Ramsey this principle is God's goodness and the goodness of God's creation. From this principle duties are derived and the defense of the duties is reducible to this first principle. While the first principle is not defensible but is the "supreme value," the duties derived from it are defensible by reference to the indefensible supreme value.

A decade later when Ramsey writes *Basic Christian Ethics*, he uses this same method. He begins by stating the need to "discover in the strange, new religious world of the Bible the source of the ethical perspectives peculiar to the Hebrew-Christian heritage." The source is:

> (1) God's righteousness and love and (2) the reign of this righteousness in the Kingdom of God. These are two sources of "Christian love." Never imagine you have rightly grasped a biblical ethical idea until you have succeeded in reducing it to a simple corollary of one or the other of these notions, or of the idea of covenant between God and man from which they both stem.[12]

The structure of this argument is the same as the "Destructive Force" essay. Once again he begins with a communally mediated first principle that expresses the "essence" of the faith, is based on "faith," and is indefensible on philosophic grounds. In the "Destructive Force" essay it is God's goodness and creation's goodness, whereas in *Basic Christian Ethics* it is God's covenant. From this first principle duties are derived which are then defensible.

This approach to Christian ethics is methodologically both troublesome and compelling. It is compelling because it recognizes the communal mediation of moral commitments and does not seek to justify them with rationalizations. But having made this recognition, this methodology is troublesome because it then distances discussions of ethics from communal mediation. Ramsey assumed his first principle required the Christian community, but this theological commitment need not be defended to the Yale University Philosophical Club. Ramsey tells them his is a "theological or Christian ethic," but the reason to tell them this is to emphasize the initial assumption of faith. Then, in good relativist fashion, he argues that others cannot dismiss his position simply because it begins with faith because they too have initial assumptions of faith. Once this is established, Ramsey need not defend his theological faith, but he can proceed via reason to deduce duties and obligations. Any objections to his method must come not by way of the initial assumption, but by the cogency and coherency of the deduced propositions. This allows Ramsey to speak to a broad audience while maintaining his theological convictions.

But do not be misled by this method. Ramsey is not constructing a scholastic argument. The basis of the whole system is still the arbitrariness of the will. Only after the "sheer adoption" of faith can the system be constructed. At its basis, the system remains fundamentally non-rational.

Rather than being indebted to a scholastic rationalism Ramsey's method appears more indebted to the Nietzchean enterprise, as Alasdair MacIntyre defines it: "all rational vindications of morality manifestly fail, and that therefore belief in the tenets of morality need to be explained in terms of a set of rationalizations which conceal the fundamentally non-rational phenomena of the will."[13] Ramsey, as well as H. Richard Niebuhr, refuse an Enlightenment justification of moral rationality. For Niebuhr, Christian ethics' first principle is "beyond ethics;" for Ramsey it is based on "sheer adoption." Is this a conscious capitulation to Nietzsche? Or is Nietzsche's primacy of will so pervasive in intellectual discourse that this methodology is unconsciously indebted to him? That Ramsey was at all indebted to Nietzsche will appear a strange claim to many Ramsey readers, yet the notion of morality being beyond good and evil is a consistent theme in *Basic Christian Ethics*. And he begins that book with two quotes, one from Scripture, the other from the *Genealogy of Morals* -- "Will anyone look a little into -- right into -- the mystery of *how ideals are manufactured* in this world? Who has the courage to do it? Come!" In his introduction to Gabriel Vahanian's *The Death of God*, Ramsey called Nietzsche, "that great genius in pain finally made mad by his perception into the inner meaning of Western culture."[14] Ramsey's work often makes cryptic reference to Nietzsche, particularly stressing the "human all too human" character of political existence. Nevertheless, the basis of ethics in a non-rational will only reflects a common Protestant (perhaps nominalist) tradition Ramsey received from H. Richard Niebuhr, and not a conscious capitulation to Nietzsche.

Whether or not Ramsey was indebted to Nietzche is not the important point, what is important is that his apparently rational system mystifies the fundamentally non-rational basis of his ethic, at its base lies the will. This has the advantage of locating moral failure away from intellectual error to sources of communal and social failure, but, for Ramsey, the methodology is still unsatisfactory. The arbitrariness of the will cannot provide a foundation for ethics. More is needed; Ramsey will seek the more by attempting to ground the "will" in the Absolute or the general will. In so doing, he becomes indebted to western civilization and American democracy. And he will also develop a sophisticated philosophical idealism for theological purposes. We will return to this point in a moment, but first Ramsey's application of this method to ethical issues should be further explained.

After establishing his methodological commitments, Ramsey constructs a pacifist position by concentrating on the second, "subordinate" principle -- "love thy neighbor whom God has given thee." He makes a distinction between "individual" and "nation" neighbors. Certain types of force, non-fatal force, may be justified "so far as it can be used out of love for one's neighbor," an example is the parent-child relationship where parents often use "coercion," and "force" in restraining children. He also concedes the moral possibility of police force. But the legitimate use of non-fatal force for the protection of one's neighbor does not justify *killing* another human being who is also a neighbor. To kill would violate the subordinate principle, and ethics primarily involves the application of principles to falsify or legitimate moral judgments. On the basis of his "subordinate principle," capital punishment, as well as war, cannot be justified.

Ramsey then speaks of the "grandmother argument." This was a common argument used by draft boards to question would-be conscientious objectors -- "What would you do if you saw a brutal man attacking your grandmother?" Ramsey replied,

> My answer is that I would, of course, use force, and if necessary shoot him, but not with intent to kill him. A man can well be laid out for months without necessarily being hit in a vital spot. Besides should I in my passion or nervousness kill him, that would not justify my having done so, though it might be a very human choice to make since we all love our grandmothers. With a sensible control of the source of weapons, an effective police force might well be organized on such a basis as I am suggesting. (p. 7)

If Ramsey allowed a type of defense for grandmothers early on, why then did he not concede the moral validity of war? He contemplates this position.

On the international scene the analysis is the same [as with the grand-mother argument] though the case is not so clearcut. England has rela-tionships and obligations both to Poland and Czechoslovakia and also to Germany. If restraint of the aggressor can be justified it must be on the grounds both of love for the national communities threatened and also of love for the *true interests* of the aggressor community. One whose only concern is for Germany, say, a refugee, might well hope that an English victory would be the purging of the Fatherland. But that the German or the English nation should be parceled up and destroyed would go beyond the justifiable use of force or the exercise of restraint upon our neighbor. For these reasons I conclude that *"destructive force is never justifiable."* (p. 7)

This quote approaches a just-war position. However, Ramsey goes on to repudiate explicitly just war as the appropriate response to England's dilemma. After acknowledging the possibility of the use of force even with respect to our "international neighbors," he goes on to speak of a "great unsolved problem." "How are nations to exercise re-straint upon nations without killing individuals?" He responds:

Here I depart from the "major" Christian tradition, which says that in a just war, one motivated by love for *all* national entities involved, one may look down the sights of a gun and with love though regret, to-wards the individual soldier, pull the trigger. Whether or not this is possible *psychologically* it seems to me plain that *objectively* such is not the case. This is a crucial point: Is destructive force in *this* case justified? I would say in the first place that just as this is a crucial case in Christian ethics, it is also the standing problem of international law. Even if it may be said to be *necessitated* by the present lack of international organization and renunciation of national sovereignty and armaments, it could hardly be said to be fully *justified*; what is *justified* ethically is the institution of these procedures of law and order together with all the neighbor-relationships in which we stand. If it were *absolutely imperative* that we have "one fight more, the best and the last" in order to establish this *absolutely desirable end* [it] might be said to justify reflexively the *absolutely indispensable* means. The question, therefore, is one of method: Is the contradictory method of war *absolutely indispensable*? The answer I am willing to act upon is *No!* and that any other method, whatever the amount of self-sacrifice it may demand, just so long as it stands a chance of not being as contradictory as war is preferable. (p. 8)

Ramsey rejects war because he is convinced of the possibility of the insti-tution of international law and order. Once again, such a conviction is commentary on the times in which he lived. Many Methodists were committed to "world federalism"; Ramsey's position is not unique. To achieve international law and order, Ramsey suggests, the means of killing one's neighbor won't work. War is self-contradictory. Pacifism will work given the appropriate conditions which Ramsey then enumerates – the realization that resort to military force is self-contradictory, the need for a change in national sentiment, and the need to take risks. As for the last Ramsey offers an illustration by applying his prescription for risk-taking to racial problems:

> Let me take an illustration, I live in the south, and I like I presume, the rest of you, believe in equality between the white and the negro races. Yet, nothing would be more disruptive to the life of my economic community than the institution of equality and democracy in the south. The only reform to which I can compare it for the east would be the socialization of all productive property. Inequality of black and white is at the very root of the society which produced me, just as unquestioning patriotism when the nation finally says, "Come!" is at the heart of our common political life. Yet, I would scrap both, for I believe that if the people could be selected either ideal condition would work. Certain whites and blacks can get along together, and different nationalities likewise, without anarchy. It is no argument against anything that if adopted instantaneously it would be disruptive, because *the very process of getting it adopted will prepare and select the people needed* to make it practically work. The danger is not that we adopt reforms too quickly; but, if they are not imposed that they are adopted too slowly. The danger is not that a nation become too quickly pacifist, but that opportunity after opportunity with which history provides for us a nation *internally prepared* to lead the way toward real international organization be allowed to go by the board. (p. 13)[15]

In this defense of "international organization," Ramsey's methodological commitment to his subordinate principle has gone by the wayside. He is not arguing for a rigid deontological commitment to non-maleficence; he is arguing that war as a means will not achieve the purpose which he holds because of his faith, the purpose of international order. Pacifism is a necessary means to that end.

Ramsey then shows why the just war alternative to his pragmatist pacifism is not viable. He offers four reasons. The first two I quote fully for they are the basis of the others.

> Let us take the phrase "just war" as indicating that combination of values or justice with the method of destructive force which most people think is tenable, and ask is the "just war" justified: *Against* an affirmative to this question I would wage the following: (1) The relativity of the very values said to justify the method of war is sufficient to invalidate the case. I take it that we are far more certain of the values lower in the scale of values than of the higher. There is more agreement that one

should have a healthy baby than concerning whether one should use physical vigor to be a good Mussolini or a good Michelangelo, more agreement about the basic value of *being* than about art, or contemplation, or freedom. A "holy war" is by definition the willingness to violate the more certain for the sake of the merely relative, and this is the opposite of what ought to be the case. (2) Secondly, even if the higher values were not more relative, i.e. even if we were perfectly sure of the absolute value of the higher ones, it would still be true that we have a greater negative obligation *not* to violate the lower than the higher. Greater commendation and *approval* attaches to the achievement of the higher values, say being a philosopher, than to merely *not killing*; but greater *condemnation* attaches to the murder than to not being a philosopher. Here the common sense moral consciousness of mankind is correct. (p. 14)

Once again the similarity with *Basic Christian Ethics* is striking. In *Basic Christian Ethics* Ramsey still ponders the problem of the relativity of superior values versus the certainty of more "basic values;" chapter three is called "Love for Superior Values." But unlike *Basic Christian Ethics*, in the earlier "Destructive Force" essay Ramsey is convinced of pacifism because 'being' itself is a necessary basic value. In *Basic Christian Ethics* pacifism is a superior value that can no longer be normative because of the relatively more important need for lower values such as order in service to the neighbor. 'Being' as a basic value is less important because, following H. Richard Niebuhr, Christianity is not as concerned with "what is the good" but "whose good" it is.[16] Neighbor love continues to define the essence of Christianity. And this primarily offers an orientation, not a substantive political program. The good may be a variety of things depending upon cultural values at the time. What Christianity adds is whose good it is. Thus, Christianity stands outside history and culture.

This argument also comes straight from H. Richard's lectures. In his lecture mentioned earlier on "Theological and Philosophical Ethics" Niebuhr discusses various "elements of great value" within philosophical ethics such as "hedonism, perfectionism, formalism or intuitionism." None of these are rejected except as ends in themselves. In response to these various ethical systems, Niebuhr states, Christians must ask not so much "What is good?" as they should ask "Whose good??" (pp. 11-12).

Following this discussion H. Richard lays out his "conversionist motif."

Christianity is interested in conversion rather than in simple rejection or compromise, or synthesis. Prophets took morality and laws of their day and gave it a new context. Jesus took the law of his day and reinterpreted it.

H. Richard then explains how Paul converted the Jewish law, Augustine neo-Platonism, Aquinas Aristotelianism, and Brunner Kantianism. Concerning the latter H. Richard says that within the tradition of American empiricism founded by Dewey "we are apt to say that what's wrong with Brunner is that he is a Kantian, and that he should be an empiricist. This is wrong. Christian ethics considers them all aspects of the truth" (p. 13). H. Richard's conversionist motif depends upon the relativity of the 'what' of the good. Christianity is a metaphysical ideal which has no determinative social teaching of its own. It is always in the position of adopting one and transforming it. In this sense, both Ramsey and H. Richard remain committed to a metaphysical idealism.

The third point against "just war" is that resort to war is "tantamount to abandonment" of those values the nation wants to maintain. That is to say, any use of destructive force whereby people are killed exceeds the limits for which a nation wars in the first place. Notice the symbiotic relationship between nation-state and the Church The telos for Ramsey's argument is international order. War violates that telos; therefore it is "tantamount to abandonment" of the values for which both the state and the church exist.

Ramsey advocates pacifism because he does not believe any value for which the nation wars could exceed the usefulness of killing. The values involved in World War II will undo this argument, for pacifism is challenged not by the nation-state at its worst, but at its best. When, in fact, the values for which people are willing to kill and die are great, then any pacifist position based on a symbiotic relationship between the nation and Christianity will not stand.

The fourth point is that due to the "superdestructive destruction" current weapons were capable of, war was infeasible even if the values involved were not relative nor abandoned. A more practical policy was peace, and Ramsey uses the example of the seventy years the Quakers ruled Pennsylvania to make his case (p. 15).

Finally Ramsey asks the question, "Can destructive defense ultimately defend?" Here he argues that history shows two things. The first is that unpreparedness invites aggression from one's neighbors and that preparing for war inevitably leads to the execution of war. Ramsey's solution to this problem is that the nation needs to prepare for peace.

Throughout this discussion one of the most striking things is Ramsey's complete acceptance of the nation-state system. Even though he challenges current manifestations of power within that system, the system itself remains a positive good. He concludes this essay with remarkable optimism about the possibility of maintaining the nation even though earlier empires had declined. He writes:

These cultures, these nations [i.e. earlier great empires] were real entities in themselves and yet they passed away. Meaningfulness is restored to the process only on the supposition, which I make, that *they need not have declined* but might have had continuous development had they been able to achieve the proper adjustment of *this world of many neighbors,* individuals and cultures other than themselves. (p. 18)

Here Ramsey endorses without qualification the possible longevity of the nation-state. The nation takes on the role of a salvific institution. Ramsey presupposes that pacifism is the way, in the end, that democratic values will survive. This is ironic in that the charge often levied at him as a just war theorist was that he provides a legitimating discourse for the nation state's policies. Although this may be so, in fact his earlier account of pacifism endorsed the nation state system unqualifiedly. His later adoption of just war was actually a qualification to this complete acceptance of the nation-state system as a positive good. The later position reflected a disenchantment with this unqualified utopianism.

The "Destructive Force" essay shows that Ramsey allowed for the defense of grandmothers, and self-defense, but he did not justify war.[17] The grandmother argument returns again in *Basic Christian Ethics,* but this time Ramsey completely reverses his argument. Now he questions the use of the grandmother argument as a basis for the right of self-defense, but he justifies war. He writes:

We need have no great sympathy for the "grandmother argument" often presented by draft boards to "conscientious objectors" to military service. Nevertheless, it is clear that modern pacifists, in withdrawing completely from resistance on behalf of national defense, frequently make greater accommodation to the supposed natural necessity of self-defense (or some multilateral ethic of defense limited to the private area where extreme violence need not be used) than ever occurred to the great thinkers who first forged a Christian theory of *justum bellum.*[18]

The "modern pacifists" to which Ramsey referred included himself. He critiques his own earlier position in "Destructive Force is Never Justifiable." He has gone from the "legitimacy of self-defense but the illegitimacy of war" to the "illegitimacy of self-defense but the legitimacy of war." While this marks a drastic shift in his moral practice, it is based on the same theoretical construction.[19] He now finds the legitimacy of warfare a more consistent result of the application of his first principle -- do no harm to a neighbor. The only decisive theological shift is that during the time of the "Destructive Force" essay, Ramsey's idealism allowed for the possibility of harmonious relations where tragic conflicts were not inevitable. Because his telos held forth the possibility of universal harmony by rule of international law, warfare was ruled an illegitimate means toward the possible telos. By the time of *Basic Christian Ethics*, he no longer held to such a position; tragedy was unavoidable; the telos shifted. All that could be expected now was an endurable order. Therefore the need for constraint and the use of force were inescapable. Of course, this is the result of Reinhold Niebuhr's influence, but even more importantly, it is the result of the consistent logic of Ramsey's own commitment to late 19th century philosophical idealism. This is an important point for it qualifies the supposed rupture Reinhold Niebuhr's "realism" represents in liberal thought. We will take this point up again when we discuss Ramsey's dissertation. Before doing so however, one more defense of Ramsey's pacifism will be mentioned; this defense is interesting because it defends pacifism against Reinhold Niebuhr's realism.

"The Current Christian Anti-Pacifism" (1941)

In 1941 Ramsey wrote an essay entitled, "The Current Christian Anti-Pacifism." Although he mentions him by name only one time, this essay has as its target Reinhold Niebuhr. Ramsey begins with this claim:

> There is a fundamental breach appearing in the ranks of Christendom that is not to be glossed over with mystical ecumenism or with exhortations to brotherly love. Both sides in this controversy find an ally in its respective secular party in American political life, and then accuses the other of having done so. Moreover, both defend themselves against this charge by asserting the hope of controlling, "converting", and Christianizing its all too human senior partner. Neither, however, examines very thoroughly the degree of the possibility that his will be accomplished. Instead, on the one hand, pacifism embraces political isolationism, and, on the other hand, Christian interventionism weds itself to our national egoistic Messianism . . . . (p. 1)

This is an astute observation. Ramsey argues that both liberal pacifism, such as that found in the Fellowship of Reconciliation, and interventionism, such as Reinhold Niebuhr's "realism," are wedded to secular America. Thus, the argument between them is really no argument. Each casts aspersions at the other side for its marriage partner while each maintains its own unholy marriage.

While Ramsey begins with this dual claim, the rest of his essay is a defense of pacifism against the "anti-pacifists." He rejects the popular claim of many ethicists and politicians between World War I and II that pacifist sentiment was partially responsible for World War I because it led people to refuse to prepare for war. The best way to avoid war, so the argument now turned, was to prepare for it. Ramsey claims that the anti-pacifists who foster such notions are self-deceived. They refuse to apply to themselves the same standards they require of the pacifists.

> Clearly, the illusion of Anti-pacifism is that it can at all control or convert the forces it is helping to set in motion. Clearly, also, this illusion is being defended by another self- deception, namely that the fault lies not in its own failure or in the inadequate Christianization of its powerful partner, but in the fact that isolationism exerts, it is said, so diabolical an influence. This, too, is the basis of that over-exaggeration of the influence of pacifism contained in the question begging verdict that by withdrawing from 'responsibility' pacifism weakens the influence of the Church and of good government, which might have otherwise (sic!) prevented the over-multiplication of evils resulting from the policies endorsed by Anti-pacifist Christian.

Ramsey rejects the claim that pacifists "must necessarily never have heard of degrees of evil, or of the choice-worthiness of the relatively better course of action within history." And he refuses to accept the claim that the pacifist "is politely invited to 'bow himself out of history' and to accept the honorific status of a purely 'vocational' and 'witnessing' Christian, while Christian warriors get busy at doing the real work of the world." He responds:

> Quite the opposite is the position really taken by this group: namely, it is by a quite well-considered choice between relative goods, and often with a full realization of the impossibility of perfection that the pacifist adopts his view and action.

Both Ramsey and R. Niebuhr agree in method; they are equally indebted to H. Richard Niebuhr's relativity of values. However, R. Niebuhr assumes pacifism is based on an "absolute" that cannot take into account "tragedy." Ramsey argues this is not the case; pacifists do not avoid the relativity of values and the conflict this creates; instead the relativity of values augments his pacifist position. H. R. Niebuhr's methodology cannot make discriminations between warriors or pacifists.

Ramsey also questions the "emphasis on self-deceiving pride" supposedly fostered by the anti-pacifists. Even though the possibility of self-deception results from the relativity of values, the claim for ambiguity because of possible self-deception can be itself a form of self-deception that has no way to "control the forces it sets in motion." Ramsey fears the consequences of the stress on ambiguity. The war cannot be blamed on pacifists who were unwilling to prepare for war because they failed to see the need to do so.

True, the pacifist movement may have grown within this period, but compare the number of pacifists who have become "reluctant" warriors with the number, if any, of the completely secular militarists and political leaders who under the influence of Christian interventionism have become "reluctant" in their warring, and the chiefly ingrown and negative influence of Anti-pacifism will be seen. Not only is there no great tendency for warriors, under Christian influence and apart from a generally secular pessimism with war's results, to become reluctant; but Germany's history seems to show a positive trend from Lutheran reluctance to participate in war to Nazi zeal for war. Perhaps we in America, with our revival of Reformation ethics, are but at the beginning of such a development. If so, the doubtful merit of Anti-pacifism will have been a destruction of pacifism comparable to the Lutheran success in stamping out Anabaptism in Germany. (p. 6)

Ramsey feared the new realism would lead to the dissolution of pacifism. He was right. He feared that the forces Niebuhr let loose could not be controlled; they would serve the war-making power of secular militarists and political leaders. He was right. This critique proves fruitful even in Ramsey's later work. In fact, this insight is responsible for his self-description of his work as an "extension within Niebuhrian realism." He developed just war norms as a discriminatory hedge against merely serving the war-making power of secular militarists. In this 1941 essay he argues that at least his pacifism acts as a hedge against that war-making power. It resulted in "reluctant" warriors, even when it resulted in warriors.

While Ramsey's criticisms are insightful, his argument is not methodologically convincing. It is primarily a type of consequentialist reasoning -- pacifism has less harmful consequences than war -- which depends on the inability to discriminate decisively between relative values. This is explicit in Ramsey's single explicit reference to Reinhold Niebuhr:

Consider this fact: A Reinhold Niebuhr in America may well come to the conclusion that he must support the less evil British imperialism as over against the excessive internal and external injustices of Germany. But, by a *precisely similar* line of reasoning a Confessional Christian in Germany might say that, despite all of the evils of the Hitler regime, only by supporting Germany today can the world be rid of a defunct, rigid, and intolerable British rule. That might be his sincere Christian end-in-view, for which both the suffering of this generation of Europeans and Christian participation in war in support of an evil power would be justified and accepted. Both the American and the German Christian, of course, would hope that once victory was secured, the tempering effect of the Christian Gospel would bring repentance, together with the surcease from sorrow and suffering; and both would think the other blind in thinking so. The very thing, therefore, upon which Christians *cannot* agree is that victory for one side will necessarily be preferable, or that it ought now, by compelling rational arguments, to be considered better.

All that can be agreed upon, and all that the interventionists can assert, is that "it is *possible* that a British victory *might* be *relatively* better." At the same time, the German Christian may well, albeit with a heavy heart for the evil involved, believe the same about a German victory. Each simply must act on his own predictions.

It is important for the Christian however, to recognize that this combination -- of the necessary admixture of good and evil in every historical possibility with the necessary uncertainty and relativity of his knowledge of the mixed eventualities of *any* historical decision -- means that he may possibly be completely wrong in the stand he takes. If this is true, there is no inherent reason why both the German and the American participationist may not be wrong and the pacifist right in his *exactly* similar prediction that it is possible that the evil resulting from the practice of his views will be relatively less than that of war. (pp. 5-6)

Because Ramsey and Niebuhr agree in method, all Ramsey can offer is the need for "tolerance." "It seems clear that if the effective unity of Christendom is to be preserved and advanced it can only be on the grounds of a tolerance that today seems fast disappearing" (p. 9). Thus the strongest claim Ramsey can make is that Niebuhr needs to be less certain than he is about pacifism's ineffectiveness.

For our insight into God's action in history we have no "crucial case" that would enable anyone to absolutize his particular generalization about what is and what is not possible within history. One can, and must, have his opinions about the processes that are going on in our time. But, not to be uncertain about these opinions is a pride and self-conceit that would limit even God to "effective" action only "beyond history."

Yet Ramsey's critique of "realism" contains more than this "humble" conclusion implies. He suggests that Reinhold Niebuhr's apparent critique of theological idealism's inability to account for tragedy is unsatisfactory. It falsifies Niebuhr's own indebtedness to idealism through a caricature of it. Because Niebuhr does not represent idealism correctly, his own "realist" theology falsely assumes a break with its predecessor. This important conclusion was neglected in "The Current Christian Anti-Pacifism," but Ramsey brought it out powerfully in his dissertation.

Bound yet Free: "The Nature of Man in the Philosophy of Josiah Royce and Bernard Bosanquet" (1943)

Ramsey's theology was deeply committed to the philosophy of idealism. His dissertation (1943) was a defense of Absolute idealism. In *Basic Christian Ethics* (1950) he wrote, "The impulse behind some of the later chapters of this book is the author's conviction that, especially in formulating social policy, contemporary Christian ethics must make common cause with the ethics of philosophical idealism."[20] In his essay for the Niebuhr festschrift *Faith and Ethics* (1957), he argued H. Richard Niebuhr conceded too much to historical relativism away from philosophical idealism, which he now called "relational objectivism." He republished this essay in 1962.

Ramsey's defense of philosophical idealism, particularly in his dissertation, is an anomaly within the intellectual climate of the 1930's and 40's. Those troubled decades witnessed first hand the failure of the Enlightenment project, and attributed its demise to its utopian views of progress and rationality. The idealist assumption of an inner consistency between self-consciousness and the collective consciousness of social institutions, particularly the state, overlooked sinful, competitive human nature, and thus naively wandered into fascism, totalitarianism, and tyranny -- or so it was assumed. The focus of ethics became the need for an anthropology that would secure the individual from totalitarianism. Thus appeared Reinhold Niebuhr's *The Nature and Destiny of Man*, Emil Brunner's *Man in Revolt*, and D. C. MacIntosh's *The Pilgrimage of Faith*.

Within this general intellectual climate, many philosophers and theologians assumed the breakdown of morality occurred because of philosophical idealism, particularly its Hegelian trajectory. Emil Brunner wrote:

> It is the delusion of the Idealistic idea of the State to regard the State as the aggregate of all human life; and it is also the lust for the power of the State, its greed, which is the reason why it would like to bring everything under its own control. Idealism has become the spokesman of this "totalitarian" view of the State, with its insatiable lust for power. It is, therefore, the duty of a Christian ethic to point out the injustice and the dangerous character of this tendency.[21]

Reinhold Niebuhr devoted a section in *The Nature and Destiny of Man* to "The Loss of the Self in Idealism."[22] Echoing Brunner, Niebuhr wrote:

> That the idealistic denial of individuality has immediate socio-political as well as ultimate cultural significance in the history of western civilization is proved by the fact that it has made a tremendous contribution

of dubious worth to the modern deification of the state. Whenever idealism seeks to escape the undifferentiated Absolute of mysticism and desires to prove that it is a counsel of historical action rather than pure contemplation, its rational universal becomes embodied in that very dubious god, the modern state.[23]

Theologians were not alone in denouncing Absolute idealism; nor were they the first. William James preceded them by two decades, and they often appear to be echoing him.

What do believers in the Absolute mean by saying that their belief affords them comfort? They mean that since in the Absolute finite evil is "overruled" already, we may, therefore, whenever we wish, treat the temporal as if it were potentially the eternal, be sure that we can trust its outcome, and, without sin, dismiss our fear and drop the worry of our finite responsibility. In short, they mean that we have a right ever and anon to take a moral holiday, to let the world wag in its own way, feeling that its issues are in better hands than ours and are none of our business.[24]

D. C. MacIntosh accepted and repeated James' criticism:

If my moral ideal for my own life is already or eternally realized in the Absolute how can I logically avoid the conclusion that the categorical imperative of the moral law is a gigantic hoax, and that life so far from being "real" and "earnest" is one prolonged "moral holiday" in the sense that there is no such thing as absolutely pressing moral obligation.[25]

Absolute philosophical idealism is blamed for the breakdown of morality because it supposedly dissolved the individual into a social structure (usually the state) and thus denied freedom, and it established a telos which denied individual freedom and responsibility. These critics share in common the Kantian assumption that morality depends on individual freedom.

The very fact that a metaphysics was blamed for moral rupture bespeaks these critics own indebtedness to a type of idealistic philosophy. Only an idealist who assumes reality is constructed by mind could also assume a metaphysics ruined individual freedom. Thus, the above criticisms do not fit with their authors' constructive position.

These critics were taken to task in Paul Ramsey's dissertation for caricaturing idealism, and failing to realize their own indebtedness to it as a philosophic precursor. While Ramsey's defense of Absolute idealism suggested "neo-Protestants" were actually dependent upon 19th century thought, Ramsey did not remind his teachers of their forgetfulness for the sake of dispensing with their constructive positions. He heralded this dependence as beneficial for the construction of an anthropology that stood as a hedge against tyranny. Thus Ramsey both was, and was not, committed to the general intellectual climate of his day.

What is "Absolute idealism?" Ramsey summarized his version of it in the following words:

> The nature of man in the philosophy of absolute idealism is usually treated as consisting simply of the doctrine that the self is a microcosm. Part-whole identity is thus held to be an exhaustive formulation of the principal elements of man's nature and situation, and, since man is in every respect a representative of a thoroughly rationalist universe, the idealistic view of man is ordinarily characterized as an excessively rationalistic one. This dissertation undertakes to show, however, that idealism regards man more as a self than as a mind, and it seeks to establish a conception of self-Other relationship as being equally as essential to idealism's understanding of man's nature and situation as the notion of part-whole or microcosmic-macrocosmic identity. . . . The finite-infinite nature of man is found to be the anthropological foundation of idealistic discussions of human freedom, the central problems of ethics, and of social philosophy, moral evil, salvation, progress and immortality. Certain abstract and metaphysical doctrines of idealism are reinterpreted in terms of its view of man. Philosophical anthropology, thus, provides a new approach to an understanding of absolute idealism. . . . The fact that the two men whose writings have been selected as the primary subject matter of this study in idealistic anthropology—Josiah Royce and Bernard Bosanquet—were leaders of Anglo-American thought of the late nineteenth and early twentieth centuries permits a favorable evaluation of the period's understanding of man. This general conclusion necessitates that the contemporary disparagement of the absolute idealistic doctrine of man be discounted.[26]

Although Ramsey's dissertation focuses mainly on an articulation and correction of Royce and Bosanquet's idealistic anthropology, its purpose is found in the final sentence of his summary. He defended late nineteenth and early twentieth century philosophy against the "neo-orthodox." In his "Introduction," he states this explicitly.

> Drawing upon the profundities of the Augustinian and the Reformation analysis of human sinfulness, and upon Kierkegaard's attacks on the system of absolute idealism, as well as upon his analysis of the conflicts of human consciousness, and influenced, whether favorably or unfavorably, by Marxism, and Freudianism, neo-protestantism considers itself to be joined in pitched battle with modern bourgeois culture, rationalistic philosophy and liberal theology. The chief issue, of course, is man, his nature, situation, and destiny. The writings of Karl Barth[27] must be given primary place as a stimulant of this development, but

Brunner's *Der Mensch im Widerspruch*, translated into English as *Man in Revolt*, and Reinhold Niebuhr's *Gifford Lectures, The Nature and Destiny of Man*, of which the first series has been published at this writing, are the most systematic and thorough presentations of the neo-protestant doctrine of man.

Ramsey agrees with the "neo-protestants" that the chief issue is anthropology. However, he disagrees that the problem lies with a liberal, rationalistic, anthropology against which these neo-protestants have set their face.

This movement [neo-orthodoxy], doubtless, has been stimulated by the tragic world upheavals of our day. The massing of totalitarian social forces, and their hurrying together into titanic struggle, oblivious of the individual man yet sucking up his every contribution into their ingenious equipment, has simultaneously impressed upon the contemporary consciousness the littleness and the bigness of man. Man has become a problem as he never was, it is said, to an age pervaded by the easy confidence that the practical attitude toward life was for man, both individually and in his groups, to forget about himself and to concentrate on and cooperate for the continued mastery of nature. Yet, it is doubtful if such an hypothetical age, in which the nature of man was not one of the chief problems of thought and of life ever existed. If not, then, contemporary anthropological discussions are apt to make too much of the supposed newness of their insights, or of their discontinuity with the immediate past history of thought, in proportion as the uniqueness of man's realization of his problematic situation is exaggerated. This may be a fault in the protagonists of a certain viewpoint, who take Augustine, or St. Thomas, or the Reformers, or Pascal, or Kierkegard as their spiritual fathers, and lump together, without serious or sympathetic study, the dominant thought of the eighteenth, nineteenth, and early twentieth centuries as having only a superficial understanding of man and as meriting entire rejection. But no age, whatever its most widely accepted spokesmen say, or by their successors are taken to have said, is without fruitful debate. There are always minority movements and protests against the orthodox thought of a time. Certain of these lesser schools may have been closer rivals of the thought that has set its stamp upon the age than a successive generation wishes to believe, or may even have its equal in influence. Moreover, no new movement ever arises without preparation. The *neo-*movements are not so new, nor, as we shall see, so alien as is often assumed to certain profound thinkers of the nineteenth and early twentieth centuries.[28]

Reinhold Niebuhr does not separate himself so thoroughly from the liberal anthropology of the 19th and early 20th century as is assumed. Ramsey's dissertation defended this claim.

Ramsey acknowledges that the neo-Protestants blame idealism for totalitarianism "by dissolving concrete individuals into abstract universals." But he argues, this is inaccurate. While indeed idealism does not countenance an individual apart from the Absolute, the "Absolute of idealistic philosophy is an Absolute of such a kind that in it the individual is real." The Absolute is a teleological whole that requires individuals be "concrete universals" for the Absolute's intrinsic purpose. Ramsey did not dismiss the prevailing question -- how do we secure the individual? He only stated that critics of idealism had misplaced objections.

Obviously, in arguing for an anthropology that identified phenomenal reality with a metaphysical Absolute, Ramsey rejected Kant's *Critique of Pure Reason*. He understands metaphysical idealism as overcoming the rift between Kant's phenomenal and noumenal self by transferring it "to the universe as a whole."[29] Nevertheless, by using Absolute idealism to assist the current intellectual climate in its quest to secure the individual for the sake of morality, Ramsey continued the Kantian quest for the freed individual. This is ironic because his defense of idealism is much more dependent on its Hegelian than its Kantian variant. The Hegelian dependence is demonstrated by the philosophers Ramsey draws upon -- Bernard Bosanquet, Josiah Royce, T.H. Green. Therefore, even though Ramsey accepts the dominant assumption that only a freed individual will be able to stand against totalitarian forces, he locates "freedom" within the community that forms the individual.

> . . . although their independent reality must be assumed, selves cannot be endowed with such isolation and caprice as to be able to make anarchy out of the "City of God." The unity and triumph of the divine plan is, therefore, the sole support of the ethical meaning of finite individuality. . . . Finite selves in community are individuated by their purposes and deeds, but, in so far as they form a united life, one can more truly affirm, "Thus the community acts in and through me," than he can say, "I act thus." . . . This is true because the ties that bind individuals in community and make them what they actually are as separate persons are the spiritual ties of memory and hope, which extend the minds of separate individuals to include and be included in common objects of the past and future.[30]

Elsewhere, Ramsey writes, "One should not be misled by the conception of organism in idealism to a premature judgment that it has no place for freedom. The freedom of man depends upon the kind of organism into which he is incorporated."[31] Freedom and morality depend upon the communal formation of "individuals" by the Absolute.

Notice what this does for ethics. It becomes self-realization because the realization of the self is also the realization of the "Greater Self." Obligation is defined as a "finite-infinite relation of the self to its own larger self."[32] And conscience is "the point of awareness by the self of its obligation to itself."[33] The universe is inherently a rational place where the Absolute works itself out (for Hegel the cunning of reason, for Ramsey providential ordering) through the particular loyalties, stations and orders of finite individuals. Freedom and morality depend upon those concrete loyalties, stations, and orders. Quoting Bosanquet favorably, and adding a few examples of his own, Ramsey wrote:

> There is an objective teleology operating both below and above any and all intentional achievements of conscious individual wills, "below" in the forces of nature, "above" in the social structures slowly evolving through history. These great constructions of history looked at as a whole have the aspect of a "design" of nature, though in all their parts they are the work of "real (or subjective) teleology" by creating finite wills and intelligences. Not any human foresight, but a kind of providential blending of human effort into a result that goes beyond any conscious purpose, has made them. In every case the individuals were serving better than they knew: The military man who persuaded the Athenians to invest the proceeds of their silver mines in ships for the navy rather than dividing it out for immediate consumption among themselves served the cause of Western Civilization by preserving Greek power beyond the great 5th century B.C. of their culture. The Greek who led the first colony to Ionia paved the way for Christianity. The British Constitution, the Church, the Roman Empire were not the work of conscious volition nor of purely irrational forces. The cause of them all, as of the achievement of a coral reef, is that the individuals find themselves in a certain relationship with their fellows such that, through whatever aims they have, their natures are expressed in a rational result that goes far beyond all conscious intent.[34]

This teleology "evolving through history" has both a positive and a negative impact on Ramsey's ethics. Positively, it commits him to a communally embodied, narrative account of ethical agency. People do not simply act existentially; the possibility for ethical activity depends upon the virtuous actions of our predecessors. This commitment remained with Ramsey throughout his life. He constantly referred to "ancient principles." Negatively, Ramsey's communally embodied, narrative account of ethical agency is too enveloping. No discriminations are made between the Athenian Navy, Greek power, Roman Law, the British Constitution and the Church. The differences between these various communities are obliterated because they are interpreted as offering a "deposit" to history that then evolves teleologically through God's providential ordering by contributing to "Western Civilization"; civilization becomes a meta-discourse that consumes the various deposits of history for its own purpose.

This idealistic commitment is found throughout Ramsey's writing. When he begins using the term "natural law," what he means is the deposit given to history by our predecessors which God's love then transforms. In 1962, in *Nine Modern Moralists*, he is still working with this basic idea in his effort to radically revise natural law.

> The excessive rationalism of the [natural law] tradition of ethics has to be replaced by an assertion of man's capacity to make moral decisions in the face of concrete, particular circumstances and cases, by his knowledge of the human essence through its basic inclination in him and the choices he is impelled to make, leaving in the wake of his acts of judgment a deposit of "natural" law that first becomes visible not to abstract reason, but in *jus gentium*.[35]

For Ramsey, Christian ethics consists of the intersection between the natural deposits left in the wake of human history with the orientation, or direction, provided by Christian love.

Several important results for ethics follow from Ramsey's idealism. He is deeply committed to vocations and orders. Christian love can work only through concrete structures of finite particularities, such as the practice of law, medicine, business, and particularly statecraft. The importance of vocations and orders, in Ramsey's work, does not originate with Luther, but with Bosanquet. However, it shapes his ethics, as Christianity is constantly in search of a concrete social policy that can only be found in one of the vocations. Another important result is that while human agency is dependent upon historically mediated, communal narratives, the human agent is not dependent upon them completely. The Absolute, or in Ramsey's terms God's providential blending, also assures that human beings transcend history. While human activity is dependent upon communally-mediated historical narratives, it also transcends those narratives. This dual anthropology is best realized politically in a "metaphysics of democracy."

Ramsey's "metaphysics of democracy" directly addresses the charge that idealism leads to totalitarianism. The Absolute works through the "general will." When the "general will" is taken to be a "super-will existing only in the totality of minds, and standing imperativistically over against any particular mind and calling for the latter's response," then Ramsey agrees that "social conservatism and even a Statism" result. Ramsey desires a different sense of the general will -- "it is one's own present possession, since, if one's real will were not as it is, the general will would not be unaltered, and thus the general will awaits its own creation by its private portions in every individual." He continues:

> In the former case, the doctrine of the general will can become the metaphysical basis for the absolute state, but in the latter rendering, it is indeed, *the metaphysics of democracy*, because it means that, making figurative use of Rousseau's expression, if one vote is left uncounted the generality is broken. Here, then in the idealistic philosophy of the state we detect not so much the footprints of the World-Reason in history, nor the *vox populi*, as taking both sides (the absolutistic and the democratic) at once, another expression of the finite-infinite self -- finite in that the individual needs to be transcended and controlled, infinite in that he can transcend and control himself.[36]

Thus, because of idealism's dual nature of human existence -- both historical and self-transcendent -- a "metaphysics of democracy" is necessary; it expresses the true nature of human being -- "bound yet free."

Here is the heart of Ramsey's position, and here is where he develops his shape to the political life that stays with him till the end. My argument is that the metaphysics of democracy that Ramsey learns from the idealistic philosophers and from Reinhold Niebuhr defines the political possibilities. The essential element is not that the community acts through the individual thereby dissolving the individual. This is only one element of his anthropology located at the finite pole. The heart of his position is that due to the finite pole, the individual needs transcended and controlled. And because of the infinite pole, the individual can transcend and control herself. This makes the metaphysics of democracy both possible and necessary. Individuals need to be transcended and controlled, and they can transcend and control themselves. The ability to transcend and control themselves will come to mean the necessity of force. Democracy is, for Ramsey, just war. It is an inevitable act of violence and its limitation at the same time. It is the only way to be political because of the transcendent anthropology Ramsey accepts.

The possibility and necessity of democracy, based on an anthropology, is similar to Reinhold Niebuhr's position in *Children of Light, Children of Darkness* when he writes that "Man's capacity for justice makes democracy possible; but man's inclination to injustice makes democracy necessary." But the critical point is that Ramsey arrives at a similar conclusion as Niebuhr from a completely different starting point. He does not begin with the notion of "sin," but with late 19th century idealistic philosophy; the same philosophy Brunner, Niebuhr, and MacIntosh blamed for the breakdown of morality and the rise of the totalitarian state.

Ramsey's dual anthropological emphasis is more honest than Reinhold Niebuhr's. Ramsey shows that this anthropology requires an "Absolute" expressed through the general will. The "freedoms" of democracy are always limited because they depend upon the expression of the will of the Absolute that can only be found in the general will. Thus complete loyalty to the general will is a necessary precondition for the various "freedoms." Ramsey points this out in 1961 when he wrote *Christian Ethics and the Sit-In*. While he himself was willing to take advantage of conscientious objection during World War II, by 1961 he finds conscientious objection as always an act of grace that can only be tolerated in so far as pacifists remain ineffective. Conscientious objection violates the general will. As long as the general will is able to absorb such people, they can be tolerated. If they actually become a threat, they can no longer be tolerated.

> The enactment of a status for "conscientious objection" to military service, or the granting of citizenship to avowed pacifists, is no exception to [the fact that no legal system contains the *legal* right to disobey, to resist, or to overturn the law by direct action or by revolution.] However much a part of American law such provisions may now be, they are always by grace of an act of Congress, which, since it is has the power to do this, has also the legal power not to do so. Apart from this, a Christian who had to decide in conscience not to obey military conscription should also understand (if his mind is clear in what he is doing and his action a fully responsible one) that the cause of the order of his whole national community will be staked (even if in very unenlightened fashion) when the full force of the law returns upon his civil disobedience. The exercise of his *moral* right of disobedience, not having been granted legal status (which would then mean that it is not disobedience), has as its obverse side the state's right to inflict penalty for disobedience.[37]

Ramsey is correct in understanding the tenuous nature of tolerating pacifists within democratic governments. His dissertation reveals the reason for this, finite freedoms depend on an Absolute act of will, embodied in the concept of the "general will." The metaphysics of democracy suggest that due to human being's finitude they need to be controlled, but due to their relation to the infinite they can be controlled. By a transcendent act of will, related to the Absolute, democracy can come into existence. But having come into existence, democracy should not deny its metaphysical basis.

While Ramsey points this out, he does not see the contradiction between loyalty to the Absolute (or general will) and loyalty to the

Christian Church. By securing the individual through the finite-infinite anthropological emphasis, and emphasizing self-transcendence, the question of the social formation of the individual is avoided. It is assumed that the metaphysics of democracy can achieve the freedom for people to both control themselves and be controlled.

Still, Ramsey provides a valuable service in his dissertation; he demonstrates the similar metaphysical premise of idealism and Niebuhrian realism. Given the intellectual climate, this is a unique claim. The uniqueness of this claim did not go unnoticed by the members of his dissertation committee. H. Richard Niebuhr told him the committee enjoyed the "freshness" of his approach.

> I am just writing this note to express first of all my personal satisfaction with the final work which you submitted, and also to tell you that all the readers were quite enthusiastic about the freshness of your approach. Professor Calhoun and I both recommend on the blanks of the Graduate Department that you be encouraged to develop a full-scale work on the doctrine of man in idealism in general using the present dissertation as the basis for such a further and more complete study. What was in my mind and I think in Professor Calhoun's mind was this: the present thesis might be well worth publishing as it stands, but since its subject is limited, dealing with Royce and Bosanquet only, its appeal might also be somewhat limited. Certainly it would be desirable that you publish an article or two in one of the philosophic journals on the basis of the present thesis, but it also seems desirable that a full-scale work on the doctrine of man in idealism in general be made available. Why this is desirable you have sufficiently pointed out in your thesis. What do you think of this suggestion?[38]

Did Ramsey take Niebuhr's advice? Perhaps *Nine Modern Moralists* is a result of Niebuhr's suggestion, although by the time it was published in 1962 the emphasis on idealism was replaced with a natural law that mantained many affinities with the early idealism.[39] Thus similarities exist between Ramsey's understanding of idealism and his use of natural law.

In 1946, Ramsey did publish an essay based on his dissertation entitled, "Theory of Democracy: Idealistic or Christian?" In that essay, he demonstrated that Reinhold Niebuhr's "realism" did not represent an epistemological rupture from late 19th century thought, but that 19th century thought was as capable as Niebuhr to take into account "tragedy."[40]

In "The Theory of Democracy: Idealistic or Christian?," Ramsey states that Niebuhr set himself "too severely against the philosophy of idealism."[41] Ramsey agrees with Niebuhr's claim "man's capacity for justice makes democracy possible, but man's inclination to injustice

makes democracy necessary," and Ramsey agrees democracy is necessary as a hedge against totalitarianism's "sucking up the individual's contribution into their ingenious equipment." But he argues that while this
claim is important, it is not novel. A similar analysis of human nature
with the correlate need for restraint was also offered by Rousseau and
idealistic philosophy. Thus Reinhold Niebuhr is uncritical as to the ori-
gins of his own indebtedness to a "metapyhsics of democracy."

While Reinhold Niebuhr argued that idealists such as Rousseau too
easily "resolved the conflict between the individual and the community,"
through "his conception of the general will,"[42] Ramsey questions how
different Niebuhr's political theory is from Rousseau's. According to
Ramsey, Rousseau's political theory is nearly identical to Niebuhr's.
Rousseau also suggests that (1) "political coercion is justified by the consent of the govern" because of the "tendency of particular wills to intro-
duce partiality in place of generality into law." and (2) that this requires
"generality of application": "because of the sinfulness of man we must be
democratic in technique as well as in the principle that rights be ac-
corded to all." Ramsey writes:

> Right is secured and sin checked only if no one has an interest in mak-
> ing the conditions more burdensome than he himself is willing to bear.
> This is achieved by generality of application. The idea of the general
> will, thus, is framed with both justice or right and sin in mind, and it
> represents a way of implementing man's capacity for justice and his re-
> gard for the common good, without being unmindful of his inclination
> unjustly to make himself an exception. Idealistic as well as Christian
> democratic theory is therefore grounded in the proposition, "Man's ca-
> pacity for justice makes democracy possible; but man's inclination to
> injustice makes democracy necessary."[43]

Idealistic democratic theory and Reinhold Niebuhr's theory of politics
look the same. In both there is a connection between the person and the
common good, an integral relation of one self to other selves. Although
this might be seen as an emphasis of Rousseau's, Reinhold Niebuhr also
suggests this relation. In both there is a need for restraint. Although this
might be seen as an emphasis of Niebuhr's, Rousseau also suggests it.
The difference between the two resides only in how one benefits from the
common good. For the idealist, "rights for the self are forms of service to
the common good." But for the Christian, "rights for the self are forms of
service to the neighbor, and ideally a Christian agent gives no express
consideration to whether he participates in, or is a mutual recipient of,
the good he does." Nevertheless, because the "common good" and the
"neighbor" are correlative terms, idealistic theory and Christianity are
identical in practice. Both require the concrete practice of democracy.

They are only different in an intention, i.e. whether we intend good for ourselves or for others. But that difference cannot be publicly displayed by the specific political act itself.

Christianity can be best expressed when coupled with a metaphysics of democracy. This results in Ramsey's quest for a social policy for Christianity. Christianity is not content with liberal democratic theory alone, and thus it is always critical of it; but Christianity also requires liberal democratic government for a faithful social policy. This is made clear in Ramsey's 1944 essay "A Social Policy for Liberal Religion" that was later included as chapter nine of *Basic Christian Ethics*.

Chapter nine of *Basic Christian Ethics*, "Christian Love in Search of a Social Policy," and chapter ten, "The Religious Foundation for Community Life," were both added at the advice of the reader assessing Ramsey's book for Scribner's, who happened to be Reinhold Niebuhr. Niebuhr thought the book had not adequately dealt with the relation of Christian ethics to social institutions.

> I have only one criticism or perhaps I should say two. The book does not deal with that side of Christian ethics which is concerned with 'institutions' or the organized social arrangements of mankind, such as family, property, government and nation. This is a defect and all the more so because most Christian ethics of recent decades have been little more than treatises upon these subjects. From the author's standpoint there is not a simply 'Christian' ethic of property or government. That is all right. But he ought to indicate from what standpoint a Christian approaches these problems. The other defect is closely related or perhaps deals with the same matter; he does not elucidate how the 'love' ethic of the Scriptures and of the Christian life is related to the rational norms of justice and the equity by which the life of the world, is ordered and its institutions organized. I would like to see another chapter or two dealing with these matters but the book is certainly worth publishing as is.[44]

Niebuhr was puzzled by the absence of a "Christian" social policy. He wanted Ramsey to be more specific in the shape institutions and social arrangements would take once influenced by Christianity. Ramsey's response was to emphasize that Christianity was not a "social policy," but that it always searched for one. Christianity was dependent upon existing social structures, which it would then transform. The democratic theory of government offered by idealism was to be used by Christian ethics because the norm of "obedient love" does not "in itself contain positive and definite enough social requirements for us to draw a Christian social policy directly out of this norm without need of searching elsewhere."[45] But neither is liberalism itself sufficient as a social policy for Christians. "Covenant Love" must transform liberalism.

In the 1944 essay, Ramsey expressed his dissatisfaction with "liberalism." It made "social policy" an end in itself.

> In the name of "social policy" liberalism in our time has abandoned any significant social policy. We have become so "liberal" in our religious and democratic thought that literally "we don't know what to do." Paradoxically, this is because we know so many things we might do, and know of no way of selecting among them, save by the process of democratic decision. Confronted by the fact that the will of the "compact majority" is often exceedingly whimsical and arbitrary, leading thinkers of our generation have labored and brought forth the theory that social action should proceed along lines dictated by "intelligent inquiry." In thus giving social decision a normative method, all normative conclusions have been abolished. On behalf of liberalism as an absolutized scientific method, liberalism as a concrete way of life has been annulled.[46]

"Liberalism," reduced to a process existing for its own sake, was incapable of providing any discriminating criteria. It was unable to distinguish between the "pragmatism of a F.D.R. and that of a Mussolini." Still liberalism was not to be overthrown for it was necessary to challenge "ethical absolutism."

"Ethical absolutism" was found in "naïve natural law theory (either in its secular, Lockean form or in its Thomistic, theistic expression."[47] Liberal social policy was a necessary alternative to "ethical absolutism," but liberal social policy alone was inadequate. "The emphasis of John Dewey, dean of American liberals, on the 'supremacy of method' in the 'construction of the good' affirms for the present only the social policy of having a social policy, leaving all other social policy to the future." Something needed to be added to liberal social policy for it to be faithfully Christian.

> The problem before us, therefore, is the formulation of a liberal social policy which will avoid, on the one hand, the vain attempt of liberalism to be liberal in scientific methodology alone without a vigorous statement of its social conclusions (an attempt vain both in that it never quite eliminates all liberal assumptions or subjects them to testing and in that to the extent that it does so it becomes quite empty and sterile). The problem, on the other hand is, to avoid the temptation simply to affirm a program setting forth ethical principles with all their needed content, as if man's perception of moral norms were so vivid and unambiguous as to make social policy a simple matter of "acting like gentleman."[48]

Ramsey's solution was the "transformation" of liberal social policy by Christian faith. This is accomplished in two ways. First through a realization of the "consciousness of sin" which qualifies all "high social principles" and "shatters their absolutization." Second, Christian faith releases one from "being fundamentally anxious about one's ultimate security," and thus allows one to "more impartially proceed to specific social decision." His primary concern is to establish a hedge against the practices of totalitarianism. Liberalism, in the form of pragmatism, is unable to do this. But neither does a natural law ethic offer a hedge. The solution is that liberalism needs to be transformed by the Christian faith. Only then are absolutisms questioned.

The result of Ramsey's insight into the similarity between idealism and Niebuhrian Christianity is that both require democratic practices. They both assert the possibility of democracy because of self-transcendence; they both assert the necessity of democracy (including forcible restraint) because of finite loyalties. The only difference between the two lies in the intention of "covenant love," which qualifies for whom the Christian serves the general will. The non-Christian serves the common good for her or his self-interest. The Christian serves the common good out of interest for the neighbor. In everyday practice, no difference exists between them; only in situations of great rupture, where loyalties conflict in drastic measures, will the difference between the Christian and non-Christian citizen issue forth in different practice.

Conclusion

We have spent a great deal of time discussing the work of Ramsey's work in the decade from 1935-1944. This is justifiable because of that decade's moral predicaments that continue to haunt and baffle us even into the present age. Ramsey's commentary offers an interesting critique: those "neo-orthodox" who assumed a rupture with predecessor thought were mistaken. "Realism" was no novel movement. The utopianism of many idealists was nothing but a surd; internal to their own philosophy was an account of tragedy and the need for restraint, which it was assumed, the times required. Ramsey surely experienced change in his move from the 1935 essay and his dissertation, but the change was basically a matter of emphasis rather than rupture. He began himself to see how "tragedy" was part and parcel of idealism's practice of democracy. This is a crucial insight. Niebuhr, as well as Brunner, MacIntosh, and James, in their well-intentioned desire to establish a hedge against totalitarianism remained self-deceptively committed to a philosophy that they themselves understood as the cultural structure that gave rise to totalitarianism. Ramsey did not seek to avoid totalitarianism by retreating from idealism; he understood that, in fact, the state captures us in ways that we cannot avoid. He realized that despite the criticisms of idealism, the "community thinks us," as much as we think against the community. Freedom is simply not so easy as a matter of an individual assertion of will. Yet Ramsey did not provide a counter-community to that of the state; he only sought to transform its practices for a barely endurable order. This is because the metaphysics of democracy, with its tragic dialectic, defines what is possible for any political action.

Ramsey's prescription is much more honest, and pessimistic, than even that of Niebuhr's or Brunner's. If he is correct, the possibilities for human existence are, at best, barely endurable. Ramsey understood that you cannot go around totalitarianism; you can only go through it.

Notes

1. "The Futility of War," *Christian Advocate*, Feb. 15, 1935, p. 202.

2. Ibid., p. 202-3.

3. Correspondence with Mayor Walter Scott, Jan. 28, 1938, Box 24, Ramsey Papers, Perkins Library, Duke University.

4. This speech is not dated. It happened sometime in 1935 while Ramsey was a senior at Millsaps. He refers to the "World War" for obvious reasons. This speech can be found in the Ramsey papers, box 35.

5. This assumes Ramsey actually used the written speech found in the collection. Given the problems his views created for him during this time, I belive that is a safe assumption.

6. Commencement Address, Box 35, Ramsey collection.

7. Ramsey papers, box 35.

8. Ibid. Ramsey often preached. He was ordained a deacon in the United Methodist Church on Nov. 29, 1943, in the Mississippi Annual Conference. His father was also an ordained minister in that Annual Conference. [See correspondence with Bishop Decell, Ramsey papers, box 6.] Garrett Seminary had requested that he "establish relationship as an ordained minister." H. G. Smith of Garrett had also told Ramsey that "ordination will help your exemption status". Ramsey had the status of 3A. [See correspondence with H.G. Smith, Ramsey papers, box 26.] However Ramsey was never ordained an elder in the United Methodist Church and gave up his deacon orders. On January 31, 1949, he wrote to Bishop Marvin Franklin requesting that his name be dropped from the Mississippi Conference. He wrote, "For some time I have felt that I should return to the status of a layman in the church, for that seems more appropriate for the work I am doing in the non-denominational privately endowed educational institutions where I now have permanent tenure." He stated that "nothing is added by ordination to my vocation at present" and that his "influence" would be "increased" if he were lay. [See correspondence with Bishop

Marvin Franklin, Ramsey papers, box 8.] Ramsey gave up his orders after the death of his father. When Ramsey was pursuing the Ph.D. his father wrote to him and told him that the most important letters anyone could ever put before his name were "Rev."

9. Correspondence with Roy Clark, 1942, Box 5.

10. H. Richard Niebuhr was Ramsey's major professor. He was also the most influential person in the intellectual practice of Christian ethics. In some sense, most of Christian ethics after H. Richard Niebuhr has been an attempt to interpret and build upon his work. Paul Ramsey and James Gustafson represent two divergent movements that both stem from H. Richard Niebuhr. Niebuhr's lectures can be found in the Ramsey papers at Duke University. At times Ramsey appears to be quoting verbatim H. Richard's position in this essay, yet he does this, unlike H. Richard, to support a pacifist position.

11. Ramsey papers, box 35. From here on I will place page number references to Ramsey's unpublished papers in parentheses in the body of the text.

12. *Basic Christian Ethics*, (Chicago: The University of Chicago Press, 1977), p. 2.

13. Alasdair MacIntyre, *After Virtue*, 2nd ed., (Notre Dame: University of Notre Dame Press, 1984), p. 117.

14. Gabriel Vahanian, *The Death of God: The Culture of a Post Christian Era*, (New York: George Braziller, 1961), p. xiii.

15. Notice the evolutionary model Ramsey is working with, characteristic of both Boston Personalism and the Social Gospel, in his insistence on appropriate selection and how the process of integration will itself take care of selection. Notice also in this quote that Ramsey admits "democracy" is not present in the South at this time. Below I will argue that Ramsey is committed to a "metaphysic of democracy." Still, this commitment did not mean he was committed to the United States without qualification. His "metaphysics of democracy" was as much a criticism of the U.S. as it was an endorsement of it. This prescription for risk-taking will be greatly lessened in *Christian Ethics and the Sit-In* once the full implications of his metaphysics of democracy take hold.

16. *Basic Christian Ethics*, p. 114.

17. Ramsey's interest in the grandmother argument was of more than purely theoretical interest. Because he was never drafted, Ramsey did not have to declare himself a conscientious objector during World War II, although, from correspondence, that was his position. This position worried his father greatly. The Methodist Church produced more conscientious objectors in World War II than any other mainline church. While it had 1,000 co's, it sent 1 million boys to the war.

18. *Basic Christian Ethics*, p. 182.

19. This theoretical construction marks a continuity in Ramsey's method throughout his life. Thus I would agree with Charles Curan's claim in *Politics*,

Medicine and Christian Ethics, (p.6) that a continuity exists in Ramsey's work on the concept of *agape.* But I would go farther and include in this continuity a basic commitment to a transformist motif based on *agape* as a metaphysical ideal. The effort to ground this method in idealism to avoid H. Richard's Troeltschian relativism results in an ontology of tragedy.

20. *Basic Christian Ethics,* p. xiii.

21. Emil Brunner, *The Divine Imperative,* (New York: The MacMillan Company, 1942), p. 458.

22. Niebuhr, *The Nature and Destiny of Man,* vol. I, pp. 76-80.

23. Ibid., p. 79.

24. William James, *Pragmatism,* (Cambridge, Massachusetts: Harvard University Press, 1978), p. 41.

25. D. C. MacIntosh, *The Pilgrimage of Faith in the World of Modern Thought,* (University of Calcutta Press, 1931), p. 130.

26. Ramsey papers, box 53.

27. Interestingly, none of Barth's writings are cited in Ramsey's bibliography.

28. Ibid., p. vii-x.

29. Ibid., p. 115.

30. Ibid., p. 25.

31. Ibid., p. 76.

32. Ramsey does not endorse this statement completely, he qualifies it by the claim that the "Greater Self," must contain some notion of the "will of God" for it to be a Christian ethic. Still, this does not change his basic commitment to idealism.

33. Ibid., p. 186.

34. Ibid., p. 120-1. The story of the benefits of the "Athenian military man" represents a continuous thread through Ramsey's work. We will see him again.

35. Paul Ramsey, *Nine Modern Moralists,* (New York: University Press of America, 1983), p. 4.

36. "The Nature of Man," p. 142, my emphasis.

37. Paul Ramsey, *Christian Ethics and the Sit-In,* (New York: Association Press, 1961), p. 93.

38. See Ramsey Papers, box 20, Jan. 28, 1943.

39. See for instance the quote from Maritain at the beginning of this book.

40. I continue to use the term "tragedy" rather than "sin," because I am convinced that Niebuhr's theological realism was not indebted to Christian notions of sin, but to pagan notions of tragedy that effectively removed God from human history.

41. "Theory of Democracy: Idealistic or Christian?," p. 253.

42. Reinhold Niebuhr, *The Children of Light and the Children of Darkness* (New York: Charles Scribner's Sons, 1944) p. 35.

43. "Theory of Democracy: Idealistic or Christian," p. 261.

44. August 1, 1949, Box 32, Ramsey Papers.

45. *Basic Christian Ethics*, p. 338.

46. "A Social Polity for Liberal Religion," *Religion in Life* 13/4 (Autumn), p. 495.

47. Ibid., p. 499.

48. Ibid., p. 500.

2

Theological Realism

What does it mean to say Paul Ramsey realized you cannot go around totalitarianism, but only through it? He recognized the totalizing force of modern political arrangements, and this made him profoundly ill at ease within modern life. Many of his critics miss this point by too easily dismissing his work as conservative reactionary. The sharp polarity of liberal-conservative in intellectual discourse, often prevents people from realizing that criticisms of liberalism do not a conservative make. Such was the case with Paul Ramsey. Although he was committed to a metaphysics of democracy, and he did desire to transform western democracy into a "just endurable" order, he was highly critical of the modern shape of western politics. In 1962 he wrote:

> The whole modern world may, without too great exaggeration, be described as a vast and ghastly concentration camp in which social forces and movements of thought combine to destroy for the individual the divine significance of his name.[1]

Here one will find no apologist for actual western democracies as the most rational form of political life!

Ramsey's dis-ease with modern social life provides critical commentary on the twentieth century and should persuade the reader that Ramsey had a much more radical edge to his work than is often credited him. His dis-ease developed because he understood modern political life as ontologically tragic, and only endurable if an idealistic anthropology grounded the self in transcendence where some freedom could be found for individuals. His effort to secure the individual mistakenly located transcendence in an anthropology rather than in Christology. Thus the early Ramsey was more concerned with a theistic grounding of anthropology than a Christological reading of human nature. In fact, Ramsey concluded his dissertation with the statement -- "the philosophic watchword of our generation may well be: 'Back to idealism and on to theism'." But by 1962, in *Nine Modern Moralists* Ramsey gives us a much more sophisticated account of his methodology that combines his idealism with a realism that is philosophically brilliant. Nevertheless, this brilliant methodology is constrained by a promethean use of tradition and an underlying ontology of tragedy that retards transformation of political existence.

Ontology of Tragedy

By "ontology of tragedy" I mean the following. For Ramsey there was only one overarching politics; political life was monolithic. And that life was grounded metaphysically in contradiction and negativity. All of political existence was based on the irresolvable dialectical tension that human beings must be controlled, and that they can control themselves. Reinhold Niebuhr's tragic dictum, and philosophical idealism, were the central determiners of this political philosophy for Ramsey.

Ramsey argued that this contradictory nature of political existence had its roots in Augustine and Aquinas. He was correct that for both of them evil was the privation of good, and this meant that in aiming for the good, evil often resulted.[2] Of all the twentieth century Christian realists, Ramsey understood this best. This is evidenced in his insistence upon the appropriate intentionality of our actions. Evil might result from our aiming at the good, but it could not be our intention. An admixture of good and evil is present in human actions since the fall. Yet for Ramsey, unlike Aquinas and Augustine, the presence of evil -- force, coercion, violence -- becomes the essence of politics.[3] Neither Augustine nor Aquinas could have allowed this. This lead both Augustine and Aquinas to countenance the possibility of Christians participating in war. But Ramsey made what they allowed as a possibility, a necessity. For Ramsey, political responsibility *required* the preparation of, and maintenance of, the use of force. This was a positive precept of charity. For Augustine and Aquinas, this was a possible legitimate act of charity, but always nuanced with the biblical prescriptions that so clearly spoke against it.[4] Perhaps because he was reacting so strongly against his own unpalatable liberal pacifism, Ramsey was much less nuanced in his insistence that warfare was necessary for political responsibility. The result was that war and political responsibility were a priori synonymous terms. What follows narrates how this ontology of tragedy came to structure a single politics for Ramsey.

Before tragedy, there was moral anguish. In 1943 Ramsey argued that Reinhold Niebuhr failed to realize that idealism could account for tragedy as well as Niebuhr's own realism. Niebuhr was not wrong, according to Ramsey, for making tragedy central; he was wrong only for failing to realize that this insight was not as disjunctive with earlier idealist thought as Niebuhr suggested. Of course, Ramsey was correct because both Niebuhr and philosophical idealism interpreted political life as fundamentally tragic. Unfortunately, Ramsey did not extricate himself from this political philosophy. Yet in 1943 good reasons were present to equate tragedy and political life; there appeared to be empirical evidence that "tragedy" constituted "human" being.

On May 19, 1943, Ramsey was once again asked to deliver the commencement address at his *alma mater*, Harrisville High School. This address marks a decisive shift from the one he gave four years earlier when he challenged the "bloody path" of Mr. Roosevelt's "dubious leadership" that desired "to put Herr Hitler in his place." Ramsey's ideal had not been actualized; with the loss of the ideal, "realism" and neo-orthodoxy prepare a way for him to make sense of the troubled times. He now addressed graduating seniors many of whom would soon be going off to war.

The 1943 commencement address is marked by a sense of moral anguish and sadness:

But what of your parents? They too have already lived through one war, and have nobly done their part therein, and, what is more important, have kept themselves fit to make a more positive contribution to peace-time society. If they can do this surely we can also. But aside from this, what has been their actual destiny? To recover from whatever initial set-back the last war gave them, to work the better part of a life-time, giving all they could to their children, and now to be faced with the possibility that you will be snatched from them or otherwise have your lives disrupted. In these days it is surely possible for a young person to look into the eyes of his father and mother with a new, sincere, and very much grown-up understanding that it is better to be yourself than one of them; that, if such be the dreadful fact, it may be better for you to die young with your dreams unexplored than for them in the high noon-time of life to lose a son in whom their hope has become fixed, to see the life of a daughter frustrated, and thereafter to live on bravely with an inexpressible loneliness. This, they will never say, for they had rather die that you might live your lifetime in peace; but it is something which *you* can somewhat understand. There is nothing quite so bad as to benefit of the object of one's hopes toward the end of one's life when it is impossible to begin anew! Could I speak for your parents tonight, I think it would be to say: "We who must live, salute you who have found the courage to die."[5]

With the United States entering the war, Ramsey experiences first hand the war's moral anguish. This creates an ambivalence in his position. Such moral anguish cannot be sustained by an isolationist pacifism. Pacifism, based on the pragmatist presupposition that it works for the nation state, cannot will the sacrifices necessary to say that you who die for the nation state are idolaters. The moral anguish is too overwhelming. How can you face boys who will soon die for the same cause for which your pacifism exists -- "our civilization" -- and tell them that their sacrifice is in vain? Ramsey could not do it. War had become too real.

Concomitant with the moral anguish of the United States entering the war, Ramsey grew increasingly dissatisfied with liberal Methodist theology. It was replaced by H. Richard Niebuhr's "neo-orthodoxy;" for the latter made sense of the moral anguish when liberal Methodist theology could not. In particular, Niebuhr's radical monotheism, already present in his work in 1943, provides Ramsey with a way to make sense of war.

In the course on "Protestant Ethics" H. Richard stated the question the Christian must ask is "what is God, the One beyond the Many, the Universal *doing*?" And to illustrate this he commented on the activity of Hitler.

> One will say when Hitler is persecuting the Jews, that there is something going on besides Hitler's activity (else I could only respond to him!) No, the innocent are suffering in order that the guilty may not be wholly destroyed, and I must respond to this suffering as for my sin!! If we are to say that when people are crucified only evil men are acting, I will get a couple of Gods!

Drawing upon this radical monotheism, Ramsey gave a speech in the summer of 1943 to the Methodist Youth Conference in Mississippi. Taking as his text Jesus' anguish in the Garden of Gethsemane and how only his faith sustained him, Ramsey wrote:

> Such faith in God is an intense personal necessity. By it a mother and father can even be reconciled to the death of a son. By it a girl can be reconciled to the evil which her brother in service is doing (without stunting her conscience by calling it altogether good). By faith in God the young man in the service himself may be reconciled to the evil that he suffers and does (not that it is evil but that it has to be done). It is impossible for such a father, mother, or sister, or the soldier himself to live wholesomely without the faith that, though the forces against which his life is thrown mean evil against him, God means it for good, to bring to pass, as may be the destiny of this day, to save much people alive.
>
> In the hour of great and costly and dirty bravery, faith in God is necessary for the facing of this hour. Moreover, whoever would lead a wholehearted life in any hour and in every moment must do so by living in faith. In every hour whether of pain or of joy, receive what life

brings you in thanksgiving to God who gives and makes everything a good and perfect gift.[6]

War and suffering are a matter of God's judgment behind the vicious activity, otherwise we would respond only to evil and create a different god who must be reckoned with. Evil itself should not be ontologized.

H. Richard's refusal to ontologize evil is theologically correct. "Evil" cannot be made a hypostasis to which Christians must respond. It always remains a surd, and thus Christians respond only to a God who judges. Yet God need not be made the agent of tragedy either. Ramsey's appropriation of this theme did not ontologize evil, but it did ontologize tragedy! If evil should not be ontologized, neither should tragedy be written into the fabric of political being, but this is exactly what Ramsey does when he makes claims such as, "By faith in God the young man in the service himself may be reconciled to the evil that he suffers and does (not that it is evil but that *it has to be done*)." Radical monotheism provided a unity to earthly, political existence, which goes beyond making tragedy understandable, it makes tragedy unavoidable. The soldier is reconciled not to the evil he does, but to the fact that given the historical circumstances in which he has been thrown, he *must* do evil. The soldier's culpability dissipates into the unavoidable structure of tragedy, which has now become a structure of being.

What must be remembered is that Ramsey did not need Niebuhrian realism, nor radical monotheism, to ontologize tragedy. His earlier commitment to philosophical idealism with its "metaphysics of democracy" already provided tragedy's structural base. Thus one vectoral influence for Ramsey's ontology of tragedy was philosophical idealism; one was radical monotheism, and another was Reinhold Niebuhr's realism. While all three of these vectors influenced Ramsey's work, he himself understood the influence of the Niebuhrs as decisive in his break with liberal pacifism. He explains this in a letter to Sid Macauley of the Christian Medical Society.

As you will see, I was among the thousands and thousands of ministers and young people who, as World War II approached, were pacifists. Also at Millsaps we were socialists, inter-racialists, and opponents of organized intercollegiate football as a brutal sport. I remember when back teaching at Millsaps, 1937-1939, after two years at Yale Divinity School, making a speech at a rally from the steps of one of the buildings and reading a telegram I had sent to President Roosevelt to stay out of the war (the occasion, I believe, was Hitler's move into Poland; but it might have been some other event).

It was against this ethos, of course, that Reinhold Niebuhr set his face, founded *Christianity and Crisis* to counter *The Christian Century*. His shattering book *Moral Man and Immoral Society* was published, I believe, in 1936, the year after I graduated from college. *The Nature and Destiny of Man* came later, and of course, that began to eat away the foundations of the position I then held.This is to say, in direct answer to your question, that I was a pacifist during most of World War II. Before Pearl Harbor and draft registration came, I was also an ordained minister — which status continued while I was teaching at Garrett (where ordination was significant) and into my years of teaching at Princeton (where it became increasingly irrelevant — and I gave it up, finding no one who thought it relevant enough to my teaching vocation even to *oppose* it!).

Those times may be difficult for you to recover, unless you have read studies of pacifism between the two world wars. It's even hard for me to remember back then. The following contrast may be of interest to you, if you are aware that in opposition to the Vietnam War many divinity school students refused to invoke that status, or ordination, and choose instead to make their witness by refusing to register for the draft or claiming particular war objection. In World War II I can remember only three or four at Union in N.Y. who felt impelled to do that, refuse to cooperate with the military by refusing to register. Thus, most of us registered, as I did, as pretheological students (and/or as ordained) *and* as universal C.O.'s. So there were few "collisions" between us and the state, depending on the draft board.

Two things were at work, I suppose, or happened to me. One was my gradual growth out of Millsaps liberalism into a more orthodox theological outlook at Yale — where the influence of the Niebuhrs had its steady effect long before any change of position on my part. The second was the "culture shock" of going to teach for two years at Garrett where I found myself in the midst of a hotbed of that same Methodist liberal-pacifist background of mine. That accomplished the overturning of my position, more than when I was *defending* it at Yale. You can say that chap. V of *Basic Christian Ethics* sets down in writing the voyage by which I came to see the fitness of a Christian non-pacifism. Some have said that there I am too hard on the pacifist. If so, I was coming down hard on a position I formerly held.[7]

Before World War II, Ramsey's theology drew upon Personalist themes. As he developed a much more sophisticated philosophy of idealism, Personalism was called into question. Once he adopted Niebuhrian realism, he abandoned any vestiges of Personalism altogether. In 1943 he reviewed Brightman's *The Spiritual Life* and Albert C. Knudsen's *The Principles of Christian Ethics*. Concerning Brightman's book Ramsey writes:

. . . without qualifying the high idealism and spiritual fervour with which every sentence of this book is fraught, many practical minded readers will find it impossible to read it without what they will fondly call a realistic reaction against its sentimentalism. . . . The book in general underestimates the context in which we know as spirit is always found, and which serves both its permanent structure of opposition, and as its only means of concrete expression.[8]

The "ideal" is now impossible because it is located within a tragic dialectic where its "only means of concrete expression" is also a "permanent *structure* of opposition."

In November of that year, Ramsey stated that Knudsen's "personalistic slant is both the strength and weakness of his views on Christian ethics." After commenting on the strengths he writes:

> Nevertheless, the personalism of the philosophical moralist in Dr. Knudsen too greatly displaces the Christian ethicist in him. This is indicated by the fact that the doctrine of vocation and of response to the "orders of creation" are postponed for their full flower until the section on practical application and find no adequate discussion in the theory of Christian ethics, and by the fact that Dr. Knudsen de-spiritualizes sin by finding its primary source in the acquired moral character of man.[9]

What could it mean for Ramsey to say Knudsen "de-spiritualizes sin by finding its primary source in the acquired moral character of man?" Sin is not, for Ramsey, primarily found in inadequate moral formation. Rather, sin is found in the "permanent structures of opposition." Because of this, theological notions of "vocation," and "orders of creation" are a necessary part of Christian ethics. Given the inescapably tragic nature of human existence, these theological notions teach us how to make life barely endurable. Even though this lesson first came from Bosanquet, Ramsey now concedes Reinhold Niebuhr's realist critique.

Ramsey's third published article, "The Manger, the Cross, and the Resurrection," shows Reinhold Niebuhr's influence (one reason being that Niebuhr gave the essay its title!).[10] In this essay, the main point is that the "cross" and not the "manger" represents the "deepest meaning of the Christian faith." Christianity is marked by the "inexorable character of history." Tragedy is inescapable. Thus, the "ideal" is not fully actualized this side of the eschaton.

Once Ramsey realizes the implications of the tragedy that marks political existence, it has serious implications for his understanding of the practice of the Christian moral life. No longer is their a blanket condemnation of war. Nor does pacifism win by default because it at least creates "reluctant warriors." Instead, Ramsey writes:

> But the "mournful Christian warrior" of the Lutheran tradition, who repentantly fights the just war, is not one who is always blubbering over his gunpowder! Rather is he one whose permanent attitude of life is directed, not toward the righteousness of his act as itself sufficient to jus-

tify him, nor toward the unrighteousness of his act as sufficient to condemn him, but toward God, the Author and the Finisher of his faith.[11]

Notice once again how Ramsey's ontology of tragedy depends upon H. Richard Niebuhr's radical monotheism. Moral legitimacy shifts from the rightfulness or wrongfulness of the act to God's justification of the actor despite the analysis of the act itself. A distinction is made between the activity of God's work on a person and the activity of the person. Justification and sanctification are sundered apart.

With the publication of "The Cross and the Manger," tragedy constrains Ramsey's work. The "reality" of tragedy shapes us, more than our ideals shape reality.

> After each [historical] event [such as war] we must always confess that we have been acted upon more than we have acted, that we have been changed more than we have changed anything, and that the ideals with which we began have not been realized in reality so much as they have been transformed to accord more with reality. By grace are we saved!

The Christian life is a struggle to actualize an ideal which can never be actualized nor dispensed with. The "ideals" have only an elencthic use; they turn us to grace where we can be healed of the contradiction of possessing unrealizable ideals. The pacifist has become the reluctant warrior has become the warrior who no longer "blubbers over his gunpowder."

As Ramsey says in the above letter to Sid Macauley, this movement from pacifism to the reluctant warrior to a warrior who willingly "wades through blood and suffering" is depicted in chapter five, "Christian Vocation," of *Basic Christian Ethics*. The title of this chapter is significant. Remember Ramsey's criticisms of Knudsen's book. There he stated that Knudsen failed to give an adequate discussion of the "doctrine of vocation" and the "orders of creation." These are important themes for Ramsey because of the inexorable tragic character of human history; some form of force, violence, or coercion cannot be avoided. Therefore, Christian theologians need to address how those who respond by force, i.e. magistrates and soldiers, will do so.

In the chapter "Christian Vocation," Ramsey stresses the negative role of modern nation states -- their role in the restraint of evil. No longer do you have the close correlation between the role of the nation state, the pragmatic role of pacifism, and the importance of pacifism for the "destiny of our civilization." The freedom the state provides depends upon the restraint it exercises -- the essential theme philosophical idealism and Reinhold Niebuhr share.

Earlier, the "Destructive Force" essay showed glimpses of the "restraint of sin" aspect of the nation-state, but within a much more limited context than one finds in *Basic Christian Ethics*. In the latter Ramsey speaks of "protective coercion" as not only justifying the use of violence, but even being a positive duty stemming from love of neighbor.[12] This then raises the question about self-protection. Although self-protection is firmly denounced for its own sake, it can be invoked for the neighbor's sake, not only as a permission, but as a *duty* .[13] This, according to Ramsey, is not a "compromise" of the task of the Christian life, but is a necessary consequence of *agape*.

> Since Christian ethics is not a legalism concerned with external deeds only or even mainly, it would be a great mistake to regard Christianity's accommodation to Constantine's empire as necessarily a compromise of its genius or a "fall" from the pristine purity of its ethic. As a matter of fact, careful examination of the first literary defense of Christian partici-pation [St. Ambrose's *The Duties of the Clergy*] in war gives striking evi-dence that underneath the obvious reversal of tactic, the general strat-egy of Christian love continued without abatement and without alteration in its fundamental nature.[14]

In 1950, Ramsey's ethic is marked by a sharp law-gospel distinction. Christian ethics rests upon an internal (gospel) and external (law) divi-sion. While certain external acts may appear to be contrary to the gospel, when their internal orientation is clarified, their consistency with grace is revealed. The inner spiritual, as opposed to the external, legal, or physi-cal, provides the legitimation for war.

> Violence and bloodshed are no doubt horrifying, especially in destruc-tive total war, but the word "unlovely" has in Christian ethics a mainly spiritual not a mainly physical meaning. A selfish act is the most unlovely thing, and an unselfish motive may lead the Christian to per-form necessary responsibilities which prove not so "nice" in terms of physical contamination.[15]

Yet who is the target of Ramsey's criticism here? What causes him to in-teriorize salvation and put forth an unacceptable internal/external dis-tinction? It is his own early account of pacifism which made the external act of killing itself the moral issue. He now sees the fallacy of that earlier move and reacts accordingly. Yet in correcting his earlier position, he asymptotically approaches ruling out the analysis of the act itself in moral terms. Later, in response to the movement of situation ethics, Ramsey will make further corrections by lessening the distinction be-tween the external and the internal. At this point, Ramsey's analysis of agape deconstructs all rules, principles, and forms of analysis of external actions.

The presence of the Kingdom of God in Jesus goes "beyond good and evil." Because this means the law is no longer relevant, Christians are now permitted "wading through blood and suffering" for the sake of their neighbor.

> Christian love transcends self-love in the same way it leaves the law behind: Everything is now permitted, everything may now be thrown away in an heroic act of self-sacrifice without a single limiting exception made on account of the remaining legitimacy of self-love or autonomous duties to the self or the inherent claims of "humanity" wherever it may be found.[16]

The "standing over against-ness" of this claim should not be lost. It qualifies not only our duties to self, but our duties to family, village, country, etc. However, Ramsey goes on to state that once you concede that "everything may now be thrown away," it also follows that "everything may still be required." Everything, that is, which love of God and neighbor demands. And here is where war is justified: ". . . love which for itself claims nothing may yet for the sake of another claim everything."[17] Just as the radicalness of the Gospel may require one to forfeit his or her life, the life of the family, or of the nation; so might it also require them to kill, maim, possibly even dash their babies upon the rocks for the sake of one's neighbor. "Participation in regrettable conflict falls among distasteful tasks which sometimes become imperative for Christian vocation. Only one thing is necessary: for love's sake it must be done. All things now are lawful, all things are now permitted, yet everything is required which Christian love requires, everything without a single exception."[18] Just as Raskolnikov in Dostoyevsky's novel *Crime and Punishment* crossed the boundary inhibiting killing, stepping beyond good and evil, so the radical nature of the kingdom present in Jesus does the same -- with this exception. ". . . the Christian [unlike Raskolnikov] does not suppose that *he* is "extraordinary," but that *his duty* is extraordinary, or in another sense ordinary, all too ordinary, human, all too human."[19]

A Christian's *vocation* legitimates crossing the boundaries erected by law. Because of love of neighbor, the Christian "wades through blood and suffering." Because of the radical nature of the Gospel, "resistance," which would be denied for myself, is offered "by the *most effective possible* means, judicial or military, violent or non-violent when the needs of more than one neighbor come into view."[20] This is a realism which is not marked by Hobbes or Macchiavelli such as is Reinhold Niebuhr's, but by Nietzche.

Once again we find Ramsey drawing upon Nietzche to explain the "human, all too human." Chapter five helps make sense of the strange juxtaposition of Scripture and Nietzche that began *Basic Christian Ethics* where Ramsey first quoted Scripture: "For you yourselves have been taught by God to love one another. -- I Thessalonians 4:9;" and then Nietzsche: "Will any one look a little into -- right into -- the mystery of *how ideals are manufactured* in this world? Who has the courage to do it? Come!" -- Friedrich Nietzsche, *The Genealogy of Moral*, I, 14."

Chapter one is entitled, "The Two Sources of Christian Love." Ramsey describes the two sources as "The Righteousness of God," and "The Kingdom of God in the Teaching of Jesus". The passage to which Ramsey refers in Nietzsche claims that language such as "God's righteousness," and "the kingdom of God" are ideals manufactured in the workshop of liars to clothe their true intention which is revenge and hate.

Nietzsche's criticism deeply affected Ramsey. How can he avoid the self-deceptive character of "Christian love" which Nietzsche knew so well? The "love of neighbor" of the "Christianity and War" and the "Destructive Force" essay were obviously tinged with self-interest; 1943 made him see that. How can he still adhere to the central character of the Christian life (I Thessalonians 4:9) and face Nietzsche's critique?[21]

Ramsey has seen something here and it is quite frightening. He has seen that the radical way in which the presence of the kingdom in Jesus challenges all our "fixed relationships" so that we refuse to kill for the nation state can also mean a willingness to wade through blood and suffering for the sake of our "duty" to the radical kingdom.

What is glaringly absent in chapter five of *Basic Christian Ethics* is any discussion of non-combatant immunity. It is simply not there even though Ramsey refers to *justum bellum*. "Christian love" uses "the most effective possible means" to fulfill duties to the neighbor. At this point war is justified more in the form of a crusade for the neighbor than in terms of its restraint through discrimination. Discrimination will be a step Ramsey will take later. Here he has shown us the *consequences* of his move from liberal theology to Niebuhrian realism. If tragedy marks human existence, and salvation is based on love for the neighbor by the most effective means, then little discriminating criteria prevent warring for the neighbors' sake from being a crusade. Later on Ramsey will place limitations on the morally detrimental potential of these logical consequences.

Ramsey has looked into where "the ideals are manufactured" and has explored the possibility that what often passes as "Christian love" particularly in the form of liberal pacifism, is nothing but the refusal to look at the blood and suffering of human existence. Along with the vectoral influences of the idealistic philosophers and the brothers Niebuhr, we must also add Nietzche.[22]

The inoffensive character of the weak, the very cowardice in which he is
rich, his standing at the door, his forced necessity of waiting, gain here
fine names, such as 'patience,' which is also called 'virtue'; not being able
to avenge one's self, is called not wishing to avenge one's self, perhaps
even forgiveness (for they know not what they do -- we alone know
what they do). They also talk of the 'love of their enemies' and sweat
thereby.[23]

Did this not characterize his Millsaps liberalism? Was it not a utopianism based on the luxury of overlooking Poland, Czecholslovakia, and
the Holocaust? Could he face how such "ideals" are manufactured and
maintain the requirement "For you yourselves have been taught by God
to love one another?" Was the tragedy too grave to warrant such a
claim?

In facing this question squarely, Ramsey developed an ethic which
ontologized tragedy. Political responsibility required force. This defines
the possibilities of political existence. But he also developed a method
which took seriously our creatureliness. If certain structures were unavoidable, then the only avenue open for Christian ethics was to work
within those structures for their transformation. Ramsey worked out this
methodology during the following decade by seeking to illumine issues
of sexual ethics, property ownership, Civil Rights, magistracy, and sol-
diering. This work culminates in his 1962 work *Nine Modern Moralists*.
There he offers a much more sophisticated ethical methodology than we
find undergirding chapter five of *Basic Christian Ethics*. By 1962 realism
and idealism have been synthesized into a useful methodology known as
"love transforming natural law."

Love Transforming Natural Law,
Or
On Making the Body, Property Owners, Civil Rights Activists,
Lawyers, Magistrates, Soldiers, etc. Barely Endurable

In 1953, Ramsey wrote to Joseph Fletcher: "Of late my thought has
been much concerned with the various types which H. R. Niebuhr delin-
eates, and so I would phrase my present point of view as "love transforming justice" which in ethical terms is the equivalent of his 'Christ
transforming culture'." From *Basic Christian Ethics* to *Speak Up For Just
War Or Pacifism* "love transforming justice or natural law" describes
Ramsey's methodology. In 1953 when he was developing this method he
was not settled himself as to what he meant by it. He goes on to write,
"Thoughts about these issues with the assistance of the types [Niebuhr]
has clarified for us has brought me to a fuller, *if still un-clear*, understand-

ing of what I meant by saying that Christian love must always be in the
ascendancy in any synthesis made with other systems of ethical insight
or judgment."[24]

This correspondence with Fletcher refers to the claim in *Basic
Christian Ethics* that Christian love must occupy the "ground floor". It
makes alliances and coalitions with other ethical views but no
"concordats". It always remains free itself. "Love," as the central characteristic of the Christian life, is not something so definitive in and of itself
that it constitutes a social ethic. It provides a direction. Therefore,
"Love" can adopt a social ethic found in the necessary structures of political existence, re-orient, and transform it.

Scott Davis describes Ramsey's methodology wonderfully:

> Conversion does not replace the natural faculties or the structure of the
> psyche. Nor does it establish in the soul a new power, distinct from
> those the individual has from birth. Rather the act of grace enables the
> individual to perceive and direct her actions toward the genuine good,
> which is God.[25]

This transformationist model has both a disadvantage and an advantage.
The advantage is that Ramsey takes seriously the material making possible present political existence. The disadvantage is that the material
structure that is to be converted is already defined as inextricably tragic.

This methodology forms the basis for Ramsey's use of "vocation."
Christian love is in search of a social policy to transform. The social
policies love transforms are primarily found in vocations such as property owner, civil rights worker, lawyer, magistrate, soldier and physician. After *Basic Christian Ethics*, Ramsey's work concentrates on both illustrating how love has partially transformed these vocations already, as
well as prescribing means by which they can be more fully transformed.

Love Transforming the Body:
"Biblical Prologue: A Crochet of Themes"

From the publication of *Basic Christian Ethics to Christian Ethics and
the Sit-In* eleven years elapsed.[26] Given Ramsey's prolific publication
record, this is an unusual amount of time. Yet this gap is misleading for
prior to Ramsey's work on issues such as property rights, civil rights and
war, he wrote and never published three chapters of a book on sexual
ethics. The three chapters were, "Biblical Prologue: A Crochet of
Themes," "Augustine and the Presiding Mind," and "Sex and the Order of
Reason in Thomas Aquinas."[27] He ends the third chapter with the claim,
"the church's teaching about the meaning of sexuality needs radical

reconstruction,"[28] and suggests that "existentialist philosophy," particularly the work of Sartre, will provide the philosophical basis for this reconstruction. Thus, he mentions a fourth chapter, "Sex and Sartre," that was not included in this particular work, but which did appear in his 1962 publication, *Nine Modern Moralists*.

Ramsey's 1953 letter to Fletcher emphasized two assumptions that were present in *Basic Christian Ethics* and are more fully developed in his reflections on sexual ethics. These two assumptions are: Christian ethics cannot avoid "synthesis with other systems of ethical insight or judgement" and because synthesis is unavoidable, "Christian love must always be in the ascendancy." This 1953 description of "love-transforming natural law" results from Ramsey's interpretation of the work of Augustine and Aquinas.

Ramsey did not assume that Augustine and Aquinas were infallible expositors of Christian faith. But because of his idealism, he did assume Providence worked through great men and their great ideas which (apolitically) stood the test of time. Augustine and Aquinas were for Ramsey central figures whose work had been authenticated by its enduring character, and thus could not be avoided. Both in his sexual ethics and in his war ethics, Augustine and Aquinas provided the backbone of his work. He did not develop his position without first examining what they had to say.

The significance of Augustine and Aquinas' ethics is that they present an account of the "natural" which is "already Christianized." For Ramsey this makes Augustine "profoundly Christian."[29] And commenting on Aquinas' grounding of the indissolubility of marriage both in marriage as a sacrament and as a natural law, Ramsey writes, "Is it not evident that the natural law upon which indissolubility seems to be based is already a Christianized natural law?"[30]

When love-transforming-natural-law is understood as Ramsey's interpretation of Augustine and Aquinas, his own method becomes much more clear. For Ramsey natural law is not a static, ontological level of being universally accessible; "natural" is always already laden with interpretation. In western Christendom, Christians had a stake in natural law because Christians defined it first:

> . . . in the older Anglo-American marriage law which endured for centuries up to nearly our own day, precisely the judges who in marriage cases spoke of life-long marriage as the 'natural law' were also the judges who in these and other decisions over and over again referred to this as a 'Christian civilization' or as a 'Christian nation.' What they said with such certainty about the law of marriage was likely a 'Christianized' natural law, or the judgment of a natural moral reason already penetrated to the root by Christian influence.[31]

On the one hand, this method is uncharitable. It advocates the continuation of a will to power over the descriptive process without publicly acknowledging this act of will. But on the other hand, Ramsey's method is quite charitable to philosophical movements of the time, perhaps even too charitable! He was so convinced of the transformative power of the Gospel, he willingly engaged any and all philosophers in debate. In this work on sexual ethics he did not simply desire a return to Augustine and Aquinas; he was critical of many of the features of their sexual ethics. He thought that a Christian ethic of sexuality needed to penetrate the philosophy of Sartre and recreate the "natural" through a Christian reading of existentialist philosophy. He uses Sartre to critique Christian tradition, and then uses Christian tradition to reread Sartre.

Because Christianity must engage other philosophical systems while maintaining the ascendancy of its own distinctiveness, Christian ethics makes common cause with systems that denied Christianity's distinctiveness. This, so Ramsey suggests, is the reason for the importance of Augustine.

> Our only concern is to understand how profoundly a 'Christian' thinker was Augustine (even if profoundly mistaken about sexuality) in what he said about fidelity itself as a charity not hesitating to dwell in the midst of what he supposes to be evil so as by any means to obtain a transforming grasp upon it. This then is not only an ethic of negative restraint, but an ethic of remedy bent in the direction of an ethic of redemption . . . . The basis of Augustine's teaching about marriage as the restraint and remedy for sin is, therefore *thematically* quite biblical. It rests the due of marriage neither upon the cohesion afforded by an interchange of self-love nor upon the so-called natural order of mutuality or the natural law of marriage; but upon the order of charity in a complete interchange which gives a quite specific work of love.[32]

Ramsey's insistence on the natural has the benefit of taking seriously our creatureliness; it has the defects of limiting creatureliness through his ontology of tragedy.

The defect in his account of creatureliness is found in his interpretation of Augustine as "profoundly Christian." Augustine is profoundly Christian not only because he "already Christianizes the natural law," but also because "fidelity itself as charity does not hesitate to dwell in the midst of what he supposes to be evil." This is an odd claim, particularly when Augustine's "The *Good* of Marriage," upon which Ramsey is commenting, was written for the expressed purpose of denying that even the polygamous marriages of the patriarchs were evil. Marriage is a good for Augustine -- "marriage and fornication are not two evils, the second of which is worse; but marriage and continence are two goods, the second of which is better."[33] Ramsey recognized that marriage was a good for Augustine; he quoted the same passage I just mentioned. What then could he mean by saying Augustine was "profoundly Christian" because he was willing for charity to dwell in the midst of evil?

One response to this question is that Ramsey only meant that charity must bear witness to evil, and transform it into good. Surely that is an appropriate, if somewhat inane, interpretation of Augustine. But Ramsey means something more; some measure of evil is unavoidable. For Ramsey, Augustine sets up principles by which the evil done is transformed by the Gospel to make it more faithful, and to make it a "good." Because he interprets Augustine through an ontology of tragedy where Christians can never be free of evil, Ramsey emphasizes the restraining order of marriage (as well as of political government) in a way incontinent with Augustine. Commenting on Augustine's claim, "Remove prostitutes from human affairs and you would pollute the world with lust," Ramsey suggests:

> Augustine seems to believe, less the whole race sink into the bird-lime, the good of society can be achieved largely by the measures of channeling the concupiscence of honest people into marriage and dishonest people into prostitution since only a few likely will choose the higher road of life-long continence. Such dark realism can only be pondered deeply before being dismissed. We shall have to go beyond this, however, before we grasp Augustine's full meaning when he speaks of faith and chastity, although in the end, this still falls under the heading of the restraint and remedy of sin, and is not, like offspring, the chief good of marriage.[34]

But Augustine's "dark realism" here is not Augustine, because he would never be able to make the analogy between continence, marriage, and fornication as Ramsey has done. This "dark realism" is indebted to Ramsey's ontology of tragedy rather than to St. Augustine.

For Augustine, continence and marriage are commensurable, but marriage and fornication are incommensurable. Fornication does not participate in the "good." Marriage and continence both participate in the good; yet continence is better than marriage. Thus marriage and continence can be compared and continence can be viewed as a "higher road," as a higher degree of perfection.

"Degrees of perfection" Ramsey finds objectionable. He denies any hierarchical ordering of the good for Christian virtue.

> . . . the imprint of Augustine [for Roman Catholic sexual ethics] in the idea of degrees of perfection, especially the inherent superiority of vir-

ginal chastity, has never been abandoned. Against the Reformation's exaltation of marriage as a sphere where the highest Christian perfection is possible, Canon Ten of the Council of Trent declared that virginity and celibacy are "better and more blessed than to be united in marriage."[35]

Interestingly, Ramsey favorably explains the history that makes Augustine's degrees of perfection possible. Augustine's hierarchy was indebted to a historical teleological ordering. Celibacy was a "higher" good, i.e. more of a participation in the eschatological reality Christ makes possible, and the hierarchically ordered degrees of perfection cannot be separated from the eschatological story of Christ's redemption.

> Augustine's portrayal of the purpose of sexuality up to the time of Christ, and after Christ the acceleration of movement toward an ultimate End, was his way of *telling a significant story* and affirming that there happens in the history of mankind and in the soul's experience something which never happened before. The form reversion from this takes in modern Christian thought is the affirmation of the goodness of sexual life and progeneration on the authority of Genesis and under the first article of the creed. Thus, knowledge of the creation, and the significance of sexuality, is given status wholly independent of the history of redemption which has rather to do with the "spiritual" ends of mankind. In contrast to all these views, it might be said that Augustine understood the creed to be a "Christological concentration," or that the beginning was understood by him from the End who had appeared in the midst of history. And that included his interpretation of the history of sexuality.[36]

Ramsey points us to the Christian narrative as a way to make sense of Augustine's ethics of sexuality, in so doing he chastises modern accounts of sexual ethics that find a base in the "natural" alone. Nevertheless, Ramsey himself finds Augustine's hierarchical ordering inadequate, and the thrust of his effort is to overcome what he perceives to be the residual disparagement of marriage because celibacy is understood as a form of higher Christian perfection. This is puzzling.

Why did Ramsey give such a wonderful account of the historicity of Augustine's degrees of perfection, and yet deny these distinctions for the sake of exalting marriage? Because he emphasizes male and femaleness as an order of creation to such an extent that he approaches making heterosexual marriage necessary for full participation in covenant. He begins his work on sexuality stating, "the creation of male and female should never be separated from the creation of man in God's image." So far, so good, but he defines this more fully:

> The desire of Adam and Eve for each other, including in its totality sexual passion, is the cure God has ordained for human loneliness.

> No one can read the Genesis story without seeing that the chief purpose of human bisexuality is the nourishment of married love and the cure of loneliness by life-in-community, including sexual community, between man and woman. . . . True, Roman Catholics say that marriage is also for the nourishment of married love. But that is said only in the shadow thrown by the teaching that the celibacy of priests, monks, and nuns is more perfectly Christian than the way of life that is open to ordinary Christians who are married.[37]

In this quote, we find Ramsey doing exactly what he accused others of in his defense of Augustine. He begins with Genesis and the first article of the creed, and from the doctrine of creation he develops a notion of "life in community" that loses contact with the story of redemption. Surely the "cure for loneliness" does not come from heterosexual marriage. Ramsey should have listened more closely to Sartre who reminded us that the family is the hell hole of togetherness! The cure for loneliness in the Christian story is Christ's body, the Church. Celibacy can be better not because celibates have conquered desire, but because their desire is ordered toward the Ultimate End, thus they participate more perfectly in eschatological reality. This does not say those who are married do not so participate; they only participate in it differently, and in such a way that they are dependent upon those who are celibate as a reminder that the Church and not the family is the redemptive community.

The assumption that because celibacy is a higher form of perfection, sexual intercourse is therefore disparaged is erroneous. Modern sensibilities might be offended by saying, "Marriage is good, and a means by which we participate in God's perfection, but celibacy and singleness are better," but the offense may be due to the leveling mediocrity created by democratic forms of government which at their worst, under the rubric of equality, seek to make everyone the same and deny distinctions of a better way of life.

So we are faced with a puzzling contradiction. On the one hand, Ramsey makes a compelling case for Augustine's degrees of perfection as based on a teleological order grounded in the Christian story. On the other hand he dismisses Augustine's degrees of perfection because of its supposed disparagement of Christian marriage. Why the contradiction? Because Ramsey was so committed to "covenant" as the biblical hermeneutic upon which ethics is grounded, and to "consent" as the necessary precondition for covenant, that he found in heterosexual marriage exemplification of biblical morality.

For Ramsey, marriage as covenant means that a "formal capacity for consent to permanent union *must be attributed to the human will* in binding itself."[38] Ramsey continues, "This is why, by contrast [to the modern period] a covenant understanding of human relations needs to be recovered if ever is to be ended the attempt to found all human relationships and especially sexual relationships upon a calculated principle of disorder."[39] The capacity for consent is a necessary a priori. It is one of the grounds for Ramsey's work in sexual, as well as political and medical ethics. Ramsey assumes that, given his theological commitments, consent is a genuine possibility; it describes reality. Once it describes reality, then it is used as a norm that legitimates a specific political order. But the notion of consent is an assertion based on Ramsey's metaphysics of democracy, and Reinhold Niebuhr's tragic dictum -- "Man's capacity for justice makes democracy possible; but man's inclination to injustice makes democracy necessary." If this basis for the assertion is unsound, then the order Ramsey legitimates has no ground.

Marriage is, like democracy, an order of creation necessarily brought about by the fall, based on "consent" and existing for the purpose of maintaining a barely endurable order. Ramsey's use of "covenant" as the possibility for "consent" is due to the primacy of liberal democracy in his work.[40] Because liberal democracy was also already Christianized, Ramsey finds in it an expression of the Christian faith. The question is, of course, has he not in this process read into Augustine and traditional Christian thought a foreign notion of "consent" which transforms the Christian life rather than being transformed by it?

Ramsey's exaltation of marriage comes at the expense of his own teleological argument for the normative role of celibacy and singleness. His combining of the importance of male or female, a "positive account of the relational or unitive function of sexuality, and one of a very high order," and the need for marriage as a restraint against anarchy nearly makes marriage a necessity to be fully human. Why does he do this? Because of two competing causes making marriage possible. The unitive end of marriage is made *possible* through the specific order of charity defined by the relationship between Christ and the Church. The restraining function of marriage is made *necessary* because of the threatening anarchy created through the fall. Unfortunately, the necessary always becomes more basic than the possible. Thus, for all his efforts to the contrary, Ramsey eclipses his positive account of the unitive end of marriage by the necessity of its restraining function. And this results from his interpretation of the fall's significance as the threat of anarchy.

Favorably quoting C.S. Lewis' interpretation of Augustine on the fall, Ramsey wrote, "Man has called for anarchy; God lets him have it." Here is the lynchpin for Ramsey's Protestant ethics; the threat of the fall is anarchy. To ward off anarchy, God provides "orders," or what Ramsey constantly refers to as "garments of skin" to preserve human existence as barely endurable. That is the best one can expect.

Yet here we need to proceed cautiously for the order that wards off anarchy can be understood much less favorably that it ever appears to be for Ramsey. If anarchy is the central threat to an endurable human existence, the "orders" are necessities. But if anarchy is not the central threat, the "orders" become the means for those in power to maintain their power. Thus, we must tread gingerly when discussing "anarchy;" we might find ourselves walking upon the head of the Leviathan!

Is anarchy the distinctive feature of the fall with which Christian ethics must be concerned? The answer to this question will situate the role of "order" in an ethical framework. Biblically, anarchy is not self-evidently the ultimate threat to God's good creation.[41] After all, the story of the fall culminates not in a tale of human-created anarchy, but in the order that made possible the Tower of Babel: "they are one people, and they have all one language; and this is only the beginning of what they will do; and nothing that they propose to do will now be impossible for them" (Genesis 11: 6). In response to this humanly created order, God becomes the agent of anarchy: "Come, let us go down, and there confuse their language, that they may not understand one another's speech" (Genesis 11: 7). Which then is the threat stemming from the fall -- order or anarchy? Perhaps C. S. Lewis was wrong, the fall does not lend itself to the interpretation, "Man has called for anarchy; God lets him have it," rather it lends itself to the interpretation, "Humanity seeks order; God graciously prevents it." If this were understood as the central threat stemming from the fall, I daresay it would deeply qualify not only Ramsey's ethics but much of Protestant ethics in general.

Still, the distinction between anarchy and order is not easily defined. Until the final note is played, what appears to be anarchical may, in fact, be order, and what appears to be order, may in fact be anarchy.[42] Any ethical purchase received by the dichotomy of order vs. anarchy needs to be open to teleological confirmation.

Without anarchy as the distinctive threat resulting from the fall, Ramsey's consistent use of Reinhold Niebuhr's tragic dictum makes no sense. Some variant of Niebuhr's dictum was used by Ramsey in a response to every ethical issue he faced, sexual ethics being no exception:

> Both experience and Scripture suggest that while man's created capacity for life-in-community and for faithfulness makes marriage possible, his propensity to unfaithfulness makes marriage necessary.[43]

The anarchy created by unfaithfulness requires some restraining order. The necessary capacity for consent makes marriage possible. But what if consent is not a possible pre-condition?[44] Then the "order" that arises to ward off anarchy is not based on faithfulness but coercion. Certainly that calls into question Niebuhr's tragic dictum.

Because he begins with an ontology of tragedy, human community, including marriage, is always constrained by the necessity of restraining anarchy. But despite Ramsey's ontology of tragedy, his sexual ethics has the benefit of taking seriously our creatureliness -- "men in their finally separate individuality are to seek only a creaturely communication with the divine." The benefit is found in Ramsey's deep commitment to the body, as male or female, for Christian ethics. But this insistence on the "body" also needed a language that defined the natural for us in such a way that the distinctiveness of Christianity was not lost. Modern conceptions of marriage focusing upon mutuality were inadequate because they sought to ground marriage in a "natural" free from an interpretive framework. From the act itself, an ethic was supposedly developed. But this reduced sexual intercourse in marriage to a bland idealism without a sufficiently specific content. In opposition to this approach, an already Christianized natural law maintained the ascendancy of an "order of charity" that grounded the "complete interchange" of marriage in a "quite specific work of love." Why is this specific while "mutuality" abstract and idealistic? Because the "order of charity" is defined by the relationship between Christ and the Church and this order (rather than offspring or human community) provides the "natural" basis for the indissolubility of marriage.

God's covenant with us becomes the basis for our covenants with each other. Our covenants with each other become the possibility for expressing God's covenant with us because God deals with us in a specific way -- "God loves in such a way that he preserves and cherishes the otherness of the other being."[45] Thus, marriage becomes a gracious possibility where faithfulness can be exercised, and knowledge of God found, rather than a restraining order where anarchy is defeated.

Positively, love transforms human sexuality by providing it with an already Christianized "natural" law that allows it to participate in God's gracious history of redemption. Negatively, love transforms human sexuality by positing limits to the threatening anarchy. The negative and positive transformations are inseparable. The problem is that what is permitted negatively for the sake of the positive becomes the rule rather than the exception. Ramsey himself recognized this:

> The law of Moses on divorce was designed to build a floor under human conduct and to protect marriage against the most open faithlessness to it. This permission was granted without abandoning the ideal of lifelong marriage. But this floor rapidly became the ceiling of human expectations. What Moses permitted was soon regarded as mandatory.

Preventing the permissive from becoming the mandatory is a problem Ramsey seeks to be vigilant against. Yet, as we turn to his ethics of individual property ownership and civil rights, we will see that he himself falls prey to making the permissive mandatory. Once again, we will see that the reason for this is because of the *necessary* place for "orders" and "vocations" to prevent anarchy in a world which has been a priori determined as tragic.

Love Transforming the Property Owner and the Civil Rights Worker: *Christian Ethics and the Sit-In*

In the "Destructive Force" essay, the 1939 commencement address, and in correspondence with Mayor Walter Scott, Ramsey expressed deep concern for the inequities African Americans faced. He understood that racism was deeply embedded in economic arrangements. Thus he wrote, "I believe in equality between the white and the negro races. Yet, nothing would be more disruptive to the life of my economic community than the institution of equality and democracy in the south. The only reform to which I can compare it for the east would be the socialization of all productive property. Inequality of black and white is at the very root of the society which produced me . . . ." In 1939, Ramsey is willing to "scrap" these economic arrangements for the sake of the realization of the ideal of harmonious relations.

In 1961, when he writes *Christian Ethics and the Sit-In*, he is much more concerned with expressing a philosophy of law concerning individual property rights than he is "scrapping" an unjust system. He admits excluding African-Americans from lunch counters is an unjust practice which needs changed. Yet he also believes that procuring justice must be balanced with law and order. This is an obvious result of the orders and vocations necessary because of the structures of permanent opposition arising from an ontology of tragedy. These necessary orders become more basic to Christian ethics than the permission to take risks because with agape, all things are permitted. Law and order is a "garment of skin" that prevents anarchy. It is given to us by God as a remedy for the fallenness of human existence. The possibility of justice for Blacks should not destroy the necessity of law and order for an endurable political life; for law and order is a necessary precondition for justice.

Through two "basic concepts of Christian Theological Ethics," Ramsey evaluates the Sit-Ins.

> 1.) God's creation of human beings for covenant, and human nature as "fellow humanity" are fundamental to any proper understanding of that natural justice on which rests our laws. 2.) The Christian understanding of the fallen creature and its *always already* broken covenant gives the justification for a regard for order as well as for justice on which any good society must be founded.[46]

Once again, the "metaphysics of democracy," with its tragic dialectic lies behind Ramsey's ethical analysis. Covenant (and implicitly, consent) is necessary for any true justice; a covenantal understanding is found in democratic government. But the covenant is "always already" broken; therefore force and coercion are necessary for the order necessary for the covenant necessary for a "fellow humanity" restricting force and coercion.

Although Ramsey descriptively concedes this tragic dialectic, he does not acquiesce to it completely. He seeks to find breaks in the structure -- "garments of skin" -- that will limit the force and coercion. For property owners, the "garment of skin" is found in the "innkeepers law." For civil rights activists, the "garment of skin" is the principle of discrimination.

The chapter, "The Created Destination of Property Right," discuses the garments of skin that makes property owners barely endurable. The title of the chapter itself divulges Ramsey's teleological approach to Christian ethics. Although he agrees that individuals must possess private property, they possess this property on the basis of the purpose for all of created objects -- that these objects will not be ends-in-themselves, but be a means by which one person is *for* another person.[47]

The purpose of creation should find expression in law. Law cannot guarantee the purpose is fulfilled, but it seeks to limit the opposite of creation's purpose as well as provide the possibility for the purpose to be fulfilled. The innkeeper's law stated that whoever opened a business "should not then discriminate among those who apply for these services he is in business to sell."[48] The innkeeper's law restricts ways property owners can use their property because of creation's purpose of being for another. It provides the possibility for property owners to use their property faithfully.

> The "innkeepers law" manifests the fact that the political order with its justice and its law and a man's proper relation to the things he owns are the external basis, the promise, the possibility and capability for covenant-community.[49]

The innkeeper's law is that garment of skin that creates the possibility for love to transform the necessary order of private property.

Civil Rights Workers must also be transformed through a garment of skin that will make their just cause properly ordered toward the creation's end. In their case, the garment of skin is furnished by the principle of discrimination. In Ramsey's discussion of "just war" in *Basic Christian Ethics* he made no reference to discrimination; love used any effective means possible. Now, love becomes more definitive in its expression. One definite expression of love is found in the need for discrimination.

Ramsey writes favorably of non-violent boycotts and sit-ins as a form of pressure Christians bring to bear upon unjust structures. He even falsely assumes that the Mennonite tradition realizes that "the nature of divine charity raises decisively the question of the Christian use of all forms of pressure." I say falsely because many Mennonites tell us that they are not opposed to "all forms of pressure," but understand the Christian gospel as mandating a particular form of pressure.[50] Ramsey, following Reinhold Niebuhr and relying upon his own earlier liberal pacifism, assumes the ideal of agape is passive non-resistance. Because the ideal cannot be actualized in a tragic world, some limits must be set to the use of force.

> . . . we must certainly assert the great difference between Christian love and any form of resistance and then go on beyond the Mennonite position and affirm that Christian love-in-action must first justify and then determine the moral principles limiting resistance.[51]

By equating the ideal with passive non-resistance, Ramsey convinces the reader that, in fact, non-violent resistance is still by necessity short of the ideal. Thus, it is not the realization of Christian agape any more than the use of force is. Non-violent resistance, as a form of resistance, still needs a moral principle that will limit resistance in an effort to be as congruent as is possible with the ideal; that principle is discrimination.

> . . . economic injury may not be deliberately and directly done to other persons as a *means* of getting at the persons who are responsible for the policy sought to be corrected. Indiscriminating boycotts are the moral equivalent of obliterating people in warfare in order to get at their government. . . .[52]

Both property owners and civil rights workers need Christian love to transform their vocations. The role of Christian ethics is to create an "interruption" in the good intentions of both groups by subjecting their practices to the searchlight of agape.

One benefit of Ramsey's approach is that the materiality of human existence is emphasized. He understands the importance of our bodies, our work, and our traditions. Unlike many people, Ramsey did not seek to "transform" the Black community into the dominant community because he understood the importance of the Black community as an order that made covenant with good possible. He reminds us that "neither male nor female does not mean the loss of particularity." And he questions current efforts toward a racially united church, suggesting that such a church would only maintain a useless white hegemony.

> The climactic changes would seem to require the Negro churches to become about as unimportant for large ranges of the actual lives of men and women as have our bourgeois white churches![53]

Thus Ramsey criticizes liberal efforts to find a neutral realm free from our particularities.

While criticizing the liberal utopia, Ramsey also dismissed all utopias. No place secure from violence is found in human existence. Democracy is the best we can do, because democracy is *justum bellum* -- ". . . democracy itself in a very real sense is nothing more than *justum bellum* . . . requiring participation in it as a form of regularized struggle between man and man."[54] But even democracy is constrained by the tragic need for force. When democracy as "regularized struggle" breaks down, then people may need to be "directly coerced."[55] Because democracy is possible, the use of force and coercion are necessary.

Christian Ethics and the Sit-In further clarifies Ramsey's love-transforming-natural law. Ramsey begins with the particular situation, in this case, private property and the Civil Rights Movement. He then seeks to find customs or laws that express in some sense the redemptive purpose for God's creation, with respect to property owners, the custom he finds is the innkeeper's law, with respect to civil rights workers, the custom is the principle of discrimination. Then Ramsey defines these customs so that the Gospel transforms them. This is a clear example of his casuistical method. Yet this is also misleading because Ramsey did not simply begin with the particular; the particular was already inscribed into a "natural" defined as tragic. Thus his conclusion, putatively drawn from particulars, is the necessity for democracy. This leads us to war.

Love Tansforming the Magistrate and Soldier: *War and the Christian Conscience*

The term "just war" is not for Ramsey simply an ethic about the use of force; it is a foundational term that describes political reality. The turn toward just war continues Ramsey's idealistic assumptions about the metaphysics of democracy. This has the fault of limiting possible ethical responses to political situations by the underlying political philosophy. Still, Ramsey's metaphysics-of-democracy-become-just-war represents a more palatable alternative to the dominant managerial technologisms many contemporary ethicists swallow. In *War and the Christian Conscience*, Ramsey's just war limitations critique dominant assumptions about ethical thought.

While Ramsey does advocate democratic process as essentially Christian, the democracy he advocates is not found in contemporary North America. Those who want to use Ramsey to defend present political configurations must consider this important fact. If democracy is just war, then the just war principles are necessary for a true democracy. The term "democracy" only denotes a legitimately moral political order if the just war principles, and particularly discrimination, are part of the fabric of that moral order. Here lies the distinctive critique Ramsey makes of modern political configurations. The just war principles are public criteria providing a limiting concept to notions of democracy. If magistrates and soldiers violate these principles, the basis of democratic society, as an already Christianized natural institution, is violated. Ramsey made this clear in his most important contribution to the discipline of Christian ethics, his 1961 publication of *War and the Christian Conscience*.

In this publication Ramsey describes the shape required for political society if it is to be truly love transformed. The shape of that political society contains two interrelated defining characteristics. First, it cannot be sustained by a "technical political reason" based on pragmatism. Second, it requires the recreation of a moral tradition that stipulates specific and limited means of violence for the preservation of a good political life.

Critique of "Technical Political Reason"

For love to transform the magistrate, argues Ramsey, the surrender of ethics to "technical political reason" based solely on prudence must first be overcome. Mere prudence, without a moral tradition with an analysis of means, can only destroy what love has transformed in the past. Thus Ramsey views the prudential ethics of Niebuhrian realists as leading reflection on the Christian moral life into the "wasteland of utility."

Prudential ethics surrendered to "technical political reason" because the tragic necessity of Christian participation in war was coupled with a pragmatist emphasis on moral reasoning. Ramsey realized the evil consequences of combining tragedy with pragmatism. Pragmatism offered no criterion of discrimination between competing goods. In so doing, it defined human beings according to possible future consequences and thus reduced them to "laboratory animals." This was the fruit of the encroaching hegemony of consequentialist reasoning.

A lack of discriminating criterion, and the reduction of human beings to "laboratory animals," had its beginning in Reinhold Niebuhr's distinction between private and public morality.

> It is true that the present dilemma is for Niebuhr only a new form of his own distinction between individual and collective morality, with the latter conceived almost entirely in terms of prudent calculation or a teleology of greater or lesser evils expected as a consequence of action. But the question is whether the problem of war today does not reveal that such an understanding of political and military morality was all along defective and that such a view, unless it regains more of the substance of what we may call a deontological analysis of the morality of action and of the means, drives on toward a reduction of human collectivity to the nature of any other collectivity from which ends and consequences are to be wrested after having been rationally projected for the determination of present action.[56]

Niebuhr's distinction between individual and collective morality led ethics into the wasteland of utility because "collective morality" was defined as a "prudent calculation or a teleology of greater or lesser evils expected as a consequence of action."

According to Ramsey, the "increasing pragmatism of the Niebuhrs" led Christian moral reflection to be dependent upon "technical political reason." This was the first of three reasons for such a dependency. The two other reasons were a capitulation to a politics of fear through an inordinate concern with the possible destructiveness of nuclear war, and the "rejection of natural law and 'middle axioms'" *for* a situational or contextual ethic.[57] The convergence of these three factors resulted in an inappropriate moral rationality which began with the "facts" and worked backwards to the "should."[58] The preeminent question became "does it work?" What *can* be done given these "facts"?, what will "work"? The "facts" define the moral landscape, placing constraints upon any imperatives Christianity offers to the use of force. Because situational "facts" rather than imperatives, or exceptionless principles from within Christian tradition, define the moral landscape, reflection from within a moral tradition is usurped by reflection based on "technical political reason."

Ramsey reverses this direction, moving from "should" to "can."[59] He wants an account of the Christian moral tradition not primarily concerned with the question of feasibility in a nuclear world. The alternative is pretentiousness.

If there are any lessons from the past, surely it is this: that we should not go about revising our moral tradition by pragmatically justifying what we are now preparing to do, but that we should frankly state -- if this is the case -- that wholly unjustifiable, immoral warfare has now become a necessity.[60]

If the pragmatist approach was the only alternative, then participation in war concedes the inevitability of doing evil that good may come. If this is politically inevitable, then either Christianity must become a sect or the Christian life itself is no longer possible, for Ramsey refused to tolerate the faithlessness of directly intending moral evil that good may come. If this were the only possibility, he rightly recognized the impossibility of sustaining Christianity.

The increasing pragmatism of some Niebuhrian "realists" suggested the inevitability of doing evil that good may come under the guise of a "realism." Ramsey gave a different interpretation to "realism" and "idealism" than did Niebuhr. Niebuhr wrote that realism "denotes":

> . . . the disposition to take all factors in a social and political situation, which offer resistance to established norms, into account, particularly the factors of self-interest and power. In the words of a notorious "realist," Machiavelli, the purpose of the realist is "to follow the truth of the matter rather than the imagination of it; for many have pictures of republics and principalities which have never been seen." This definition of realism implies that idealists are subject to illusions about social realities, which indeed they are.[61]

For Niebuhr, idealism is "characterized" as "the esteem of its proponents by loyalty to moral norms and ideals, rather than to self-interest, whether individual or collective."[62] Notice how this commits Niebuhr to "facts" supposedly free from their embeddedness in narratives formed by moral norms and ideals. To Paul Ramsey's great credit he saw how this position made Christian theology dependent upon the "experts" who define the facts.

Ramsey reversed the Niebuhrian polarity. He characterized the "idealist" as one who "finds his way under the lure of such goals as the greatest happiness of the greatest number, etc."[63] This turns Niebuhr's definition of "idealism" back on itself. While for Niebuhr, idealism was characterized by a type of deontological commitment refusing to bend in the face of the harsh reality of political life, for Ramsey idealism is marked by a "deontological" commitment to utilitarianism. Niebuhr's "realism" fits better within Ramsey's description of "idealism."

Certainly Niebuhr's realism was not merely a form of utilitarian calculation. Rather than primarily advocating a utilitarian approach to ethics, Niebuhr recognized the power configurations involved in the political order against sentimental appeals to "love." Still, Niebuhr's approach does lend itself to a consequentialist ethic. He himself writes, "one may well wonder whether an approach to politics which does not avail itself of the calculations of justice, may be deemed realistic."[64] Of course, this claim does not entail utilitarianism, and calculations of justice are immensely important. However, "calculations of justice" come too easily to Niebuhr within his own system. His emphasis on power suggests that everyone is driven by an inordinate self-interest. Conceding the centrality of this realist account of power, how are we then to calculate justice? Is justice for Niebuhr not an approximation to the best possible balance among competing forces? How is this to be "calculated" when, at the same time, Niebuhr tells us that our calculations themselves will be driven by self-interest?

Ramsey's definition of "realism" maintains the importance of Niebuhr's analysis of power, but he is leery that prudential moral reasoning is so easily capable of appropriate calculations to ends such as justice. A "realist" writes Ramsey

> ... is one who knows that there are many ways that may reasonably be supposed to lead [to our goals], ranging all the way from the noblest to the most wicked political decisions and actions; and he reminds the calculative idealist that in politics he had better know more than this about right and wrong conduct. No properly ethical statement has yet been made so long as our moral imperatives are tied to unlimitedly variable ends. Nor has a properly ethical statement yet been made so long as the means are unlimitedly variable that are supposed to lead to fixed, universal ends, even the ends determined by *agape*.[65]

For Niebuhr, realism denoted taking into account "all factors" into a calculation of justice in the development of a response within a social and political situation tainted with sinful self-interest. Ramsey doesn't deny the importance of this, but he extends it to include an analysis of the "intrinsic" nature of the means employed to reach a specific, limited end rooted in a moral tradition.[66] If the ends are "unlimitedly variable," then regardless of any moral imperative, responses in social and political situations will be constrained by a proportionality based on the variable ends. If the end is "fixed" but the means remain "variable," then we will still be led by the principle of proportionality through calculating the variable means to achieve the fixed goal. In the first possibility "what works" offers no discriminating criterion because the "what" is tied to a myriad of possible ends. In the second possibility, even when the "end" is secured, without an intrinsic analysis of the moral nature of the "what," no discriminating criterion is provided. The means used can invalidate the fixed end regardless of its worth. In both cases we are led into the "wasteland of utility."

How can we escape what Ramsey rightly sees as a morality driven by the winds of calculating effectiveness? Any ethic constrained by the language of "either deontology or teleology" will simply not allow his criticism. If, as with Reinhold Niebuhr, realism is a species of a teleological ethic and idealism of a deontological ethic, then Ramsey's attempt to "interpenetrate means and ends" will be discredited as "unrealistic." Ramsey wants to dislodge Niebuhr's analysis of power from his pragmatist account of moral reasoning. But he also wants to maintain the centrality of the analysis of power and reconfigure it within a tradition of moral reasoning as much concerned with "right conduct" as with prudential calculations. Something more than Niebuhr's analysis is needed, and the more is a moral tradition that will provide an intrinsic analysis of means. This contributes to his call for a re-creation of a moral tradition based on the "principle of discrimination."

Recreating a Moral Tradition

To overcome a pragmatist ethic driven by effectiveness Ramsey appeals for the "re-creation" of a "moral tradition."

> At the same time (if means and ends interpenetrate), there is need for a recreation, in both thought and feeling, of the moral tradition of civilized warfare in the right *conduct* of war and the moral limitations to be placed upon means.[67]

A "re-creation" of a traditioned non-combatant immunity supersedes a tradition of Niebuhrian pragmatism.

> A symptom of what we have to recover from is the widespread opinion that rules for noncombatants is only a detail added incidentally to the theory in the Middle Ages, a dispensable relic of the age of chivalry or of the pageantry wars of the eighteenth century; and that prudence will be sufficient to guide us in the conduct of war or the limitation of war.[68]

How do we "recreate" a moral tradition? What does Ramsey mean by "tradition"? This is a serious problem for Ramsey because he never gives us an adequate account of tradition, and his ethical reflection requires it. He does give us a brief description of what he does not mean by a moral tradition, and from this what he does mean is implicit. He writes:

... the political experience and ethical analysis summarized in the so-
called just-war theory cannot be dealt with all in one lump, as if it were
a simple system of moral rules for the classification of cases, subject to
no significant historical development, freighted with few ambiguities,
there to be accepted or rejected as a single, if ancient or "classical," formulation of one possible position in Christian ethics, with no significant
decisions to be taken *within* this tradition itself.[69]

The Just War tradition is not a text of rules to be applied to produce a
particular conclusion. Instead it is an ongoing historical discussion.[70]

The need for a moral tradition leads Ramsey to be more confident
about the justice by which people war than the justice for which they
war. The latter, *jus ad bellum*, requires experts who must claim the ability
to calculate adequately present circumstances and future consequences.
To rely on such experts is the way we surrender to technical political reason. The former, *jus in bello*, is known with more certainty because it
depends upon past tradition rather than future consequences. This leads
him to focus on *jus in bello* rather than *jus ad bellum*. He does not deny
the importance of justice leading to war, but the justice in the conduct of
war is less ambiguous and relative than the justice for which people war
because the former is more firmly rooted in Christian tradition.

Ramsey's emphasis on *jus in bello* appears in his genealogy of "just
war" drawing upon St. Augustine:

At least at the outset, the just-war theory did not rest upon the supposition that men possess a general competence to discriminate with certainty between social orders at large by means of clear, universal principles of justice, as to be able to declare (without sin's affecting one's
judgment of his own nation's cause) one side or social system to be just
and the others unjust. . . . My contention is that Christian ethics may at-
tribute to ordinary men, and to their political leaders, a capacity to
know more clearly and certainly the moral limits pertaining to the
armed action a man or nation is about to engage in, than they are likely
to know enough to compare unerringly the over-all justice of regimes
and nations.[71]

Because of the relativity of "justice" for which people war, Ramsey's
development of just war norms is anomalous within the just war tradition in that he allows for "justice" to exist on both sides. He does not tie
just war norms to a particular form of "justice" based on *jus ad bellum*
principles. The relativity of "justices" in the earthly city within which the
church makes pilgrimage results in a strong anti-utopian emphasis. The
Church has no stake in a single polity, or in a single depiction of "justice."
All the Church can do is transform the political societies in which the

Church finds itself. However, a truly transformed and specifically just political existence is impossible this side of the eschaton.[72]

In his chapter "Turn Toward Just War" in *The Just War*, Ramsey depicts this view of political society.

> The political life of mankind goes on perennially under the sign of the verdict at Babel.... Each man calls to another, every group and nation calls to the others as they build in every age the City of Man. Each tries to communicate to the other workers his plan for the whole edifice. They strive for vision of the whole, and for agreement on this. Excellent plans these are, some better than others. But it turns out that each thinks he is making the plan for the center of the tower, and he imagines his neighbor to be working on some less worthy part of the project. The vision every man and every nation has is "a view of the universal"; it is not "a universal view."[73]

Ramsey's recreation of a traditioned noncombatant immunity depends on the relativity of justice. "Justice," as the goal of political life "under the sign of Babel" is always relative. Thus, to war for "justice" is to fix means to an "unlimitedly variable" end. While the justice for which people war is relative, the justice which is to define how Christians war is not relative but an "unchanging principle."

> In any discussion of the claims of reason to direct statecraft against or in modification of the claims of necessity, it is of first importance to distinguish the unchanging principles which govern the use of force from the practice which these principles (if there are any) require from age to age because of the changing shape of warfare. ... This is the principle of *discrimination,* and in it there are two ingredients. One is the prohibition of "deliberate, direct attack." This is the immutable, unchanging ingredient in the definition of justice in war. In order to get to know the meaning of "aiming discriminately" *vs.* "aiming *in*discriminately," one had to pay attention to the nature of an action and analyze action in a proper fashion. The second ingredient is the meaning of "combatancy-non-combatancy." This is relativistic and varying in meaning and application.[74]

Ramsey's development of the principle of discrimination is not based upon a presumption *for* justice as a goal for a transformed political society. Nor is it based on a presumption against the use of violence or killing. Instead it is based on a presumption against allowing the neighbor to suffer *in*-justice within specifiable limits. What justifies participation in warfare -- love for the sake of one's neighbor -- also limits it because one has a myriad of neighbors which must be taken into account. The principle of discrimination stands as an "objective generality" over and against one's subjective intention. To attack deliberately and directly non-combatants oversteps the boundary for which Christians participate in war. A neighbor is violated rather than defended.

The shape of political society is bounded by the principle of discrimination. For the shape to retain its figure, a moral tradition must be recreated. Yet at this point a sleight of hand has taken place in Ramsey's work. While a specific moral tradition actually gives Ramsey this political shape, he places its genealogy in an *intrinsic* analysis of "love."

In *War and the Christian Conscience*, he claims that what "love requires" now has *intrinsic* limitations placed upon it. "The conscience schooled by Christ which first compelled Christians to justify warfare at the same time prescribed for them its moral limits." Indeed what love requires does now have limits placed upon it, unlike in *Basic Christian Ethics*, where love used the most effective means possible. But by suggesting "love" has *intrinsic* limitations, Ramsey implies that an analysis of love itself can generate the criterion of discrimination.[75] Such is not the case. Ramsey's formal definition of love as being for the neighbor has insufficient content to develop limitations on what love requires.

An analysis of the intrinsic limits "love," *in and of itself,* places upon the required participation of Christians in war is simply not the way in which Ramsey developed these norms. He was emphasizing "love" long before he emphasized discrimination. "Love" itself did not suggest to Ramsey the use of these norms. Father John C. Ford and the Roman Catholic moral tradition did.[76]

Rather than arising from an intrinsic analysis of "love's" requirements, just war norms were presented to Ramsey from an essay by Fr. John C. Ford, "The Morality of Obliteration Bombing." Ramsey's analysis of love's requirement cannot be separated from the social production and reproduction of just war norms in Catholic tradition. The irony of a Methodist social ethicist from Mississippi appealing to the Catholic tradition, even before Vatican Council II, should not be lost on the reader.

Paul Ramsey was thoroughly Protestant. He was the son of a conservative Methodist preacher, raised in the south in the early part of the 20th century. True to his Protestant heritage, in 1952 he wrote a letter to Dean Acheson vigorously protesting the appointing of an ambassador to the Vatican "because the claims of the Roman Catholic Church [were] unacceptable to Protestants." What claims were "unacceptable"? In a letter to James Nash of the Massachusetts Council of Churches Ramsey claims that Roman Catholic moral theology was "rigid, minimalist, and juridical" because it was "tied to the confessional." And as late as June 19, 1967, in a paper, "Christian Social Ethics in a Changing World," Ramsey spoke out against "ecclesiastical positivism and legalism," particularly the kind perpetuated by the "Roman Catholic magisterium." For

Ramsey's thoroughly Protestant bones, Roman Catholic ecclesiology was unacceptable.

Ramsey's anti-Catholic sentiment suggests the anomaly of the inordinate influence on him of Father Ford's defense of just war theory.
When Ramsey developed just war norms for Protestant social ethics in the 50's and 60's, he desired to leave behind the authoritarian ecclesiology of the Roman Church and its morality tied to the confessional. He did this by claiming just war was as Lutheran and Calvinist as it was Roman[77], and by claiming it was part of the *jus gentium* now inscribed in the "western tradition of civilized warfare."

Father Ford's decisive influence occurs at this point. He provides a principled morality separated from the need for an ecclesiological context by removing discussions of warfare from the context of the confessional. Ford wrote,

> The morality of obliteration bombing can be looked at from the point of view of the bombadier who asks in confession whether he may execute the orders of his military leaders, or it may be looked at from the viewpoint of the leaders who are responsible for the adoption of obliteration bombing as a recognized instrument of the general strategy of war. The present paper takes the latter viewpoint. It is not aimed at settling difficulties of the individual soldier's conscience.[78]

Father Ford removes just war from its ecclesial context, and he situates it within a discussion of "international law, the law of humanity, and the natural law."[79] On the basis of "natural law rights" alone, without discussing the place of the confessional, he invokes the principle of noncombatant immunity. Just War is no longer primarily an ecclesial practice "tied to the confessional."

Just war within the context of natural law as opposed to the confessional assuages Ramsey's anti-Catholic ecclesiological sentiment and grounds just war in rational inquiry, in the supposedly neutral forum of the "law of humanity." This fits better Ramsey's own Protestant view of the Church. Yet neither Ramsey nor Ford consider if an "epistemological rupture" occurs with this re-situation of just war norms. That is to say, do just war norms situated within the practice of the confessional have one meaning and just war norms situated within the context of international law have another? Certainly in the work of a theologian such as Victoria, the practice of the confessional is explicitly presupposed in his development of just war norms. While the development of just war norms by the Dutch canonist Hugo Grotius does not presuppose this practice. Should ethicists see continuity between Victoria and Grotius simply because they both use the term *justum bellum*? Grotius places just war in the context of an unalterable natural law that needs no church even to read the "natural" law.

For Grotius and Fr. Ford, just war norms no longer require the practices of the Church to make them intelligible. They both seek to find a "non-sectarian" grounding for these norms. Thus, they are grounded in the Law of Nature.[80] Although Ramsey discussed "natural law" prior to *War and the Christian Conscience*, he did not portray it in such a favorable light as he did in that book. Now he even suggests the problem with Protestant ethics is that it rejected natural law for "contextualism."[81] But in *Basic Christian Ethics*, Ramsey called the natural law " a sub-Christian source of insight."[82] Ramsey now embraces "natural law" as a means to challenge "technical political reason," and to create a moral tradition with intrinsic limitations to warfare and violence.

While natural law introduces a new element in Ramsey's work, it is still only a variation on an old theme. Love transforming natural law is both a continuation and a criticism of H. Richard Niebuhr's Christ transforming culture. It is a continuation because both Ramsey and Niebuhr assume that we already participate in political structures such as war. Because the structures are unavoidable, the most that can be done is limit them through transformation by the "ideal" or the "ethos" of love. As early as 1940 Niebuhr made this clear in his lecture notes.

> The Majority Church no longer held the [pacifist] position, possible when it was a minority. When the Church accepted responsibility for the common moral life (a highly moral thing) it no longer could present its ideal in pure fashion. It used natural law distinctions, justifying defensive wars. This distinction is exceedingly difficult to make in practice .... We ought not to begin with the distinction of natural law and gospel; but begin and end with gospel, with response to God and not to the self.... There is no way to get out of the world of political coercion: we must accept the fact that we are participating in the world of war. Life not only is, but has its character from the events of the past. We participate in Japanese aggression. Japan is what it is because we are what we are. I certainly cannot pretend that I am not participating in the class warfare. ... The question is since we are participating, how shall we participate, how shall we limit it?[83]

The "structures" are unavoidable. No matter what we do we cannot avoid complicity in war. Therefore the question is not "if," but "how;" not if we should participate, but how do we do so in such a way that the structures can be transformed. H. Richard Niebuhr found natural law distinctions a way to avoid the brute fact that we do participate in these structures. Ramsey found in natural law distinctions a way to participate in the structures faithfully.

For Ramsey the "structures" now have a name -- natural law. And the interplay between transformation and natural law defines how he develops the relationship between Christianity and the wider society. Love transforming the natural law makes two important contributions to Christian political theory. First it corrects "the implicit absolutism of loyalty to earthly kingdoms." No "natural" order is sufficient in itself to be the object of complete loyalty; it must always be transformed. Thus Ramsey's position contains a constant element of political critique. But it makes a second contribution which Ramsey says "has less frequently been pointed out."

> . . . since the nature of that City in which men together attain their final end is divine charity, as a consequence even earthly cities began to be elevated and their justice was infused and transformed by new perspectives, limits, and principles.[84]

"Love transforming natural law" implies the transformation of the earthly city by the presence of divine charity in its midst because Agape is the end to which all history "naturally" moves.

"Love" is not simply an internal motivation. It is to be more than a motivational quality of a person's life. It exists through the structures by way of principles, providentially embedded in history through the process of civilization. In 1970 Ramsey wrote a letter commenting on the transformative role of agape.

> If Christianity adds only motivation then we should simply say that there is no such thing as Christian ethics but only an ethics otherwise known and formulable. *Agape* is a norm and not only an inner spirit; in shadows cast by Christ-like love we also know something more of man: sinfulness. In speaking of the nature and meaning of love, of "love transforming justice," of the theological virtues, we are speaking of the distinctive or revealed dimension in the Christian moral life. I do not believe these are revealed ethical *propositions,* but a life and a relationship -- which then can and must be followed out in moral judgments, e.g. concerning marriage Ephesians 5; concerning the immunity of noncombatants from direct attack evolving from what *agape* requires in situations of conflict; concerning the worth of a neighbor for whom Christ died; such as he ought absolutely never be made a means to certain other ends or to the ends of others; a controlling awe-full sense that we should not play God over the future.[85]

Certain given structures are unavoidable, i.e. marriage, reproduction, situations of conflict, etc. Christians must live in these structures. The question is how they do so. They do so by principled moral judgments that transform the structures.

Lest the reader too quickly accept this position, be reminded that for Ramsey transformism was not easily accomplished. He recognized the deep problem with H. Richard Niebuhr's categories; transformism too easily became synthesis. In *War and the Christian Conscience* Ramsey writes:

> ... when Richard Niebuhr's book [*Christ and Culture*] first appeared almost everyone in American Christendom rushed to locate himself among the "transformists": naturalists, process theologians, personalists, idealists, Lutherans and Anglicans who were sometime Thomists, as well as those you would have expected. It was as if the "typology"or clustering of Christian approaches to man's work in culture and history had suddenly collapsed in 1951, so universal was the conviction that, of course, the Christian always joins in the transformation of the world whenever this is proposed. At least as a corrective, it is of first importance to maintain a clear distinction between loyalty to Christ and our responsibility to uphold the orders of society, especially if it is our view that it is precisely Jesus Christ through whom we can and may and must act within the world.[86]

Ramsey is critical of the transformationist position when it's primary task is interpreted as "the transformation of the world whenever this is proposed." Such a use of "transformism" slides back into the early prewar utopianism. Similar to his criticisms in the "Current Christian Anti-Pacifism," Ramsey views this usage as legitimating a too easy synthesis of the distinctiveness of the Christian life with American culture.

Ramsey even suggests that Christian ethics was skewed because of the unchallenged assumption that the Christian's primary task was the transformation of culture whenever possible. He calls this "Calvinism gone to seed." He sees it in the 1958 World Council of Churches' study document on "Christians and the Prevention of War in an Atomic Age."

> In a curious way this document stands squarely within the tradition of just-war theory, and yet not so squarely there, because of an unsureness and ambiguity introduced throughout, I can only say, by the Calvinistic impulse to transform the world gone to seed in an inarticulate pacifism that has in mind at every point the final and complete prevention of war.[87]

While H. Richard Niebuhr's theology caused Ramsey to accept the inevitability of the earthly structures, he realized that the popularity of the transformationist motif also led many to slide back into the liberal Protestant pacifist position he adhered to prior to 1943.

This slide back into liberal Protestant pacifism was marked by a too close identification of the "sphere of the Church" with the "sphere of the

State." Ramsey's conversion from pacifism gave him a more critical view of the State. Whether pacifists or just warriors, ethicists who rushed to transform culture wherever possible collapsed this distinction and lost this critical view. The WCC document slides into this identification on the basis of the transformationist motif.

> It threatens to identify the sphere of the Gospel with the sphere of the State in so far as while commingling with the latter Christian responsibility receives its justification only proleptically from a quite transformed state of affairs in the there and then.[88]

Possible future consequences of transformation construct a too close identification of the two cities in the here and now.[89]

Still, while Ramsey saw many problems with the transformationist model, this did not deter him from identifying with it. It remained central to his approach to Christian ethics, and he defended it against those who were critical of it.

One such critic was John Howard Yoder. In 1963 after reading Ramsey's critique in *War and The Christian Conscience*, he wrote to him saying he thought they were in agreement. The problem, as Yoder identified Ramsey's critique, was "in identifying the real uniqueness of the 'conversionist' approach to culture." Yoder wrote:

> Before building further on my agreement with you at this point, I felt it would help to check whether I understand the reasons which you imply without spelling them out for this difficulty, especially with respect to Augustine and to Calvin. Certainly there is some sense in which St. Augustine "converted" the pre-Christian heritage which he brought from his philosophical timing to his faith. In fact, is this not just what you say in your own ethics text? The difference would then lie not in the effort to "convert" a part of his pre-Christian heritage, but rather in the remaining element of Manichean dualism, through which, in the doctrine of original sin, his distrust of the material world carried through.

To this Ramsey replied:

> My point is that the Augustinian and the Calvinistic traditions are genuinely "conversionist," but that it is almost impossible to communicate this today because "conversionism" is uniformly identified with a progress view of history and of man's action in time. I refer to this again on page 93 as "the Calvinistic impulse to transform the world gone to seed . . . " I mean the interpretation of the "conversionist" point of view as if the effect of one transformation is to be added to another, and yet another, until man's life in history is utterly transformed from what we

know it to be. In contrast to any such view I think that Richard Niebuhr was quite correct in identifying the Johannine Gospel, St. Augustine, and Calvin as conversionists. They believed no such thing, but their modern adherents almost inevitably fall into such beliefs. I would, perhaps, disagree with you in interpreting the recalcitrant element, which prevents a progress interpretation of this position, in terms of a "remaining element of Manichean dualism." In fact, I think that it can be shown that most modern Christian thought is far more dualistic than ever were these great formulators of the conversionist position.[90]

Ramsey criticizes modern adherents to "conversionism" for holding to the same liberal utopianism he himself had held. He critiques his own early theme supporting his liberal pacifism that "our" task is to apply Christ's ideal to society and actualize it. Still, Ramsey's just war position maintained a version of this theme. Due to the relativity of values, Christianity is not a structure itself; it only transforms existing structures through the new direction created by the Gospel. Various cultural formations give substance to that direction.

Ramsey's use of the transformationist motif neither collapsed the "sphere of the Church" with the "sphere of the state," nor created a disjunction between them. Acting in the world means there are given structures -- practices with their concomitant rules which are inescapable -- necessities. These structures, practices, relationships, etc. are the material means which the Gospel transforms creating space for the righteousness of God in an alien world.[91] And this righteousness is found in God's covenant with Israel, and in Jesus Christ. "Christian ethics and Christian political theory must be decisively Christocentric. . . . Jesus Christ must be kept at the heart of all Christian thinking about justice -- and precisely that sort of justice which should prevail in the "world of systems," in this world and not some other."[92] Only through Jesus Christ, "*can, may*, and must [we] act in the world." Christology provides the possibility of righteousness even within the "world of systems." But this "world of systems" also provides the only context within which Christology is expressed.

Transformism, according to Ramsey, is not the Christian life molding culture into its own image and thereby progressively creating a better world. Rather, it is where the determinative power of the Gospel meets the indeterminacy of historical cultural-social-political contexts, and the Gospel issues forth in the possibility of faithful Christian response -- but always within the constraints of these earthly structures. For Ramsey, that interaction is best accomplished through just war norms.[93]

While Ramsey assumes the Christian perspective truly transforms the inevitable structures of earthly existence, he does not assume that Christianity itself is a political structure. Surely this is why he opposed the Catholic Church as necessary for the production of just war norms. This is clearly demonstrated in his understanding of the merely personal rather than political view of the early Christian movement.

> The change-over to just-war doctrine and practice was not a "fall" from the original purity of Christian ethics; but, however striking a turning-full-circle, this was a change of tactics only. The basic strategy remained the same: responsible love and service of one's neighbors in the texture of the common life. The primary motive and foundation for now approving Christian participation in warfare was the same as that which before, in a different social context, led Christians out of Christlike love for neighbor wholly to disapprove of the use of armed force. Christians simply came to see that the service of the real needs of all the men for whom Christ died *required more than personal, witnessing action. It also required them to be involved in maintaining the organized social and political life in which all men live.*[94]

From Jesus to post-Constantinian Christianity *agape* as the "primary motive" remains the same. But whereas pre-Constantinian Christianity was merely "personal witnessing action," post-Constantine Christianity becomes "responsible" for the structures, "the political life in which all men live." Ramsey's equating the early Christian position as one of "personal, witnessing action," as opposed to the later adoption of "social responsibility" is questionable. It assumes a private/public distinction peculiar to modernity. He needs this distinction for the adoption of the preventive role of the state and for the importance of "vocation." The responsible and public role is contrasted with the "a-responsible because personal" account of the early church's pacifism. Thus he fails to see that the early Church was a political configuration which lost its identity once it was absorbed into an empire.[95]

One can't help but see here the role of Troeltsch's *The Social Teaching of the Christian Churches*, particularly his claim that the "preaching of Jesus and the creation of the Christian Church were not due in any sense to the impulse of a social movement."[96] When the early Church is understood as concerned with the "personal" as opposed to the social, then the role of "vocation" takes on tremendous significance. It calls forth the language of "responsibility." That is to say, once you have sufficient power for a single overarching politic, then you must exercise your power responsibly, even if it requires sacrifices of "personal" integrity, for the sake of others. This will involve you in vocations that were not open to the early Christians, but are now positive duties.

War and the Christian Conscience was Ramsey's attempt to transform the office of magistracy, just as *Christian Ethics and the Sit-In* sought to transform property ownership and the Civil Rights struggle, his essays on sexuality sought to transform the body, and as we shall see his works on medical ethics sought to transform the health profession. In all of these works, Ramsey is seeking to interpret H. Richard Niebuhr's "Christ transforming culture" in such a way that " Christian love must always be in the ascendancy in any synthesis made with other systems of ethical insight or judgment." Although Ramsey fails to understand Christianity itself as a social structure, he does develop a brilliantly complex methodology which is best expressed in his 1962 work, *Nine Modern Moralists*.

Love Transforming Natural Law: *Nine Modern Moralists*

From the publication of *Basic Christian Ethics* to *Nine Modern Moralists*, Ramsey developed H. Richard Niebuhr's transformationist theme. He continued the quest for a transcendent grounding of human nature that would secure the individual, but his reflections on sexuality, property, civil rights, and warfare led him to emphasize the necessary structures through which agape worked. Two theologians became central to his work -- Jacques Maritain and Karl Barth.

A recurrent theme for Ramsey is Karl Barth's claim that creation provides the external basis for creation, and covenant is the internal basis for creation. By "creation," Ramsey includes the body and sexuality, private property, the political order, the state and its laws, and other various vocations. These aspects of creation provide the material means by which the "covenant" is lived out.

But what does Ramsey mean by "the covenant?" Is it a general category establishing an abstract ethical principle? Yes -- insofar as it is understood as "fellow humanity" where what it means to be for another is not spelled out. But the purpose of Ramsey's analysis of the body, property, and vocations is to produce an ethic that takes seriously the materiality of human existence and avoids abstraction. The covenant upon which Christian faith is predicated employs creaturely, bodily means for our participation in it. Of course, the covenant does exist without us because the Trinity provides its internal basis. Yet creation gives us concrete opportunities to participate in the covenant.

This is surely Ramsey's central point; given this point, his analysis of the body, property and vocations fruitfully expresses our covenant participation. Had he simply made this point, his ethics would have avoided the cumbersome discussions of theoretical method that lead ethics astray into a metaphysical wasteland. Alas, the temptation to cover ethics with a metaphysical garment of skin seduced Ramsey as well. Thus, while admitting his indebtedness to Barth's theology, he also lodges a rather severe criticism of Barth that creates room for his own philosophical development of love transforming natural law.

> The development of a philosophy of law and an analysis of "natural justice" on the basis of covenant creation is imperative even for a Barthian theological ethics. It is not enough simply to speak of "church law" or the human law developed within the community of believers as "exemplary law" that may provide indirect guidance for the political order where "some form of law is sought and found in an attempted movement from the worse to better." Before and while this may be true, creation-covenant may provide criteria for this movement of secular law from worse to better.[97]

Dissatisfied with Barthian claims such as "what the Christian community owes to the world is not a law or ideal but the Gospel,"[98] Ramsey sought something more (or less?). He did not disagree with Barth that by the Church being the Church, it renders service to the world; but he saw no danger in rendering service to the world through giving that which was not the Church, i.e. a "law or ideal," insofar as it was transformed by love.

What is the danger in creating a philosophy for the "world?" Unlike the majority of liberal Protestants (and current liberal Catholics), Ramsey was not concerned that the Barthian Church/world split would abandon the world and make the Church "sectarian." As he mentioned on many occasions, he was more than willing to be "sectarian" if the need arose, or if it were possible to do so, for the sake of the faith. But Ramsey was too Barthian to make the false assumption that the effectiveness of the Church's ministry was found in its relevance to the world. Ramsey did not find the "sectarian" appeal dangerous; he sincerely held that Christianity could address the world, using the world's categories such as law, statecraft, and medicine,[99] and transform those categories so faith would not be endangered. For this reason he could put together two most unlikely bedfellows -- Karl Barth and Jacques Maritain. His indebtedness to, and advocacy of, both their positions should send any systematic theologian into a fit of apoplexy. Both can be advocated by Ramsey because of "love transforming natural law." This position receives its most extended development in Ramsey's *Nine Modern Moralists*.

Nine Modern Moralists narrates the natural law's radical revision. Ramsey states, "what is attempted here is certainly not the complete construction of a Christian social ethic. Yet everywhere the thread of connection should be discernible. The unifying theme may be stated as 'Christ transforming the natural law'."[100] By "Christ transforming the natural law" Ramsey has in mind the revisions of the natural law he himself devised during the decade of the fifties. For this reason, the structure of *Nine Modern Moralists* is significant. What the reader finds here is something of an intellectual autobiography. The chapters are a compendium of influences on Christian ethics in general, and Ramsey's work in particular, post World War II.

The shape of the argument follows Ramsey's development since his dissertation. First, Dostoevski's theism provides the substance for Ramsey's clarion call sounded at the end of his dissertation, "the philosophic watchword of our generation may well be 'back to idealism and on to theism'." Dostoevski's theism answers the question, "What does it mean for a human being, possessed as he is of human or 'finite freedom' to attempt from his heart to live by and live out the thought that for him there is no God?"[101] "God" establishes limits or boundaries against which humanity fights in vain. A Raskolnikov character who steps over these boundaries will find that due to his own essential nature, his step is an act of self-destruction. Thus, the chapters on Dostoyevski, like *Nine Modern Moralists* itself, develop an anthropology where "the most significant thing about a human being is his reference to the Transcendent."

While Ramsey develops an anthropology, it is intended to be a Christocentric one. He agrees with Barth that Christian theology suffers from "independent anthropological statements." But for Ramsey this does not call into question anthropology, it only results from "an insufficiently Christianized way of interpreting man's existence before God." It results from the effort of allowing the "natural" alone to describe humanity. In contrast to this, Ramsey understands his own anthropology as a Christianized one.

Ramsey has conceded Barth's criticism of anthropology -- to a degree. As we saw earlier in *Christian Ethics and the Sit-In*, he still desires to develop an ethic beyond the limits of the Church's dogmatic.

> Still there may be a danger that some who follow Barth's lead will fail to elaborate fully a doctrine of man or to articulate an ethic which results from the proclamation of the gospel and which may serve to clarify the church's proclamation. In short, it may be said there is peril in making too few *dependent* anthropological statements.[102]

Nine Modern Moralists is Ramsey's attempt to honor Barth's critique of independent anthropological statements, and at the same time develop an anthropology, Christocentrically dependent. Thus, to put it in terms which do not do justice to the complexity of his thought, he seeks to make Barth and Maritain lie down together. This intent is expressed in the term "love transforming natural law."

Given Ramsey's commitment to philosophical idealism, the reader should be suspicious that Ramsey's anthropology will be Christianized. After all, the anthropology was in place long before the Barthian emphasis. Be that as it may, Ramsey's stated purpose is to give us an anthropology "always viewed in the light of Christ;" he does not seek simply to inscribe philosophical idealism, or a bland theism, into Christianity.

What we find in this 1962 exposition is a remarkable success at a difficult enterprise. The enterprise is difficult, for as Ramsey himself suggests, the effort to "transform" other philosophical discourses often ends in an unacceptable synthesis.[103] But neither is "transformation simply replacement of the moral law." A moral law can exist in a given culture, independent of Christianity such as "rape is wrong," which does not explicitly depend on Christianity, but which Christianity can inscribe within its own narrative. Jacques Maritain provides for Ramsey the conceptual tools by which this is accomplished, although even Maritain's work is not simply synthesized into Ramsey's; he transforms Maritain's integralism by removing it from a Catholic ecclesiological context and situating within a Protestant ecclesiology that emphasizes freedom of speech.

Before allowing Maritain to present a "natural law" to be transformed, Ramsey moves from Dostoevski's theism and examines Marx's materialism, Sartre's atheistic existentialism, Reinhold Niebuhr's theistic existentialism, H. Richard Niebuhr's transformism, Tillich's monistic natural law, and Brunner's dualistic natural law. Each of these moralists furnishes Ramsey the opportunity to defend his transcendentally grounded anthropology and show the necessity for some natural law.

Ramsey's transcendentally grounded anthropology receives an obvious criticism from Marx's materialism.[104] In response to Marx's materialism, Ramsey makes a telling admission.

> This is a difficult point for me to make, for it happens that I hold another philosophical view of human nature. Yet I have to admit that what the Bible affirms is not the primacy of the spiritual over the material, or the power of ideals in history, but the rule of God over all. It affirms that "God comes first, and not man," but it is not the least concerned to argue that thought precedes the act in man's individual and historical existence.[105]

This is a telling admission because Ramsey states that his own anthropology is not materialist. In his dissertation he did hold to the primacy of the spiritual over the material, and of thought over act. The very structure of *Nine Modern Moralists* continues to presuppose the "power of ideals in history." Yet Ramsey now admits that Marx's materialism is more "biblical" than his own idealism. And he suggests that the claim "God comes first and not humanity" cannot be equated with idealistic philosophy. These admissions qualify his methodology. No longer will he begin with an ultimate principle and work from it as H. Richard

Niebuhr taught him. Now he begins with particular responses and works from there, such as he did in *Christian Ethics and the Sit-In*. Ethics begins with the material at hand rather than with universal principles.

While this admission qualifies Ramsey's method, it does not qualify his anthropological foundation. Finally, for Ramsey, "Marxism departs significantly from the Bible in denying the importance of the Divine appointment to which man is called." And that is because Marxism denies the grounding of the self in a transcendent reference. Without this, Ramsey is convinced, totalitarianism is waiting at the door. Thus he falsely suggests that "the lack of any transcendent point of reference deprives the Marxist of any capacity for self-criticism,"[106] and falsely assumes that a theistic grounding of anthropology provides a hedge against totalitarianism rather than a legitimation for absolutist practices.

If Marx's materialism presents a modification within Ramsey's anthropological framework, Sartre's atheistic existentialism completely rejects it.[107] With Sartre, the transcendence of the human being does not reflect the Imago Dei so much as a hell from which there is no escape. Ramsey recognizes this and writes,

> Man is a Look-looking, and then by virtue of the Other he becomes a Look-looked-at, to escape which he can only look back and transform that other Look in turn into a Look-looked-at. He is a transcendence-transcending which becomes then a transcendence transcended and in return transcends that other transcendence. He is a surpassing-surpassed and then surpasses that surpassing; a pursuing-pursued which then, as a pursued-pursuing, momentarily overcomes that other pursuit.[108]

Ramsey agrees sufficiently with Sartre to use his existentialism as a critique of Buber's I-Thou intersubjectivity as well as Kieerkegard's and Niebuhr's analysis of anxiety.[109] This criticism represents Ramsey's faithfulness to Barth (and unfaithfulness to Niebuhr.) The notion of "transcendence alone" cannot insure a Christianized anthropology. Something more is needed and the more is not to be found until the final chapter when, as a criticism even of Maritain, Ramsey writes, "the naturalistic interpretation is not yet an adequate account of morality; the question to be raised is whether there is not needed some more *explicit theological* premise *active* in the moral life itself in order to sustain any such ethic or to comprehend it."[110]

What Sartre does provide Ramsey is an essentialist anthropology, even if it is only *opto ergo sum*. Thus, for Ramsey, even Sartre gives some account of a "natural law." Moreover, if Sartre's atheistic existentialism offers a natural law, then how much more will Reinhold Niebuhr's theistic existentialism despite his protests to the contrary. As Ramsey writes on his chapter on Niebuhr:

> Fortunately or unfortunately, we today have a way of finding out whether anything akin to the traditional theory of natural law still remains central in a man's thought or to what extent this still governs what he has to say about man and morals. We can compare him with a viewpoint which in fact drops out altogether every remnant of the natural law and breaks decisively with the Western tradition in this regard: the viewpoint of atheistic existentialism. By contrast with Jean-Paul Sartre, the divergence of views among Christian theologians appears as only a family quarrel over the *meaning* of the natural law or the moral law God gives us for living in his human family.[111]

Ramsey now introduces the work of Reinhold Niebuhr, H. Richard Niebuhr, Tillich and Brunner to show how each of them are natural law theologians even if they quarrel over the meaning of the "natural."

Niebuhr is a natural law theologian because he understands "love as the law of human freedom and justice as the application of this law."[112] Yet Ramsey makes an important critique of Niebuhr's "natural law as love." Niebuhr "adjectifies" love in terms of self-sacrifice and thus "gains too easy a victory, and by a somewhat mistaken strategy, in his campaign to demonstrate the (relevant) impossibility of love." For Niebuhr then, according to Ramsey, love does not sufficiently exist in the structures of earthly existence.

Rather than love as self-sacrifice, Ramsey writes, "Love is just love."

> Love is just love, the genuine article, for which perhaps one univocal word should be reserved. The word "love" is surely not deserving of use for the self's relation to itself; . . . love is a bond of life with life by which one person affirms the being and well-being of another.

"Love" is a substantive that defines one's commitment to one's neighbor. Because this is "love," we need on occasion to "sacrifice the sacrifice" through our participation in vocations and communities for the good of our neighbors. In a passage we have seen before, as early as the dissertation, Ramsey writes:

> . . . are not nations, in the light of their total task in behalf of their own people and all the future generations and their possible contributions to the community of mankind, duty-bound to "sacrifice the sacrifice"? At least we can all be thankful that Themosticles persuaded the Athenians to use the funds from a newly discovered vein of silver in their mines, not for democratic distribution and consumption, but for building a stronger navy by which they were able to hold off the power of the

despotism from the East for a few more decades in which Greek culture came to flower.[113]

The seeds for the undoing of this argument are found in Ramsey's own work. We already witnessed the powerful critique he made of Niebuhrian realists who failed to interpenetrate means and ends and based moral decisions on future "possible contributions." Yet, in this argument, Ramsey acts the part of the worse Niebuhrian pragmatist. Future consequences legitimate Themosticles' actions, even if retrospectively.

Clearly Ramsey is correct in his criticism of Niebuhr's adjectification of love. But his own "substantiation" of love is woefully inadequate. All it denotes is a purely formal relation between the self and the neighbor that holds out the neighbors "well-being" as the purpose for the relation. This is deeply troubling because this defines the thrust of biblical morality for Ramsey, and it is purely formal. The problem with mere form is not that it is amoral, but that it is immoral. Form always encapsulates some space, even if that space is emptiness. An empty life or an empty relationship is immoral because its content is barren. The content will either remain barren or be replaced with other contents which then get legitimated because of the form. Insofar as Ramsey does not give a specific shape to the Christian life, but only this formal account of a relation, his position potentially legitimates non-Christian contents. This is proven to be the case once we see that the form is filled in with the content of free speech.

Ramsey offers another important critique of Niebuhr; Niebuhr's method follows more decisively a traditional theory of natural law than does even Maritain's. Because Niebuhr proposed that "justice 'points toward' and finds 'fulfillment' in love," Ramsey suspects his notion of justice may be "grounded in structural reason and nature, independent of love which transcends these things." Thus Niebuhr has an absolute natural law -- the law of love, which exists outside history and culture, and then there are "principles of equality and justice by which love takes shape for application to historical situations" akin to the *jus gentium* and finally there is civil law.[114] If this is the case for Niebuhr, then Ramsey finds him "more the rationalist than Maritain the Thomist."

Ramsey dispenses with this notion of natural law in Niebuhr and finds elsewhere in Niebuhr's work a more acceptable natural law that grounds justice fully within the law of love. This is the Niebuhr Ramsey finds useful as a radical revisionist of the natural law because,

> it is of considerable importance to establish once for all that the relevant principles of social ethics have their ground and source in the law of love, and not in the concession of a degree of validity in the older forms

of natural law nor simply as the products of technical reason contriving temporary "schemes" of justice.[115]

If Reinhold Niebuhr can speak about justice without speaking about love, then he is subject to the Barthian critique of offering independent anthropological statements. Yet if "justice" can be spoken of "in light of Christ," then Ramsey can develop, so the argument goes, Christologically dependent anthropological statements. Once again we are moving from Barth to Maritain.

For Ramsey, the question is this -- does the conversion Christ calls for deconstruct all fixed norms (a position Ramsey held in *Basic Christian Ethics*) or can "absolute or unchanging truths" exist even "in light of the absoluteness of God in Christ." In other words, must Christ always transform culture, or is there present in cultures and trans-culturally "relationally objective norms" that could be "permanently valid." While Maritain's work holds forth "the universal and permanent validity of certain ethical principles or hierarchy of values relative to the structure of man or to his mode of being in the world,"[116] H. Richard Niebuhr's reliance upon relativism made ethics dependent upon culture. Ramsey moves toward Maritain and away from H. Richard's relativism because "the ethics of the natural or moral law" maintains the possibility of a trans-cultural reality even if it is always known culturally.

> It cannot be too strongly emphasized that there would never have been any reason prevailing in culture if men of the past who placed a degree of confidence in reason had been persuaded theirs was only cultural or historical reason.[117]

Yet this quote falsely assumes on the one hand that truths exist outside of culture, and on the other, that within the particularities of cultures Truth cannot be found. The first assumption is a residual effect of Ramsey's idealism; the "men of the past" create ideals that withstand the test of time and are truthful regardless of culture or history because they are grounded in something which transcends culture and history. This "grounding" is made explicit in Ramsey's statement, "men of the past who have championed right against wrong have ordinarily conceived their task as having in view what was most decidedly not the work of their own minds alone."[118] The second false assumption and the first one are connected. Because something must exist trans-culturally for it to be true, then if something can be demonstrated to be culturally or historically particular, it cannot be True.

The problem with such an understanding of truth is two-fold. First it assumes Christianity is not a culture; it is not a social history produced and reproduced in each generation. Second it implies a split between

"Christ" and Jesus peculiar to liberal Protestant Theology. The Christ of faith is a metaphysical reality that exists beyond the particularities of Jesus of Nazareth and is therefore not bound by those particularities. Ramsey perpetuates this split when he charges H. Richard Niebuhr with making Christ "subject to a religious and a historical relativism -- so much so that the reader may occasionally wonder whether in the long run Christ transforms relativism or relativism transforms Christ." Certainly at this point, Ramsey left Barth behind. Barth's revolution in theology insisted on the inseparability of Christ and Jesus. God does, in fact, become found in the religious and historical relativism of a Jew from Nazareth. As Barth constantly reminded us, we must never forget that when God assumes flesh, it is Jewish flesh God assumes. Rather than grounding anthropology in a transcendent reference, Ramsey should have stressed the "humanity of God." This gives us a Christological reading of human nature, with all its cultural and historical vicissitudes, instead of seeking a foundation outside of history for an anthropology. It also requires a historical and material account of those practices that preserve this reading of human nature. Central to the Christian Gospel is the assumption that one need not look outside culture and history to find God, but God is only found in a particular culture and history subject to all the vicissitudes that entails. And that history cannot be named "western tradition," but only Judaism and the Christian Church.

This is not to say that Ramsey's criticism of H. Richard Niebuhr's relativism is inappropriate. He rightly saw that the way H. Richard had framed the question marginalized the presence of Christ in history. But H. Richard could frame the question of the "enduring problem" as the relationship between Christ and culture only because he also worked with a liberal Protestant Christology that separated "Christ" from "Jesus."[119] Think how differently his book would have been had it been called "Jesus and Culture." Thus while Ramsey correctly critiques this marginalization of Christ from history, he does not see that the problem lies with the way the question is framed, and Ramsey continues to ask the same question, "The chief problem for Christian social ethics is how we are to understand the relation between the law of nature and the righteousness of the covenant."[120] This question is a variant of Niebuhr's question -- how do we relate Christ and culture, which is in turn a variant of Troeltsch's -- how do we relate the essentially religious and non-social Jesus and early Church with a social ethic? The problem with Troeltsch's question is that it began with the assumption that the early church was not a social movement, but a religious and ethical ideal.[121] The question then becomes how does this ideal relate and influence the social order. Thus at the beginning of this question was the assumption of the essence of Christianity as something independent of cultural and historical political realities.

Ramsey perpetuates Troeltsch's question. On the one hand we have the natural law, the knowledge of which is always subject to the relativity of history. On the other hand we have the righteousness of the covenant -- the "immediate presence of God." The temptation for those who live within the righteousness of the covenant is to "ignore the fact that they live within the ordered forms of *some* natural community which is based, in part at least, upon agreement as to inherent principles of justice based on creation."[122] For Ramsey, this "natural community" based on consent is first and foremost the nation-state. Yet what Jew would fail to understand the synagogue as just such a "natural community?" And what Christian would not understand the Church as the same? Why is church and synagogue not an "ordered form of natural community," but the state is? Why should the state be so privileged over these other communities? And what kind of "natural community" is "based upon agreement?" The question assumes that a natural community will be a democratic institution in charge of ruling a people. Thus, the question boils down to the relationship between the Church and the United States' political government, and the practices of liberal democracies constrain the question of Christian social ethics. That this is so is evident in Ramsey's work where he finds the intersection between the righteousness of the covenant and the natural community preeminently taking place in "the court," or wherever there is "unlimited discussion of free men."[123] Here the form of his definition of love gets filled in with the contents of J. S. Mill's liberalism.[124]

In his chapter on Tillich and Brunner, Ramsey gives two answers to his question. Tillich resolves the tension between the natural and the righteousness of the covenant by eliding both into an ontology. But "Tillich's ontology blunts the transformation of steadfast love."[125] Brunner, on the other hand, resolves the problem of righteousness and the natural by not resolving it at all; his is a dualistic account. Neither Brunner nor Tillich satisfactorily resolve the question of covenant righteousness and the natural. Nevertheless, Ramsey finds in both Tillich and Brunner an appropriate direction. For neither of them begins with "justice" in and of itself,[126] but with a "justice" that has been "already transformed" by love.[127] This is a theme we witnessed in the chapters on sexual ethics. Herein lies a distinctive feature of Ramsey's ethics; he realized that the very description of the "natural (or justice)" presented for transformation within Christian ethics could not help but be transformed even in its presentation. To assume a "natural" independent of the distinctiveness of Christianity, or grounded in ontology, was a subterfuge. Ramsey closes down any space for a dualistic account of natural political existence and the righteousness of the covenant.

In closing down this space, through the help of Maritain, Ramsey "wrecks" the traditional deductive theory of natural law:

> ... knowledge of the natural law no longer is a matter of reflecting upon essential human nature in abstraction from variable factual conditions and social relationships. Knowledge by connaturality, congeniality, inclination arises only vis-à-vis quite concrete conditions of fact.[128]

The natural law for Ramsey is ontologically intrinsic to the being of every person; it is a "permanent *nisus* or tendency of the soul of man."[129] Yet, as we have just witnessed, the natural law is only known in concrete, historical situations. This is a wonderful use of Maritain. Ramsey has given us a "natural" that is not a category of a universal rationality, but is an inclination known only in the specific activities of people. He gives us an account of an essential human nature, but it can only be known through particular practices.

This is quite illuminating; and should put to rest the popular criticism of Ramsey that he worked from a traditional deductive theory of natural law, and a universal account of human nature. The way Ramsey develops it, we need not fear an essential human nature. Essential human nature creates problems only when we assume it results from a neutral epistemology, and thus the epistemology becomes secondary to the ontology. Ramsey quite rightly realizes you cannot begin with the ontology of the natural law; the ontology is only a necessary assertion making possible the knowledge of the natural. Basic inclination causes a person to act (or not act) in one way or another, but this is known only when the action or inaction occurs. Thus the "inclination" is known *post facto*, and these *post facto* inclinations become "deposits in our law" that create a tradition and operate as a pedagogue for training in moral virtue.[130]

The emphasis on ontology is a result of Ramsey's shift toward realism, but the ontology does little work for him. He does not develop a traditional deductive natural law schema based on that which *is* universally true. Instead, he goes the complete opposite direction and begins only with a rationality known *in media res*. Thus, he neither privileges realism over idealism, nor idealism over realism. His ontology is only necessary for the possibility of his epistemology that finds the "natural" in the "prism of the case," becomes expressed in law, and then changes as new cases are encountered. In a brilliant philosophical move, Ramsey avoids the twin problems of nihilism and foundationalism. He refuses to elide all reality into language, while at the same time he rejects making linguistic descriptions merely phenomena grounded in a deeper real, or mere propositions directly corresponding to the real.

The central difficulty I find in Ramsey's work has nothing to do with his development of natural law, but with the tradition that reads the natural for him. Ramsey makes two crucial criticisms of Maritain's work. First, Maritain himself does not follow through on the implications of the natural law known only by inclination. This criticism leads Ramsey to his brilliant philosophical move. But the second criticism is troubling. Maritain still depends upon the Roman Catholic Church for the publication of the natural law, and Ramsey finds this unacceptable. With this second critique Ramsey re-opens the old space for a potentially neutral "natural," and undoes the brilliant philosophic critique he gave us.

Ramsey has already made linguistic descriptions central to his account of the natural through the need for concrete particulars. But language can never be abstracted from a social context. Thus when he criticizes Roman Catholic natural law from "guaranteeing the conclusion in advance" and removing "the matter from the province of rational inquiry and discussion which were said to be quite sufficient to establish it,"[131] he re-visits the possibility of a natural law known through a universal rationality rather than inclination rooted in a tradition. Then Ramsey falsely assumes that "unlimited discussion" will serve decisions about the natural better than a sociological positivism. And the context for the unlimited discussion becomes the western tradition of jurisprudence, which is identical with Ramsey's "Protestant view of the Church."

> . . . a possible Protestant view of the fundamental nature of moral and legal decisions based on natural justice (or law) has a great deal in common with the jurisprudential understanding of judicial reasoning and moral decision in legal cases. Both accent personal responsibility for making decisions without submitting the matter to any ecclesiastical or sociological positivism.[132]

What we have here is another deceptive sleight of hand. Ramsey believes he has moved the context for natural law from an "ecclesiastical or sociological positivism," to a neutral realm of unlimited discussion. What in fact he has actually done is exchanged one sociological positivism, the Roman Catholic Church, for another, the United States Judiciary.

Notes

1. *Nine Modern Moralists*, (New York: Unversity Press of America, 1961), p. 19.

2. See Augustine *Enchridion*, chap. IX-XI, and Aquinas, *Summa Theologica I,I* q. 49.

3. See Ramsey, *The Just War*, pp. 7-8, "the use of force is the *esse* of politics, and it is inseparable from the *bene esse* of politics." Contrast this with Aquinas where evil can only have an accidental cause, I.I, q. 49 art. 1. If anyone objects to my argument that I am neglecting the fact that Ramsey does not find the use of force as an evil, I would stand with Aquinas in arguing that "evil" is not simply a matter of human action, i.e. fault, but also a matter of pain. Thus, the infliction of pain is evil. Is there a use of force which does not inflict pain? My argument here does not argue for pacifism, but it argues against Ramsey's making force and violence the essence of politics through an ontology of tragedy. This is what is unacceptable.

4. For a further discussion of this see chapter four where I give evidence of Ramsey's selective appropriation of Augustine on just war. For an example of a nuance on the use of force Ramsey looses with respect to Aquinas see *Summa Theologica II*, Q. 40 art 1, reply to objection 2.

5. Ramsey papers, box 35.

6. Ibid.

7. Ramsey papers, box 16.

8. Ramsey papers, box 35. "First Church Review," Jan. 2, 1943.

9. Ibid., "Garrett Tower," Nov. 1943.

10. The title to this essay is not Ramsey's but Reinhold Niebuhr's. Niebuhr needed an essay and Ramsey sent him this one. Niebuhr took it, gave it this title, and published it. April, 1943, *Christianity and Crisis*.

11. Compare this quote with that on p. 188 in chapter five, "Christian vocation," in *Basic Christian Ethics*. Ramsey claims that this chapter depicts, in personal terms, his transformation from pacifism. It will be discussed in detail below.

12. *Basic Christian Ethics*, (Chicago: The University of Chicago Press, 1977), p. 176.

13. Ibid., p. 177.

14. Ibid., p. 172. Notice that Ramsey understands a continuity to Christian tradition concerning participation in war because Ambrose as well as earlier thinkers were only offering a "general strategy of Christian love." This essentializing of tradition will be critiqued in chapter four.

15. *Basic Christian Ethics*, p. 182.

16. Ibid., p. 162.

17. Ibid., p. 171.

18. Ibid., p. 184.

19. Ibid., p. 179.

20. Ibid., p. 165

21. An important reason Ramsey used Nietzche's critique was also to suggest that even though agape as a norm was generated from Jesus' false eschatological understanding, the norm was nevertheless valid. This is his "genetic fallacy" argument which he later understood as a mistake. He felt as though he could honestly look at how agape was manufactured and still hold to it as the essence of the Christian life.

22. See also Ramsey's introduction to Vahanian's *The Death of God*.

23. Nietzche, *The Genealogy of Morals*, (New York: The Modern Library, 1977), I, 14.

24. Ramsey papers, box 8, correspondence with Joseph Fletcher, March 5, 1953, (my emphasis).

25. Scott Davis, "'Et Quod Vis Fac': Paul Ramsey and Augustinian Ethics," *Journal of Religious Ethics*, vol. 19, 2, p. 47

26. Ramsey did publish two edited works during this eleven year period, the Niebuhr festschrift and Jonathan Edward's *Freedom of the Will*.

27. A version of the chapter on Augustine was published in the *Journal of Religious Ethics* 16/1.

28. Chapter three, p. 103.

29. see chapter two, p. 41.

30. chapter three, p. 88.

31. chapter two, p. 52.

32. chapter two, pp. 41-2.

33. Augustine's "The Good of Marriage," p. 20.

34. chapter two, p. 39.

35. Ibid., p. 77.

36. Ibid., p. 80-1.

37. chapter one, p. 2, 6, 11-12.

38. chapter three, p. 68, my emphasis. How interesting that someone who was editing Jonathan Edward's *Freedom of the Will* could make this claim.

39. Ibid.

40. In *Nine Modern Moralists*, the work to which we are headed in this chapter, Ramsey claims, "Without identifying Christ with liberal democracy, it may be affirmed that the growth of democracy in the 17th century was due in part to the Christ transforming culture motif in Puritan Protestantism."

41. See Jacques Ellul's *Anarchy and Christianity*, pp. 45-85. Although it is interesting, and very suggestive, I do not find Ellul's argument convincing. I do find it more convincing than C. S. Lewis's.

42. see John Milbank's *Theology and Social Theory*, (Basil Blackwell, 1990).

43. chapter one, p. 15.

44. For a critique of the language of "consent" in male-female sexual relationships, see Catharine A. MacKinnon's "Privacy v. Equality: Beyond Roe v. Wade," in *Feminism Unmodified*.

45. chapter one, p. 9. Had Ramsey a more fully developed doctrine of the Trinity, this point could have even been more powerfully made. The covenant upon which creation rests is not simply the covenanting activity of God with Israel and in Jesus, but the love of Father, Son and Holy Spirit. The Trinity is, as John Milbank suggests, "The transcendental coding of difference as peace." Thus Ramsey's point could be more powerful in that God not only loves in such a way that God "cherishes the otherness of the other" created beings, but God in Himself is a cherishing of the otherness of the other persons. See Milbank's *Theology and Social Theory.*

46. *Christian Ethics and the Sit-In,* (New York: Association Press, 1961), p. xiii.

47. Ibid., p. 18.

48. Ibid., p. 17.

49. Ibid., p. 18.

50. See John Howard Yoder's "The War of the Lamb," in *The Politics of Jesus,* (Grand Rapids, Michigan: William B. Eerdmans Publishing Co. 1972).

51. *Christian Ethics and the Sit-In,* p. 113.

52. Ibid., p. 107

53. Ibid., p. 63.

54. Ibid., p. 104

55. Ibid., p. 105.

56. *War and the Christian Conscience,* Durham, North Carolina: Duke University Press, 1961), p. 146

57. Ibid., p. 3

58. Ibid.

59. Ibid., p. xxiii

60. Ibid., p. xxii.

61. Niebuhr, *Christian Realism and Political Problems,* (Fairfield: Augustus M. Keller Publisher, 1977), p. 119.

62. Ibid., p. 120.

63. *War and the Christian Conscience,* p. 6.

64. Niebuhr, p. 132.

65. *War and the Christian Conscience,* p. 7.

66. Ramsey's claim of analyzing "intrinsic" means must be approached cautiously. While he seems to be saying that you analyze the act itself, he never analyzes the act apart from the "specific limited end." Thus his "intrinsic analysis" is not so much an analysis of an act separated from an end, but an analysis of an "act" within the context of a specifiable end. That end is given by his Christian tradition.

67. Ibid., p. 8

68. Ibid., p. 159.

69. Ibid., p. 16

70. This is not the last word to be said concerning Ramsey's use of "tradition." In the final chapter, I will further explain how he used "tradition." There I will critique the Promethean power it offered him.

71. Ibid., p. 32.

72. Ramsey calls this "Augustinian." I will challenge this reading of Augustine. Also, while in theory, Ramsey supports no "single polity" because of the relativity of justices, in practice this relativity results in a commitment to the nation-state system as a competing balance of forces.

73. *The Just War*, (New York: University Press of America, 1983), p. 178-9. The difference between "a view of the universal" and "a universal view" comes from H. Richard Niebuhr. Niebuhr's relativism required no universal view. Ramsey's critique of Niebuhr's relativism did not extend to a political order which envisioned political society as something other than a relativistic competing balance of forces.

74. Ibid., pp. 397-8.

75. In the next chapter, we will see that Ramsey actually sees this limit to political society as part of a natural law intrinsic to political society. In so doing, he privileges democratic governments as divinely instituted in a way that does not fit with the best of his own analysis

76 . Ramsey says this himself in *Speak Up For Just War Or Pacifism*. "The fundamental move, out of Christian love, to *resistance* of evil was made in my *Basic Christian Ethics* (1950; ch. 5 pp. 153-57, 166-90), before I had read the landmark article by John C. Ford, S. J. on 'The Morality of Obliteration Bombing," which decisively influenced my chapter on "The Genesis of Noncombatant Immunity" in *War and the Christian Conscience*. Speak Up For Just War Or Pacifism, p. 72.

77. see *The Just War*, p. xii.

78. Fr. John C. Ford, "The Morality of Obliteration Bombing," *Theological Studies*, V, 3 (Sept. 1944), p. 268.

79. Ibid., p. 269.

80. Which for Grotius not even God can change. See Grotius, *The Rights of War and Peace*, (Westport, Connecticut: Hyperion Press, Inc., 1979), Bk. I, chap. I, X.

81. *War and the Christian Conscience*, p. 3.

82. *Basic Christian Ethics*, p. 76.

83. Ramsey papers, box 35.

84. *War and the Christian Conscience*, p. xxi.

85. Letter to Fr. Pesce, March 11, 1970.

86. *War and the Christian Conscience*, p. 113.

87. Ibid., p. 93.

88. Ibid., p. 110

89. This criticism is necessary to keep in mind in any fair examination of Ramsey's controversial book, *Who Speaks For The Church?*, (Nashville: Abingdon Press, 1967). It will be examined more closely in the next chapter.

90. Ramsey papers, box 31. Notice how Ramsey failed to comment on Yoder's central point about "materiality."

91. The use of "material" is obviously mine, but I think it consistent with Ramsey. The question is if the "materiality" upon which the Gospel as ideal worked was too rigidly defined and the Gospel itself was not understood sufficiently as "material."

92. Ramsey, *Basic Christian Ethics*, p. 17.

93. Interestingly, this interpretation of Ramsey's transformism has a close ally in John Howard Yoder. In *The Politics of Jesus*, Yoder writes, 'The pattern [of the politics of Jesus] is thus uniformly one of *creative transformism*, The early Christians accepted the common sense analysis of Stoicism that the ethical duties of the Christian could best be stated with reference to living up to the meaning of one's role in society. Yet the meaning of that role was changed in its form by the encounter with the apodictic imperative style of Old Testament law, and changed in substance by the stance of servanthood derived from the example and the teaching of Jesus himself. His motto of revolutionary subordination, of willing servanthood in the place of domination, enables the person in a subordinate position in society to accept and live within that status without resentment, at the same time that it calls upon the person in the superordinate position to forsake or renounce all domineering use of his status. This call is then precisely not a simple ratification of the stratified society into which the gospel has come" (my emphasis, p. 190-1). Unlike James Gustafson who argues that Yoder "develops Christian and biblical ethics very differently from Ramsey" (*Theocentric Ethics*, (Chicago: University of Chicago Press, 1984), vol. II, p. 88), I think Ramsey and Yoder's development of Christian ethics is so similar that it is quite difficult to adjudicate between Ramsey's just war and Yoder's pacifism. Unfortunately, overlooking the similarity of their two positions because of the difference of their views on war has precluded a more thoroughgoing searching of the theological similarity upon which their two positions rest.

94. *War and the Christian Conscience*, p. xvii (my emphasis).

95. See John Howard Yoder's *The Politics of Jesus*. Yoder's claim that the early Christian movement is a politic so deeply qualifies the discipline of Christian ethics that few have either understood it or attempted to take it seriously. Thus the discipline continues to be bound by Troeltsch's distinction between the early Christian movement as personal and the post-Constantinian church as social.

96. Ernst Troeltsch, *The Social Teaching of the Christian Churches* (The University of Chicago Press: Chicago and London, 1981) p. 39.

97. *Christian Ethics and the Sit-In*, p. 22.

98. Karl Barth, *Church Dogmatics,,* IV.2, (Edinburgh: T & T Clark, 1978), p. 721

99. One reason he thought this could be done was because these categories traditionally belonged to the church first, thus they contained seeds for another transformation.

100. *Nine Modern Moralists*, p. 2-3.

101. Ibid., p. 11. The second chapter on Dostoevski was first published in 1951.

102. Ibid., p. 56.

103. See Ibid., p. 171.

104. The essay on Marx was first published in 1959.

105. *Nine Modern Moralists*, p. 61.

106. Ibid., p. 64.

107. This essay on Sartre is, most likely, the essay Ramsey referred to in his aborted book on sexual ethics.

108. Op. cit., p. 80.

109. Ibid., p. 74.

110. Ibid., p. 226. This "theological premise" is problematic. What we will find is that the problem Ramsey runs into is that his more active theological premise is an extreme notion of Protestant grace that overlooks the fact that grace needs a history and social context. Ramsey will not concede the Roman Church as that context, but he does concede the U.S. Supreme Court as the context.

111. Ibid., p. 111.

112. Ibid., p. 130. There is some interesting correspondence between Ramsey and R. Niebuhr over situationalism. When Ramsey was soliciting essays for *Norm and Context in Christian Ethics*, (New York: Charles Scribners' Sons, 1968) he wrote to Niebuhr asking for an essay. On May 18, 1966 Ramsey wrote, 'The occasion, but only the occasion (like steam from the kettle) of this project was Joseph Fletcher's *Situation Ethics*. Perhaps I am overly exercised about what I regarded as a sort of flight from careful, disciplined reflection. We are swapping our birthright for a pot of message, it seems to me. Yet there is no point, and it would not be responsible, to produce a sort of *Honest to God Debate*, which is going to be more ephemeral that the original book by far. What is needed is a renewed probing of the issues and problems Fletcher's book and a number of other books and articles are raising in a somewhat superficial and sensational way." Niebuhr responded, "I have serious reasons for my negative attitude toward Joe's contextualism. I think it is taken too seriously. I trust you with your interest in both AGAPE ethics and Natural Law to do justice to the problems of the essentially Bartian antinomianism." Ramsey asked for a more definitive refusal and Niebuhr responded: "You mention my negative reply to the invitation to contribute to a symposium on Joe Fletcher's book. I was not interested partly because I thought so little of Joe's book; and partly because I am

bored with emphasizing the whole Catholic tradition of Natural Law norms which Protestants should have taken more seriously long ago." Interestingly, Niebuhr assesses his own work as "emphasizing the whole Catholic tradition of Natural Law."

113. Our Athenian military man appears again, Ibid., p. 138.

114. Ibid., p. 128.

115. Ibid., p. 125.

116. Ibid., p. 173, see also 209-210.

117. Ibid., p. 171.

118. Ibid.

119. This is evident by the separation in Niebuhr's *Radical Monotheism* between the Lordship of Jesus Christ and the Lordship of God.

120. Ibid., p. 181.

121. Troeltsch, *The Social Teaching of the Christian Churches,* vol. I, p. 40.

122. *Nine Modern Moralists,* p. 181.

123. Ibid., p. 230.

124. Notice also in the introduction to *Who Speaks for the Church* where Ramsey develops his notion of the church primarily upon the work of Mill rather than any theologian.

125. Ibid., p. 185.

126. Remember that for Ramsey "justice" is the application of love to the "natural," thus "love transforming natural law" or "love transforming justice" are terms he can use almost interchangeably.

127. See op. cit., p. 186, "My thesis, already announced is that love has already transformed Tillich's concept of justice . . . ," and p. 200 "This, in fact, has already happened in Brunner's own analysis of justice. His also is a love-transformed understanding of justice. There is no other way to explain the difference between what he says "natural justice" requires and what Aristotle would probably have said."

128. Ibid., p. 220.

129. Ibid., p. 216

130. See Ibid., p. 195.

131. Ibid., p. 227.

132. Ibid., p. 213.

3

Protestant Casuist

The criticism that ended the last chapter is not extrinsic to Ramsey's own work. As he turns his attention to issues in medicine in the 1970's, Ramsey himself opens the door for such a criticism by his stinging critiques of the United States Judiciary. Neither the church nor the state could sustain the moral tradition from which Ramsey worked. This fact brings into focus a sad state of affairs in Paul Ramsey's work; he needed a particular moral tradition, capable of sustaining *agape* as the telos for human existence. In the fifties and sixties he thought a judiciary that allowed free and unlimited discussion would provide the institutional structure for that tradition's exercise. By the seventies Ramsey no longer placed confidence in the United States Judiciary as providing space for the practice of the moral life. Where then does one go?

Ramsey was a casuist who worked from a particular tradition, but who did not have any institutional practices to sustain that tradition. He was a particularist forced to use the leveling, generalized putatively universal language of modernity in hopes that his particular tradition might find some room in the modern era. The end result is that his work is much too particular to Christianity to be useful as a common, universal politics of speech, and it is much too universal to be useful as a politics of speech for the creation of an alternative Christian community. Yet Ramsey's work does offer an alternative to the dominant ideology undergirding much of ethics, and his work waits for the creation of those institutional practices that will give it life.

For the purpose of rehabilitating a Christian ethics rooted in tradition, and challenging Christian ethics acquiescence to a secular cultural discourse, Ramsey reclaimed casuistry. "Casuistry" was a pejorative word in Protestant social ethics. Many Protestant ethicists understood "casuistry" as signifying the attempt to secure a certain particular action through a deductive application of principles. Although Ramsey allows for deductive reasoning, his method is much richer than a mere deductive process. It was a principled casuistry.

Protestant ethicists have been wary of any principled ethic. Principles led to the creation of systems which insured certainty by logical consistency, but were unable to deal adequately with the "real world." Principles constrained ethical discourse by creating a logical, deductive system that effectively removed the operation of grace from human affairs.

Freedom from "principles" defines the main thrust of Protestant social ethics in this century. Karl Barth sarcastically writes:

> [Special Ethics] gives precise and detailed information about good and evil in relation to what man has done or intends doing. And in so doing it does not tyrannise him, since the principles controlling its decisions may be tested by anyone before the court of his own conscience. If only he knows and recognises the relevant law, he is able should he ever doubt the direction given him by the moralist, to convince himself whether the latter is right and whether he may or must stand by his positive or negative judgment. As a rule, however, everyone will be grateful to the moralist for the superior knowledge with which he is able to relieve him of the often very oppressive task of making his own orientations and decisions.[1]

For Barth a deductive, principled approach is idolatrous. It assumes the place of God by claiming to know good and evil and to systematize such knowledge in the form of principles.

Emil Brunner shared at least this presupposition with Barth, "devotion to abstract principles" resulted in "un-freedom."

> But even now we have not reached the ultimate thing which has to be said about the "curse of the Law." *Legalism is unfreedom,* and this, not merely in the sense in which everyone is conscious of sin in the representatives of a typically legalistic righteousness -- as inflexibility, feverish intensity, devotion to abstract principles, but in a far deeper sense. The Good that one does simply from a sense of duty is never *the* Good. Duty and genuine goodness are mutually exclusive. Obedience due to a sense of unwilling constraint is bondage, and indeed the bondage of sin.[2]

Abstract principles were a sign of faithlessness because they violated the unencumbered freedom necessary for Christian living.

Reinhold Niebuhr also inherits and perpetuates this legalism-freedom dialectic with the concomitant result that "law equals unfreedom." Jesus rejects "Hebraic legalism."[3] And instead of the "legalistic" route, Jesus, like Reinhold Niebuhr, takes the "prophetic".

The criticisms of legalism in both the gospels and the epistles give an indirect insight into a prophetic rather than legalistic interpretation of life. The criticisms take the following forms: (a.) No law can do justice to the freedom of man in history. . . . (b.) No law can do justice to the complexities of motive which express themselves in the labyrinthine depths of man's interior life. . . . (c.) Law cannot restrain evil; for the freedom of man is such that he can make the keeping of the law the instrument of evil.[4]

A logical consequence of this freedom-legalism dialectic was Joseph Fletcher's *Situation Ethics* where love was free in every momentary decision to decide a course of action regardless of past precedents. Fletcher simply took the discourse he inherited and popularized it. A great deal of nuance was lost with its popularization, but Fletcher's alternatives in moral reasoning -- legalism, antinomianism, situationalism -- maintain obvious similarities with the way others before him set the discourse.

Casuistry as an Alternative Discourse

In Fletcher's work, "transformation" took a direction that alarmed Ramsey for the important reason that Fletcher saw the seeds of situationalism in Ramsey's *Basic Christian Ethics*. In 1965 Joseph Fletcher wrote to him, ". . . what your *Basic Christian Ethics* planted in my noggin years ago has a great deal to do with what is in this book [*Situation Ethics*]." Fletcher thought he had an ally in Ramsey. Love must be free to transform any situation. No principles were to be in ascendence over it. And this was the distinctive characteristic of Protestant social ethics.

Ramsey quickly distinguished his position from that of Fletcher's. First he published *Deeds and Rules in Christian Ethics*, and then he edited a book with Gene Outka, *Norm and Context in Christian Ethics*. Both of these works attempted to salvage an agapeic ethic from Fletcher's consequentialist reasoning. In responding to Fletcher Ramsey reconsiders the freedom-legalistic dialectic, and finds that principles do not inhibit freedom; they provide resources for both moral and immoral action. As Ramsey said in *Ethics at the Edges of Life*, those who make the rules, i.e. establish law and principles, "manifest who and where we are." Thus the assumption that we can be free from principles is illusory and dangerous.

In explaining to Fletcher his differences with the situationalists, Ramsey wrote:

> The reason I *must* , however reluctantly deal more extensively with Robinson and Lehman is because the candid issue between us is whether *agape* is expressed in *acts only* or in *rules also* , which question is generally begged; or else the structures in which human beings live are attributed to other than uniquely Christian sources of understanding (natural law, etc.) while Christians go about pretending to live in a world without principles. The latter *was* about my position in *Basic Christian Ethics*. I have come to see that *agape* can also be steadfast.[5]

Once again, Ramsey emphasizes the "structures." The world in which we live is always already structured, i.e. it always comes with principles, rules and law that define who, what, and where we are. If we assume the world is not so structured, we will only wittingly and unwittingly reproduce in our lives those principles that structure the world. Fletcher failed to see the structures, and thus, says Ramsey, "Fletcher is simply a sign of our times."[6] In opposition to the principles that structured modern life, Ramsey employed a principled casuistry. His casuistry was an alternative discourse within the dominant ethos of Christian ethics.

In response to Fletcher's work, Ramsey distances himself from the extent to which he previously freed love from all social structures. This was a necessary move because Fletcher rightly drew the conclusion from *Basic Christian Ethics* that Ramsey was an ally. Ramsey had written, "No matter how strongly we have insisted that Christian love cannot get along without searching for a social policy, the final word must place the accent again on freedom, freedom even from the social policies Christian love may have found in times past."[7] But Ramsey saw the problems with love freed from structure; *agape* became a slave to "other than uniquely Christian sources."

The principled structures through which *agape* works was not only developed in 1965 as a reaction to Fletcher. We have already seen how Ramsey's development of an ethics on the body, property, and war found "already Christianized natural structures" in which *agape* can live, move and have its being. *Nine Modern Moralists* narrated the conceptual way this worked. In the mid-sixties, as a response to the situationalist debate, Ramsey further clarifies his methodology, developing a type of casuistry that does not exclude the possibility of exceptionless principles. In so doing he finds more promise in a principled ethic and "casuistry" than the major thinkers before him in Protestant social ethics.

Ramsey found two important things. First, Barth and others had set up a straw position which they then too easily knocked down. They equated a deductive, principled approach with "casuistry." Ramsey challenged that equation. That challenge resulted in a casuistry which used principles, but did not tie them to a unilinear deductive method. Casuistry prevented a mere deductive rationality because the principles served the purpose of defining and clarifying the moral terrain. They could not insure, by way of a logical and systematic application, the production of particular actions. "Exceptionless principles" were then possible because they only help us define and clarify what is going on. They let us know that we are a people who do not rape or murder. We may not know completely what rape or murder is yet, but we know that we are never to participate in those activities. Beginning with a principled definition of who we are to be, Ramsey then utilizes his casuistry to assist us in knowing when rape and murder occur. These principles neither destroy freedom nor necessitate legalism.

The possibility of exceptionless principles, culturally mediated, also tied Ramsey's understanding of human agency to the past rather than to an "open future." Principles such as do not rape, steal or lie depend upon Ramsey's own covenant keeping with Christian tradition. Donald Evans makes clear the fact that the reason Ramsey does not see certain qualifications within principles as "exempting conditions," but as "extension or explication of the meaning" is because he was committed to a particular tradition. Evans writes,

> Consider for example, Ramsey's claim that "there could be no good charitable reason for saying that picking someone else's apples to save life belongs among the meanings of 'theft,' or for saying that mere verbal inaccuracies of speech to save life belong among the meanings of 'lying.' These were extensions and explanatory principles 'conditioned by principle itself'". I agree that it would be uncharitable to use the words "theft" and "lying" in this way if we think that our moral (legal, religious) tradition forces us to hold that theft and lying are exceptionless (unrevisable in their wording). But if we do not think this about our tradition, or have no such tradition, if we do not hold an exceptionless rule in these matters, then charity does not require us to give such an elastic meaning to "theft" or "lying."[8]

Evans rightly understands that Ramsey's casuistical use of exceptionless principles requires a commitment to his tradition. If that commitment is not present, no pressing need exists to view qualifications within principles as explications and extensions of meaning rather than "exempting conditions." Ramsey's covenant with Christian tradition makes exceptionless principles possible; Ramsey's concern that an agapeic ethic supposedly freed from principles resulted in agape's captivity to non-Christian sources makes exceptionless principles necessary.

In rethinking the use of principles, Ramsey's second conclusion is despite all the Protestant railing against casuistry, a rigid casuistical approach still defined it. The implicit, rigid casuistry of Protestant ethics was all the more insidious for it was unarticulated, and masqueraded under the honorable name of "freedom."

Because Church social pronouncements depended more on a concern to be relevant to "modernity," than to reflect critically from and to the Christian tradition, Ramsey stated that a casuistry constrained Christian ethical reflection that privileged a "secular sectarianism" and abandoned church people. Principles such as atomistic individualism, a disembodied rationality, and an engineering technologism were defining the moral terrain, but under the illusion of freedom, ethicists were operating as if those principles were not present. A great deal of Ramsey's work consisted in exposing this privileged secular sectarianism. Responses, and mainly criticisms, to the Dun Report, the Quaker pamphlet, *Towards a Quaker View of Sex*, National Council of Churches and World Council of Churches pronouncements on Viet Nam, the United Methodist Church's Board of Church and Society statements on abortion, the Roman Catholic Bishops' pastoral *The Challenge of Peace*, the United Methodist Bishops' pastoral *In Defense of Creation*, constitute a major portion of his works. He did not defend a "conservative" social position over and against these "progressive" pronouncements. He desired to show how the worst form of Christian casuistry, embodied in most of these documents, subverted an adequate delineation of the moral terrain upon which Church people had to exercise practical wisdom. He wanted to replace this mode of proceeding, which under the illusion of free moral choice perpetuated a rigid deductive approach to Christian ethics, with a more refined, and tradition-dependent, account of Christian casuistry.

A wonderful statement of this is found in a letter he wrote in 1970 concerning abortion:

> Now, I myself believe that the church is today actually a sect, and better act like one in today's world. But this properly should be a *religious sect*, not a series of political-interest-action sects. . . . To continue to act (in interest-action groups) as if our primary task were still to speak to overall social problems is to presume a Constantinian or pan-Protestant position still to be the case; this itself is a prescription for evacuation bit by bit in ever renewed efforts to stay relevant to an increasing secular society. . . . The latest (to me) distressing example of this is the pell mell race to issue statements on abortion, without first seeking the broadest and deepest discussion of this issue in distinctly Christian terms, not as a secular solution of various social and human problems.[9]

The drive to be "relevant" to pressing social issues within the confines of an un-confessed secular social structure turned the church into a secular sect abdicating its responsibility to speak a grace-informed word, formed from Christian tradition, to perplexing social problems.

Undergirding these secular sectarian statements was a denigrated form of casuistry based on personal liberty of conscience in its existential particularity. Assuming such an individual conscience, social pronouncements took on an air of moral definitiveness inimical to the Church's casuistical tradition. Once convinced that personal moral freedom undergirded social-action pronouncements apart from any external constraints, then such "openness" allowed for rigid definitions of right and wrong which bound conscience more than traditional Christian ethical reflection ever intended to do.

Ramsey thought the dominant Protestant theoretical critiques of casuistry as a constraining deductive system were at the same time the way the church went about discussing social ethics. This is explicit in his essay "Protestant Casuistry." He writes, "[T]he way Protestants think about social questions today seems inconsistent with their theological theory that casuistry must be rejected." He goes on:

> In "social ethics" as this is done by Protestant moralists and in social action pronouncements, casuistry, or getting down to cases, is often eschewed in the realm of personal moral choice. At the same time, statements about right and wrong in any of the realms of social policy are made with great alacrity; and these are regarded as incompetent or held in deep suspicion unless the proposals are formulated with enough detail to be supported before a Congressional committee and unless the moralist can demonstrate how they can be made to work.[10]

Notice the two claims in this quote. First Ramsey argues that Protestant moralists eschew casuistry. Instead they advocate personal choice -- a vulgarized form of liberty of conscience. Second he notes that even while they eschew casuistry they also pronounce definitive statements about right and wrong. While confronting casuistry head-on under the pretense that it destroys individual response, Protestant casuistry allowed a rigid form of it, similar to that which they already caricatured, slip in the back door. This rigid form of casuistry makes definitive statements about right and wrong with an "alacrity" that would shame the most legalist of all the casuists.

Ramsey's critique of the rigidity of Protestant casuistry sets a context in which to read his *Who Speaks For The Church*; for in this book he reacts against the rigidity with which Protestant social ethicists attempt to constrain the consciences of Church people. Because they speak with definitive alacrity, they convey the idea that to be Christian is to respond politically in this way and no other. They produce a text, some social action pronouncement, which is to be applied upon the life of the Church resulting in a particular action. Thus he writes, "Of late, however, ecumenical social action pronouncements have presumed to encompass the prudence of churchmen in their capacities as citizens."[11] Ramsey is not saying that the Church should not be involved in politics. Rather he is saying that the "social action curia" (Protestant social ethicists) should not see their role as the production of particulars by way of pronouncements. They should not assume a rigid, vertical approach to the moral life. This he calls the "Church and Society syndrome" -- "numerous particular pronouncements on policy questions to the consequent neglect of basic decision and action-oriented principles of ethical and political analysis."[12] This "syndrome" has two effects, first is the one already mentioned -- it is oppressive, restrictedly binding conscience. Second, it creates illusion. The production of particulars is not the role of the Church moral theologian.

Ramsey makes a distinction between the "competence" of church people and that of politicians. He argues that "maximalist church pronouncements . . . seek to assume in the name of the church decisions that belong in the realm of the state."[13] He also writes, "Let the church be the church and let the magistrate be the magistrate. Let both keep their distances. May there be less confusion of these roles."[14] Needless to say this is not the way to get invited back to sit on social action curias within the life of the church. But this is too easily misunderstood. Ramsey is not unqualifiedly endorsing a sectarian withdrawal of the Church from political affairs or an unqualified Constantinian endorsement of the machinery of the state. In fact, he is making a descriptive claim about who actually makes governmental decisions. Many theologians, working under the rubric "what God is doing in the world," falsely assume "that statesmen and other leaders are anxiously waiting for the church to give them more from the storehouse of its political wisdom."[15] They are not and it is illusory to imagine otherwise. In fact, such an assumption undercuts the ability of the church to speak for the church to the world and exercise its own practical wisdom. Falsely assuming political leaders are concerned, church agencies give concrete advice which becomes nothing but an abstraction because it is of no use to people who constitute the Church. They create "texts" which are to be imposed upon church people apart from the necessary exercise of the formed judgment of those people.

The original title of *Who Speaks for the Church* was *Speaking for the Church*. This original title was changed by the editor. The original conveys better the idea that social action committees usurp their role by applying specific texts, claiming to speak a word they cannot for they are not the church. When this occurs, no place is left for the necessary exercise of practical wisdom by the people who constitute "church".

... by concentrating on particular conclusions that can be reached, and by intervening with these in the discussion of a Christian's citizenship and the decisions that must be reached in the various sectors of society, we turn the church inside out. Christian address to the world becomes identified with a number of specific partisan positions that may or may not be correct. The church becomes a *secular* "sect" in its ecumenical ethics set over against the world as it is, instead of becoming truly a Christian sect concerned to nurture a distinctive ethos set over against an acculturated Christianity or against a culture that is no longer Christendom. This is surely a form of culture-Christianity, even if it is not that of the great cultural churches of the past. This is, indeed, the most barefaced secular sectarianism and but a new form of culture-Christianity.[16]

When such a specific text is imposed, speaking foremost to the magistrate, the "distinctive ethos" cannot be nurtured. The exercise of practical wisdom is usurped.

What practices will be capable of nurturing the "ethos" to prevent the Church from becoming a secular sect? Which tradition provides Ramsey with these practices? In continuity with *Nine Modern Moralists*, Ramsey still believes that the free exercise of unlimited discussion will best nurture Christianity's distinctive ethos. In *Who Speaks for the Church* Ramsey cites the work of John Stuart Mill, and claims that "freedom of expression and debate and . . . maximum conflict of opinion" will best provide the necessary practices.[17] Thus Ramsey seeks to correct the church with liberal political theory. Ramsey rightly recognized the problem with the church pretending it was the magistrate; the "Church and society syndrome" created a void in the Church's life by failing to "clarify the church's address to the world." But he falsely understood liberalism as the necessary corrective.

I have put the best possible face on Ramsey's distinction between the Christian ethicist and the magistrate. In my interpretation, this distinction is primarily descriptive. The distinction prevents Christian ethicists from assuming that the magistrate waits for them to make public policy. But of course, for Ramsey this distinction also has a normative element to it. Here is where it becomes deeply problematic as Ramsey himself, in conversation with Michael Walzer, later admits.

While the development of Ramsey's casuistry cannot be separated from the situationalist debate, neither can it be separated from his reflections on the Viet Nam War. In 1968 Ramsey published a collection of essays that reflected on the war, entitled *The Just War: Force and Political Responsibility*. In that same year he published his fullest account of casuistry, "The Case of the Curious Exception." In *The Just War*, Ramsey's casuistry had led him to countenance the moral viability of the deterrent effect of bluffing based on the threat of the ambiguity in a counter-force nuclear strike.[18] He later changed his mind on this issue.[19] In his *Just and Unjust Wars*, Michael Walzer condemned Ramsey's acceptance of the bluff.[20] When Ramsey read Walzer's criticism, he confessed that one reason he countenanced the bluff was because he had made the distinction between magistracy and church ethicist too rigid.

> The last upper step in my graduated deterrence I some time ago abandoned, namely the Bluff that we might do such huge immorality even in retaliation. This was introduced as a possibly moral position in the first place because and only because I did not consider it the task of a religious ethicist to tell statesmen what may or may not be *feasible* and politically *necessary*. I guess I relaxed my ascetic distinction between defense postures I could condemn as a religious ethicist and those I would renounce as imprudent, even stupid, as a citizen.[21]

This is an important midrash on Ramsey's own work. He suggests that he himself had been sectarian by assuming that he did not have more to tell the magistrate based on his own theological convictions. And he suggests that the sharp distinction between the two had led him to his problematic conclusion about the bluff.

Walzer also critiqued Ramsey for the way in which he used scholastic distinctions to legitimate moral action. Walzer wrote, "He multiplies distinctions like a Ptolemaic astronomer with his epicycles and comes very close at the end to what G. E. M. Anscombe has called 'double-think about double effect'."[22] Ramsey was unwilling to concede this criticism of his casuistic ethic. In fact, he thought that Walzer, if he was going to remain a just warrior and not a pacifist, needed to cultivate more of a sense of the casuistic method.

> I predict that if you continue to put your intelligence to work on the issues in *Just and Unjust Wars*, you will either become more pacifist than you now are or else you will have to explore more fully some of the scholastic distinctions I have multiplied and employed in my effort to conceptualize a possibly moral deterrence.

Ramsey realized that his own just war stance required a casuistic ethic. Casuistry provided a way for Ramsey to negotiate a tragic world without simply conceding the need for "supreme emergencies" where immoral actions are allowed because of their good consequences, even if only for a limited time.

The fullest account of Ramsey's casuistry is found in "The Case of the Curious Exception." Here he defends the possibility of exceptionless principles. Associating casuistry with exceptionless principles should appear anomalous to anyone familiar with the term "casuistry." It is usually associated with terms such as dissimulation, equivocation, mental reservation, probabilism, probabiliorism, equiprobabilism.[23] Often it is depicted as developing the skill to find exceptions to legalistic principles by considering circumstances. Indeed, Joseph Fletcher, who is the ethicist *par excellence* advocating exceptions to moral principles based on circumstances, stated, "Casuistry is the homage paid by legalism to the love of persons, and to realism about life's relativities."[24] In *Situation Ethics*, he even said he was doing "neo-casuistry."[25] H. Richard Niebuhr also said, "Casuistry is the accommodation of the ought to can."[26]

While Fletcher and Niebuhr interpreted casuistry as an acknowledgment of freedom from legalism, Karl Barth found casuistry to be too rigid a method. He equated it with a "*summa* of ethical statements" which set the "moralist on God's throne."[27] Ramsey responded against both positions. Niebuhr and Fletcher were wrong to think casuistry ruled out exceptionless principles and merely accommodated "ought" to "can." Barth was wrong to think casuistry was only the rigid application of a "text" of principles to situations.

In "The Case of the Curious Exception," Ramsey defends both exceptionless principles and his casuistical method. Exceptionless principles and a casuistical analysis are mutually supporting; for principles embedded in a tradition make the moral life possible, but the meaning of the principles is not completely accessible before confronting particular situations. The principles provide the basis for first determining how we are to act, i.e. we are a people who should not murder. But by using the principles for a casuistical analysis of a particular situation, the meaning of the principle is further clarified. To defend both exceptionless principles and casuistry, Ramsey challenges both Fletcher's and Barth's accusation that principles cannot deal adequately with real life experiences because they "prescribe" possible responses by a rigid deductive methodology.

Fletcher believed he was standing with Barth in allowing the punctiliousness of God's Word as it comes to the person in the situation to be determinative for ethical reflection. Therefore Fletcher writes, "unlike classical casuistry, this neocasuistry repudiates any attempt to anticipate or prescribe real-life decisions in their existential particularity."[28] Ramsey argues that criticisms of casuistry made by such theologians as Barth and Fletcher falsely equate classical casuistry with a deductive process. Having established a straw position by caricaturing casuistry, they then too easily dismantle it. But, suggests Ramsey, they have dismantled nothing.

Many criticisms of Ramsey overlook this central point -- casuistry is not merely deduction. In a paper entitled "Methodological Alternatives for Religious Ethics and Public Policy," David P. Schmidt critiqued Ramsey by equating his casuistical approach with a deductive process. "Ramsey's approach," he argues is "best understood as a study of Christian love in light of the nature and authority of norms, principles, and rules in ethical theory."[29] Certainly this is true, but Schmidt continues:

> One important feature of this effort is his account of Christian love as a moral principle which grounds a deductive schema of moral reasoning -- an approach which owes much to traditional Catholic models of casuistry.[30]

Ramsey disagrees that this is either his understanding of casuistry or the traditional Catholic model. In a response to Schmidt, he writes:

> I altogether deny that "deduction" is how one proceeds to cases. Casuistry, yes; deduction, no. That there may be a kind of *linear* movement in applied ethics, I allowed, i.e. one step, then another, in clearing the moral terrain where possible. The "prolongation" or extension of Christian love into the concrete actualities of our lives; the "subsumption" of cases, exclusion of others, from righteousness; in the end, proceeding by graced and biblically informed reason -- I guess I have used all these formulations, and more. To the effect, for example, that one describable sort of killing of a fellow human being *falls within* possible justification as a class of instances of the Christian moral life in action; and another describable sort, never.

Ramsey rejects not only equating his casuistry with deduction, but also making such an equation with regard to traditional casuistry.[31] His reclamation of casuistry points to a different reading of the tradition, for certainly Schmidt is correct that many people do understand (albeit falsely) "traditional models of Catholic casuistry" as deductive.

Ramsey's response to Schmidt is commentary on "The Case of the Curious Exception." This quote nicely expresses the shape of his casuistry. It is a "linear movement," "clearing the moral terrain" for the "extension" of "Christian love," moving toward the "subsumption of cases".

What does it mean for ethical reasoning to be "linear"? This claim is intelligible against the background of a claim made by I. M. Crombie. Ramsey challenged Crombie's account of ethical reasoning where we begin with general principles and descend to more specific ones on the way to a particular.

I. M. Crombie wrote an article called "Moral Principles" for the British version of the situationalist debate.[32] He began by noting "truistic moral principles" such as the Golden Rule. Then he "descended" from these general rules which are "always valid but elastic in interpretation" to more specific principles.

> The golden rule lives in a very exalted and rarefied logical atmosphere, and there are many steps between it and the settling of practical questions. . . . We shall leave [this principle] there and come down the mountain to the level at which we meet with principles which are still very 'open' and 'elastic', and therefore very uncertain guides to action, but less open and elastic than the golden rule.[33]

The "principle of beneficence" was the next principle "down the mountain." Crombie continued his downward journey until he came to definite action-rules. While the "golden rule" is "always valid but elastic in interpretation," the "definite action-rule" was "not always valid but rigid in application." That is to say, once the ethicist had determined an instance when the definite action-rule was valid, a necessary action followed.

The application of a definite action-rule produces a particular action. That is why Crombie placed the "action" and "rule" together with the hyphen. According to Crombie, we can only endorse an exceptionless principle when we maintain "freedom of manoeuvre" in the application of a definite action-rule. We can only agree to say that adultery is always wrong, when we have the freedom to apply this principle to this particular. If such freedom does not exist then we cannot endorse exceptionless rules.

Ramsey opposed the shape of Crombie's moral reasoning because it constrained principles into a deductive system which was an easy mark for Barth's criticism. A "definite action-rule" asks casuistry to do what Protestant caricatures of it had criticized; it was asking for the "production of the particular, " a "subsumption- ruling rule". This was to ask for the impossible. "An *application*-governing rule would be a project for putting out of commission the actual production of particular deeds by absorbing them utterly into the principles."[34] Ethical reasoning contains no subsumption-ruling rule. Theory is not capable of this. It only surrounds the particular by describing morally relevant features so that we might understand what is going on. Practical wisdom is still needed for the subsumption of cases.

In opposition to Crombie's vertical image, Ramsey asserts a horizontal one. We move toward the subsumption of cases, but ethical reasoning itself never produces, by way of logical deduction, a subsumption of a case, i.e. a particular. Ethical reasoning is "clearing the moral terrain," removing irrelevant features involved in *understanding* the particular at hand. It does not produce the particular; it "surrounds" the particular. In the end practical wisdom, not ethical reasoning, is responsible for the particular action or inaction. Ethical reasoning, practical wisdom, and the particular do not follow logically one from the other by descending in logical fashion. They all exist on the same plane. Each requires the other.

If this spatial imagery is not kept in mind, then Ramsey's "component stages" within moral reasoning will be viewed as a mere deductive account of moral reasoning.

> Our model of the component stages in moral reasoning can, therefore be stated as follows: ultimate norm (*agapé*, utility, self- realization, etc.); general principles; *defined*-action principles, or *generic* terms of approval and *generic* offense terms; *definite*- action rules, or moral-*species* -terms; then the subsumption of cases.[35]

While this "model" appears to be a formal taxonomy, it is not when the spatial imagery is maintained. We do not move *downward* from the ultimate norm, but *across* from general to specific. Thus the ultimate norm is not left behind in articulating moral-species-terms. Instead it is only more fully expressed. The moral species term is not grounded in the ultimate norm. To the contrary, there is an interdependence between them. The articulation of the moral species term further clarifies and expresses the ultimate norm. Yet the ultimate norm makes possible the articulation of the moral species term.

Crombie's vertical "descending" view of casuistry assumed the predominant Protestant understanding of casuistry as too "scholastic." He was asking a theory to accomplish more than it could. Ramsey's horizontal approach emphasized description and tradition. The descriptions we use in surrounding a particular assist how we can respond. Actual responses were dependent upon our moral formation grounded in the traditions that constitute who we are that allow us to describe this particular in an intelligible way. Such descriptions then render further intelligible our tradition embedded principles.

While Ramsey's casuistry was a reaction to Crombie's deductive model, it was also a response, both positively and negatively, to the work of Karl Barth. Ramsey thought that Barth persuasively did casuistry even though Barth himself rejected the term.

Barth described casuistry as follows:

> Special ethics" [read casuistry] is sometimes taken to mean the understanding of the command of God as a prescribed text, which, partly written and partly unwritten, is made up of biblical texts in which there

are believed to be seen universally binding divine ordinances and direc-
tions, of certain propositions again presumed to be universally valid, of
the natural moral law generally perceptible to human reason, and finally of particular norms which have been handed down historically in
the tradition of Western Christianity and which lays claim to universal
validity. . . . On this presupposition the task of special ethics consists (1)
in expounding the statements of this law -- on the analogy of a country's
law -- in relation to the plenitude of conditions and possibilities in
which human action takes place, and then (2) in applying it to the individual cases, which means either assessing what has been done, or making a regulation or issuing a prohibition, commandment or permission
in respect of future action.[36]

To an unsympathetic reader, the above could be a description of
Ramsey's work. Barth satirizes this account. It provides "formal clarity,"
he argues, and "everyone will be grateful to the moralist for the superior
knowledge with which he is able to relieve him of the often very oppressive task of making his own orientations and decisions."[37] The problem
with casuistry is that it forces the believer out of her existential milieu
where she must respond with nothing but the claim of God's Word upon
her.

Barth gives three decisive reasons against casuistry. First, the moralist "sets himself on God's throne" by claiming to "distinguish good and
evil" through a "*summa* of ethical statements compiled by him and his
like from the Bible, natural law, and tradition." Second it universalizes
the "command of God" through rules and forms, thereby denying the
command's particularity. And third it is an "encroachment in relation to
man's action under the command of God." The individual must be free,
not with respect to "choice, preference, or selection," but to obey the
claim God commands on this particular person.[38]

While Barth's "special ethics" could describe Ramsey's work, it does
not because Ramsey avoids allowing casuistry to fall into the trap of the
logical application of a pre-*text* to particular situations for the production of moral certitude. Barth failed to see that casuistry is not only a
textually-emphasized form of rationality. And his dismissal of "rules
and forms" is not only inadequate but destructive of Christian ethics.
Indeed Barth himself does not escape "rules and forms" when he goes on
in III/IV to do "special" ethics.

"Texts" do not produce action or the need for inaction. This is the
role of practical wisdom. For Ramsey the moral reasoning of casuistry
certainly contains a "textual" moment. It "is always a matter of *surrounding* the particulars of actions by increasingly specific general terms -- i.e.,
increasing illumination -- for the direction of concrete actions."[39] Insofar
as this "textual" moment exists, deduction is a part of ethical reasoning.

Yet this textual moment is only the basis upon which we understand what is going on. Notice the spatial imagery once again. Ethical reasoning "surrounds" the particular. It is on the same plane with that of the concrete particular. It provides intelligibility, but it cannot simply be applied to individual cases with the result that a particular action must now be done.

Ramsey has not equated casuistry with deduction. Therefore, Barth's [et. al.] criticism of casuistry is invalid. "Many learned men make the common mistake," Ramsey writes in reference to Barth and Thielicke, "of supposing that a telling objection can be brought against casuistry by pointing out the distinction between the articulation of moral principles and the application of these principles to concrete cases."[40] This criticism would be appropriate *if* casuistry attempted to accomplish the task of *resolving* the particular through the application of a text. But this is not the task of the casuist.

What then is the casuist's task? An answer to this question is found in Ramsey's criticism of Thielicke. He set up casuistry's insurmountable problem as the inability to synthesize a conclusion by way of deduction with subsumption by way of induction. In the "transition from conclusion to subsumption," "conclusion arises from a process of deduction, whereas subsumption proceeds from that which is inductively apprehended". Ramsey found this an unacceptable way to think about casuistry because it assumed that the purpose of principles is to lead by way of deduction to an assured conclusion. Such is not the casuist's purpose for Ramsey never assumed that principles were to replace the role of practical wisdom.

> Whether or not "conclusion" or "deduction" are apt words to designate that prior moral reasoning, it has to be stressed that "subsumption" was always the great work of "prudence" or "practical wisdom," which as Plato says even a philosopher needs in order to be able to find his way home at night. He would have to know the meaning of "housekey" and "going up one flight (and not down to the basement)" (these are neutral action descriptions) and of "no drinking while driving" (this is a non-neutral action description, an offense term). If he pretty well knows the *sort* of thing this prohibits, then he would have to subsume his own case under it. It looks as if there are only *defined*-action rules, and that to ask for something more definite than this is to ask for the action itself. What Crombie has proved the impossibility of falls outside ethical *reasoning* and beyond the play of principles and rules. It is the actual practice of morality.[41]

Ethical reasoning contains a textual moment. It "clears the moral terrain." This activity moves between general and specific as it describes the "sort" or "kind" of prohibition or permission. A particular action does not follow of necessity from these descriptions. We are not here confronted with a practical syllogism where a necessary action follows from the major premise through a minor one. Ethical reasoning "specifies" certain kinds of action. But, "such specification of action is never a *particular.*"[42] What is a particular? It is the "subsumption of a case."[43] And the subsumption of a case is not a matter of the application of a text alone, but primarily of practical wisdom.

Notice in the earlier quote on component stages of moral reasoning that the series of stages is interrupted by "then" which separates the "subsumption of cases" (the particular) from the prior ethical reasoning. The prior ethical reasoning is not disjunctive from the subsumption of the case. Nor does it deductively lead to the subsumption of the case. If the latter were possible the "then" would not be necessary and Ramsey could not distance casuistry from deduction. To avoid this he states that "subsumption" is the actual work of practical wisdom and not theoretical reasoning. Therefore what we have is a complex interrelation between theory and practice where principles guide, but do not produce, practice, and practice in turn defines, and clarifies, what the principles actually mean.[44] Oliver O'Donovan states this nicely when he writes:

> For Ramsey, . . . the moral rule is a 'moral species-term', a tool of reasoning which is capable of embracing even the unpredictable particular case and rendering it intelligible. But as we apply the species-term to the particular case, we come to understand not merely the case but the term, too, better than we did before.[45]

However, it must be remembered that practical wisdom, and not theoretical reasoning, is responsible for "application." The exercise of practical wisdom requires a tradition where people are formed to embody the principles that will then render intelligible particulars. The articulation of principles cannot insure the practice of the moral life, only the embodiment of those principles can.

In challenging the notion that casuistry was a deductive process where a system of principles entailed the production of a particular action, Ramsey challenges the freedom-legalism distinction. No longer can one critique casuistry as the rigid application of a text to a particular. Principles do not constrain and deny freedom. In fact, they are necessary for freedom. Some principles structure reality; the question is whose principles do we embody? If this question is not asked, and if agape is not in-principled, then a free space for the practice of the moral life cannot be found.

Ramsey's reclamation of casuistry is not a cry to return to "casuistry" as *the* paradigm for all moral rationality. For example, Ramsey's casuistical approach should not be seen as correlative with the recent revival of casuistry by Albert R. Jonsen and Stephen Toulmin. They set "casuistry" as a method against any form of exceptionless principles. The latter is marked by "theoretical argument" leading to the "tyranny of principles," for it "seeks eternal, invariable principles, the practical implications of which can be free of exceptions or qualifications." Against this deductive schema they invoke "practical reasoning," "which pays closest attention to the specific details of particular moral cases and circumstances."[46] But Ramsey's casuistry does not set itself against exceptionless principles. Instead, his casuistry, unlike that of Toulmin and Jonsen, assumes a coherent tradition from which the casuist works.[47] Embedded in that tradition are principles and rules that regulate practices.

In fact, in his *Ethics at the Edges of Life*, Ramsey criticized Jonsen's purported ability to create "consensus at the surface of action-decisions" among a group of people representing divergent moral perspectives. Ramsey suggests that the divergent moral perspectives were not as diverse as appears. He writes, "In other words, conceivably a diversity of private beliefs was buried under initial broad agreement about how cases should be managed."[48] That word "managed" has a great deal of significance; Ramsey recognized that the "art" of management established the categories by which ethical decisions were addressed, and therefore the "consensus" did not represent the overcoming of particularity through some innate moral sentiment about the rightness and wrongness of certain actions. Instead it represented the hegemony of managerial practice over more substantive ethical reflection.

> Did the movement at the level of practice and management determine the substantive moral principles needed to justify itself? What then is the meaning of a moral policy except to justify decisions actually being taken? The serpent, tail in mouth, goes round and round.[49]

Ramsey's casuistry did not exist at the surface level of "action-decisions." It went much deeper within the principles that form practices within traditions. Ramsey sought to address pressing moral issues without sacrificing the particularity of a moral tradition.

Casuistry and Medical Ethics

By thinking through specific issues in war, economics, sexuality, and civil rights, Ramsey found it necessary to employ discriminations such as direct vs. indirect, tragic vs. wicked, perfect vs. imperfect voluntary, principles vs. action-decisions, killing vs. allowing to die, etc. These casuistical discriminations were not attempts to circumvent Christian morality; anyone who assumes that has not given Ramsey's work a fair reading. Ramsey utilized his well-honed casuistry to render complex issues morally intelligible so that a space could be secured for the practice of the moral life. He recognized that "moral persons need social space."[50] Social space for moral persons was increasingly diminished due to a variety of problematic premises that structured modern political existence, and reduced the practice of the moral life to private preference. In the latter part of the 60's and throughout the 70's Ramsey's well-crafted casuistry turns toward issues in "medical" ethics. The practice of medicine provided wonderful material for Ramsey's casuistry for two reasons. First it was a practice steeped in tradition, particularly Jewish and Christian. Cases were easily "prismatic" for someone who worked from a decidedly tradition-dependent approach. The tradition could be used to highlight morally relevant features of the practice. This is the reason I placed "medical" in quotes above. Ramsey did not think the practice of medicine itself, as a vocation, was capable of furnishing resources for the practice of morality. He constantly sought to show that "medical ethics is consonant with the ethics of a wider community."[51] By that, I assume he meant medicine's scientific basis was incapable of producing the resources for a moral medical practice. He certainly denied that an adequate ethics can be found in the "science of genetics itself or in the truth it discloses concerning the biological world."[52] And the "facts" science produces were incapable of disproving Christian ethics.

> Christian ethics . . . is not found among the contents of any natural science, nor can it be disproven by any of the facts that such sciences know. It is a fruit of intending the world as a Christian.[53]

Christian ethics was not dependent upon the practice of science. In fact, science was incapable of realizing its own problematic premises, and if left to itself, it would only diminish space for the Christian moral life. Medical ethics needed to be connected to a wider ethics.

When Ramsey employs his casuistry to render the practice of medicine intelligible, he does so by inscribing those practices within the Christian tradition. In correspondence with his editor for both *The Patient as Person* and *Ethics at the Edges of Life* Ramsey makes it clear that he seeks to clarify issues within medical practice through exposing them to the searchlight of his religious convictions.

> It may be the case that in the Bampton lectures [as opposed to the Beecher lectures] I make more direct and frequent appeal to religious warrants. That may be because some of my colleagues within the field of theological ethics claimed to discern a significant shift in my premises in the *Patient as Person* in comparison with earlier writings. In any case my problem is how *at the same time* to clarify and deepen and correct

understanding at the level of the premises *and* to render the specific issues more corrigible to moral reasoning. I don't think I would sacrifice one of those goals for your editorial deftness or the royalty, if a given suggested change seemed finally to require that.[54]

Ramsey's effort to "render the specific issues more corrigible to moral reasoning" wedded the practice of medicine to his theological premises and divorced it from the premises of modernity. Thus the second reason the practice of medicine provided such wonderful material for Ramsey's casuistry was because he found modernity's problematic premises, against which he practiced casuistry, readily evident in medical practice. In each of his three major works on medical ethics, he tried to create social space for the practice of morality by exposing what had usurped that space.

In *The Patient as Person* the problematic premises are the reduction of the person to a means for a scientifically engineered future, the loss of the distinction between allowing to die and putting to death, and the "ubiquity of the fear of dying" that creates the need to engineer life at all costs.[55] These three premises are obviously related. The manufacturing of the future reduces people to means in the hands of technological managers. The preservation of life deemed worthy for technological preservation becomes the telos of human existence. The elderly and the handicapped are no longer surrounded with protection; they lose social space.

To create a counter-space, Ramsey lifts up the notion of "consent as a canon of loyalty." He asserts that "no person should be used as a subject without his will." Here, with the language of consent, we are once again on familiar ground. As already demonstrated, consent played a key role in Ramsey's political, sexual, and medical ethics. No one should object to the importance of consent in political, sexual and medical practices *if* the only alternative is tyranny, rape and coercion. Yet setting up this alternative is problematic for it makes consent an a priori necessity. Then the important questions of which social formation will provide for a genuine consent? or is consent even possible? are preempted. As he does in legitimating western democracy Ramsey's honorable search for consent reads back into human nature its possibility. Once again, Niebuhr's tragic dictum allows for this possibility.

Man's capacity to become joint adventurers in a common cause makes the consensual relation possible; man's propensity to overreach his joint adventurer even in a good cause makes consent necessary.[56]

Do all men and women have this capacity? If the second part of the tragic dictum is true, but the first part is false, then will not the notion of "consent" only sanction the "overreaching" because the same capacity for relation justifies both parts of the dictum?

In the first chapter of *The Patient as Person*, Ramsey highlights the Articles of the Nuremburg Tribunal to emphasize the role of consent in medical ethics. The Articles begin, "The voluntary consent of the human subject is absolutely essential." The Articles continue by delineating some of the necessary conditions for consent to be possible:

> This means that the person involved should have legal capacity to give consent; should be so situated as to be able to exercise free power of choice, without the intervention of any element of force, fraud, deceit, duress, overreaching, or other ulterior form of constraint or coercion; and should have sufficient knowledge and comprehension of the elements of the subject matter involved as to enable him to make an understanding and enlightened decision.[57]

Anyone who has pondered a "dark realism" as Ramsey so often did, should certainly be suspect that such conditions could ever be met. While consent as described by the Nuremburg Articles, if possible, would be important for a moral medical practice, the question is if this notion of consent is possible. If it is not possible and in place at present, and we base our medical practice on the assumption it is, then the assumption only serves to justify what is occurring on grounds still unarticulated.

Ramsey's realist critique questions the possibility of fulfilling these conditions for genuine consent. While something similar to Habermas's ideal speech event would be necessary for consent to be possible on the grounds described by the Nuremburg tribunal, Ramsey's work does not allow for such a possibility. It is precluded by his constant emphasis on the relativity of justice(s). Does the possibility of a genuine consent require the creation of the Enlightenment's autonomous person? Then Ramsey's criticism of modernity's atomistic individualism and the social conditions necessary for consent to be genuine appear to be in contradiction.

Nevertheless, we should not too hastily dismiss the place of consent in Ramsey's work. He himself recognized the difficulty with children, prisoners, the oppressed, and the mentally and physically challenged being found in situations that fulfill the necessary conditions for consent. Thus Ramsey used consent negatively as a tactic to free these groups of people from experimentation. In fact, a great deal of Ramsey's work emphasizes that certain groups of people must be excluded from medical research because they cannot consent.

> If we are not persuaded that *because they are children* children cannot consent (nor should anyone else consent in their behalf) to experiments primarily for the accumulation of knowledge, we at least should be convinced that such experiments ought not to be performed upon children in orphanages, reformatories, or homes for the retarded *because they are a captive population.*[58]

While for purposes of therapeutic research others can give consent on their behalf based on the concept of the reasonable person, children in orphanages, reformatories and homes for the handicapped constitute captive populations who cannot give consent for non-therapeutic research. While Ramsey used consent negatively, he also used it positively. Without exploring the conditions of consent's possibility, Ramsey generated norms based on "a reasonably free and adequately informed consent," and the "concept of the reasonable man."

> . . . neither the law nor medical ethics can get along without the concept of the reasonable man. The test of what an informed and prudent adult would reasonably be expected to have done to himself or his child affords some limits, *provided that* the child qualifies as a subject of investigation because of his own need.[59]

And based on this concept, even prisoners were capable of "consent."

> . . . it is not impossible to arrange things so that a man in prison may freely volunteer to become a joint adventurer in an experiment for the sake of the knowledge and good to come, and not for the sake of the reward. It is not impossible to protect his will from duress to cooperate in such medical undertakings. [60]

Regardless of whether or not prisoners should or should not be used in medical research, do we want to use consent as a way to justify their participation? How could prisoners ever be expected to fulfill the Articles of Nuremburg Ramsey cites? For that matter how could the unemployed, the working class, migrant workers, and a variety of others who live in situations of duress, and who do not have sufficient resources to resist the lure of rewards to be "willing" participants in medical research? The assumption of consent, even with all the qualifications Ramsey offers, simply cannot describe adequately the practice of medical research. Even though Ramsey uses consent for a normative practice, the invocation of Niebuhr's tragic dictum also assumes consent is descriptive of a possible state of affairs. And this despite Ramsey's criticism of modernity as a "vast and ghastly concentration camp"!

Rather than consent as a canon of loyalty, the strength of Ramsey's position is found in loyalty itself. Ramsey suggests that people make claims upon our lives regardless of their ability to consent to covenant. "True, the small patient or retardate cannot enter into the covenant making for medical progress as a human enterprise. However, this does not excuse parents, guardians, or researchers. They can still keep covenant with the child and with the individual retardate."[61] But covenant based on consent, and covenant based on claims others have on us regardless of the possibility of consent are two different things. The first notion of consent is similar to liberal contract theories of government; the second is much more biblical. God chooses Israel despite their consent, and God continues God's covenant even when they refuse to consent.

The strength of Ramsey's position does not lie in "consent" but in the fact that, given who God is, those who represent the edges of human existence have special claims on us as a people. Life is sacred not in and of itself, but because it is a gift from God, and therefore it is related to God. This was clear in *Basic Christian Ethics* -- " . . . from viewing man as a theological animal we are driven to regard all truly human worth as derivative, not inherent. Christian interpretations of man's dignity affirm something about man in relation to God, not just something about man *per se*."[62] This position has the benefit of finding sacredness not in anything intrinsic to humanity, but in God's election, and that election is always mediated socially. Thus neither the intellect, nor the will, nor even the capacity to consent make the human being sacred, but God's call.

A shift occurs from *Basic Christian Ethics* to *The Patient as Person*. No longer is sacredness found in God's election, but now it is intrinsic to humanity. " Just as man is a *sacredness in the social and political order*, so he is a *sacredness in the natural, biological order*. He is a sacredness in bodily life." Here life appears to be sacred in itself, where as before it was sacred because of its relation to God. Is this just a shift in emphasis? Or is it an effort to circumvent a medical ethics that bases care on the capacity for minimal relatedness? While it is probably both a shift in emphasis and an effort to base care on a person's existence despite her ability to "relate," it also signifies a shift in the social relation of sacredness. The individual becomes sacred despite social relations. Once this is coupled with consent, Ramsey's position appears quite similar to liberal political theories of government.

As I have mentioned on many occasions, Paul Ramsey was immensely critical of modern liberal government. Why then did he make so much of the use of consent? One reason is because he needed some way to safeguard those who were at the edges of life; consent could provide some safeguard. But this would work only if the capacity to consent existed. Another reason is because Ramsey sought to find a language accessible to as many people as possible despite their theological convictions and "consent" appeared to cross over communities and traditions. The use of "consent" represents an effort to create a meta-discourse that is accessible to people despite their own particularities. What in fact it does create is one more particular "politics of speech" that engulfs all others under its overarching framework.

Ramsey developed this meta-discourse because he conceded "pluralism" as a description of contemporary reality. "There is, in any case, no way to avoid the moral pluralism of our society."[63] Insofar as he, even reluctantly, accepted this, Ramsey fell prey to modernity's totalizing claims that seek to eradicate all alternative social spaces.

The idea of "pluralism" is made possible by a totalizing politics of speech capable of domesticating all real differences into its own universal language. Ken Surin has described how this dominant ideology works with respect to "religious pluralism."

> The McDonald's hamburger is the first 'universal' food, but the people — be they from La Paz, Bombay, Cairo or Brisbane -- who eat the McDonald's hamburger also consume the American way of life with it. Equally, the adherents of the 'world ecumenism' canvassed by the religious 'pluralists' align themselves with a movement that is 'universal', but they 'consume' a certain way of life. Not quite the American way of life itself . . . but a single overarching way of life which has become so pervasive that 'the American way of life' is today simply its most prominent and developed manifestation; namely the 'life' of a world administered by global media and information networks, international agencies and multinational corporations. The dominant ideology of this new world reality declares that nations, cultures, religions, and so forth are simply obsolete if they are maintained in their old forms as fixed and intractable 'particularities'. It is this new world reality and its ideological concomitants (e.g. the 'global gaze') which both makes the McDonald's hamburger into a universal food and sustains the 'world ecumenism' advocated by the exponents of 'religious pluralism'. It creates the *episteme* or 'paradigm' which renders both sets of phenomena intelligible.[64]

This same *episteme* also creates the need for some type of non-particular category like "consent" so that an author can supposedly speak broadly in a "pluralistic" society.

That Ramsey accepted "pluralism" as descriptive of modern political life is all the more surprising because he reminded us that the overarching managerial categories establish the parameters of ethical debate, and thus secure "universal" conclusions regardless of peoples' particularities. As I already mentioned, he criticized the Sonoma Conference at precisely this point. And in *Fabricated Man* Ramsey recognized that the lack of ethics in genetic control is the result of the "replacement of categories appropriate to the ethical evaluation of behavior or of moral agency by categories appropriate to the elaboration and evaluation of *designs*."[65] Genetic research worked within an episteme of "engineering consequences." This presumption Ramsey calls a "modern thought form" or "the unspoken premise of modern man." Clearly Ramsey has identified one of the fruits of modernity's politics of speech; managers and engineers are now the central characters constructing a monochromatic future. Yet Ramsey failed to see that pluralism and the illusion of "consent" constitute the building blocks they use.

The role of consent in Ramsey's work is doubly troubling because his second problematic premise of modernity is the "combination of *boundless determinism* with *boundless freedom* in all our thoughts."[66] Ramsey understood that in modernity human nature was reduced to technological manipulations to "control the future" that only resulted in a self-imposed, and self-created determinism. This problematic premise usurped the teleological understanding of human nature before the modern period.

> The boundless determinism and the boundless freedom contained in this thought are not solely or mainly a product of science. They are rather a widespread cultural phenomenon or thought-form characteristic of man in the modern period. Dostoevski discerned this to be true. Where there is no God, no destiny toward which men move and which moves in them, then self-modifying freedom must be the man-God.[67]

The teleological anthropology Ramsey seeks as an antidote to modernity assumes Christianity would be the dominant ideology and practice. It assumes institutions would be the bearer of these practices. And it assumes that this telos would actually make a difference in peoples' lives whether they are bound to the particularity of institutional Christianity or not. All those assumptions are gone forever, if they ever were present. Christianity cannot be a politics of speech accessible to the common good despite particular loyalty. When Christianity seeks to become this, it is reduced to one more totalizing ideology that cannot help but distort the true nature of the Christian life. Better the fiction that pluralism describes contemporary reality than underwriting the fiction that a generalized Christian anthropology can be used as an antidote to modernity's managerial technologism! The latter is too powerful at engulfing all generalities into its engineering power. Only by countering with a clear alternative can the necessary social space be secured.

Although his effort to ground an alternative social space in an anthropology overlooks what institutions will bear the practices that preserve this understanding of human nature, Ramsey's casuistry does point us in the direction of an alternative social space. This is made evident by

Stephen Toulmin's negative, and Alasdair MacIntyre's positive, responses to Ramsey's medical ethics.

Ten years before Stephen Toulmin co-wrote *The Abuse of Casuistry*, he reviewed Ramsey's *Ethics at the Edges of Life*.[68] He wrote:

> As with much contemporary bio-ethics, Ramsey's methods of argument are basically casuistic. To say this is not to condemn or criticize his procedures. On the contrary, the ancient art of casuistry -- by which moral reasoning works its way from case to case, beginning with rights and wrongs about which we feel no doubt and proceeding to more difficult cases by analogy with those first clearer cases -- has fallen quite unjustly into disrepute in the last 200 years.[69]

Toulmin affirmed this method because it overcame the inability of "principles" to provide agreement when people have "quite different underlying commitments." However, he criticized Ramsey's use of it due to Ramsey's pessimistic view of human nature, his "Methodist preacher" mode of rationality, and his "faith in the social efficacy of legislation."

> . . . I do not myself believe that the roots of ethics in human nature and experience are nearly as shallow as Ramsey implies. Fundamental moral sentiments could never be destroyed by a handful of Supreme Court rulings unless deeper and more powerful agencies were also at work.[70]

For Toulmin, casuistry is a *method* for overcoming the contingencies of our various differences through case by case analogical reasoning. This method operates on "fundamental moral sentiments" which legislation is not capable of destroying.[71] But Ramsey's reclamation of casuistry is not a method moving from case to case by analogy without a priori commitments. Toulmin correctly understood that Ramsey assumed a handful of Supreme Court rulings did establish principles that became embodied in people and further decreased space for the practice of a Christian morality. And Ramsey believed that these principles usurped others necessary for his casuistic analysis.

Alasdair MacIntyre presents a more positive explanation of Ramsey's casuistry that takes into account Ramsey's a priori commitment to the Christian tradition. He reviewed *Ethics at the Edges of Life* along with Sissela Bok's *Lying* and Charles Fried's *Right and Wrong*. He writes:

> Where Paul Ramsey rests his final appeal on the biblical, tradition [Bok and Fried] appear to rest theirs in the end on some undeclared private, personal preference. Ramsey's premises may be unargued but his reason for accepting them is at least clear; at the root of his argument is an appeal to faith and an appeal for obedience to divine law. Nonetheless

what he has to say must be of compelling interest to everyone concerned with the moral problems of medicine, life and death, and not merely to those who share his faith. This is not only by far the best book of the three, it is probably the single most important text in the area of medical ethics written in modern times.[72]

MacIntyre claims Ramsey has two "central achievements." First he exposes the often unarticulated presupposition that "18th century individualist moral philosophers speak through the mouths of living justices and lawyers." Thus, contra Toulmin, the language of institutions such as the Supreme Court, as well as the Academy, do perpetuate a specific morality as well as construct reality and fundamental moral sentiments. And secondly, "Ramsey deepens our understanding of certain key distinctions."

MacIntyre's review in 1978 is particularly interesting in light of Ramsey and MacIntyre's exchange in 1977 in the essay "Can Medicine Dispense with a Theological Perspective on Human Nature."[73] MacIntyre argued that a theological perspective on human nature is dispensable for medicine. Naziism subordinated ethics to the German nation. This is intolerable. We cannot allow ethics to be subordinated to a theological perspective either, so the argument goes. If "norms of ethical practice" are derived from the Lord of the Christian Church rather than the Lord of the Nazis is not helpful; we are still left with what appears to be an arbitrary claim. MacIntyre asks, "How are we to decide between these claims?" He responds:

> A central part of the answer is surely that Christianity passes a number of ethical tests that Naziism fails. Yet this argument presupposed just what Ramsey denied, namely, that ethics cannot be subordinated to religion, but does indeed provide an independent criterion by which religions are to be judged. Yet one ought to note that in this Ramsey, although he may have Kierkegaard on his side (the most dubious of allies, I should have thought), is at odds with much Christian and even more Jewish theology. Catholic Christianity has classically been commended by apologists because its revelation is congruent with our natural knowledge of the good for men.[74]

MacIntyre's later works, particularly *Whose Justice? Which Rationality?* makes his comment here seem similar to the position he wants to critique rather than affirm. Even in light of his *After Virtue* this statement appears anomalous. Yet in this article MacIntyre refers to his "forthcoming" *After Virtue*.[75] At least at this point, MacIntyre still has a stake in moral philosophy as something distinct from theology. MacIntyre asked if "medicine can dispense with a theological perspective on human nature?," and responded yes. Ramsey responded, ". . . as a theological ethicist [read: as opposed to a moral philosopher] I approach grappling with MacIntyre's essay with a certain divine nonchalance."[76] Ramsey's reliance on biblical tradition meant he had little at stake in MacIntyre's question. The grounds for his own position were secure regardless of a philosopher's concern to ground medicine in something supposedly more universal than a theological tradition.

The irony of this interchange between MacIntyre and Ramsey should not be lost on the reader. MacIntyre is soon to be famous for his criticism that independent ethical criteria do not exist apart from a traditioned-formed, narrative-dependent community capable of sustaining, through its internal practices, the virtues necessary for the extension of that community. Ramsey, on the other hand, was known as a Protestant natural law theologian. Here we find MacIntyre arguing for the advantage of natural law because it establishes independent ethical criteria against Ramsey's subordination of ethics to theology.

> Let Ramsey provide one decisive position on a question disputed in contemporary medical ethics; let him provide one belief about the Lord of heaven and earth; and then let him show us how the former is derived from the latter. Until he does this, what he is asserting will remain quite unclear.[77]

MacIntyre's criticism of Ramsey in 1977 gives way to praise in 1978. No longer does MacIntyre desire "independent ethical criteria" unless one understands a "traditioned narrative dependent community" as such. With *Ethics at the Edges of Life*, Ramsey represented the type of moral reflection MacIntyre came to endorse. It required explicit communal presuppositions. Ramsey's casuistry requires MacIntyre's "tradition."[78] Ramsey's development of casuistry does not develop "independent ethical criteria." It is not a cry to return to "casuistry" as *the* paradigm for all ethical discourse upon which consensus can be built despite people's particularities. About such criteria Ramsey had a "divine nonchalance."

Ramsey rightly diagnosed the problems with modern culture. He recognized how the principles structuring reality placed in jeopardy those who lived at the edges, who were not suitable means for future engineering. He sought to transform that structure by an insistence on a theological tradition where life is pure gift that finds its sacredness only in its relation to God:

> . . . no one has "standing" in the moral universe to tell whether he should ever have been or not. Life is not a good; it is an inexplicable gift. . . . It is a duty of parents and physicians and the human commu-

nity in general to sustain the life of a defective infant — who is not born dying and who cannot refuse treatment.[79]

Life as a gift from God means that discriminations based on "quality of life" can only have a minor role in medical practice. The six months of a Tay-Sachs baby's life cannot be compared with someone else's seventy years and be found of less worth.[80] This giftedness has its basis in Ramsey's theology. "Giftedness of life" was a shorthand way for him to tell the Christian story.[81] The life of a Tay Sachs baby was sacred, and should be treated so, because that life participated in the giftedness of creation that finds its basis and telos in redemption. Yet Ramsey assumed an anthropology that grounded the self in transcendence was necessary as the vehicle to sustain life's giftedness.

Although Ramsey's casuistry does point us in the direction of an alternative social space, his effort to ground that alternative social space in a transcendental anthropology overlooks what institutions will bear the practices that preserve this understanding of human nature. The lingering question is not if we have an appropriate anthropology, but how are people formed in such a way that this understanding of the human appears natural rather than some other? What practices and institutions will be capable of securing the respect for life as a gift? In *Nine Modern Moralists* Ramsey rejected the "sociological positivism" of the Roman Catholic Church for a judicial system which he supposed would allow for free and unlimited discussion. Once we had freedom, so Ramsey thought, a better understanding of human nature would emerge. But by the time Ramsey wrote *Ethics at the Edges of Life*, he no longer expresses such hope about the judicial system. He suggests that the court is a "hierarchical magisterium" and "imperial judiciary" that "sacralized secular concepts" and is incapable of the type of moral reasoning he hoped in *Nine Modern Moralists* they would make possible.[82]

This places Ramsey in a quandary. If the sociological positivism of the Roman Catholic Church is unacceptable, and the law and the courts fare no better, where is the institution that will form people into the necessary anthropology to stand against modernity? During this time, Ramsey reconsidered the role of the Church. In 1976 he wrote a letter to Thomas Ulshafer expressing a change of opinion concerning his earlier anti-magisterium sentiment.

You might have in mind that the lecture that composed those [last] two chapters [of *Nine Modern Moralists*] were given in 1958. That will set in historical perspective the criticism that I brought against Maritain, my confidence at that point in time that *agape* and natural justice both freed from authoritative church interpretation could continue in full-fledged partnership, my present doubt about that and my question whether

> Catholics at least ought not now find more in Maritain's position than I did then. For -- as I see it -- what has happened is in Catholic thought a growing denial of a distinctive Christian ethics (my exodus morality) accompanied by increasing "socialization" of the person to the whole extent of his being.[83]

Here in 1976 Ramsey criticizes Catholic moral theologians for becoming in part what he wanted them to be in 1958 -- less ecclesially authoritarian, and more committed to the society at large as the interpretive framework for understanding human nature. Still, even though Ramsey reconsidered the role of the Church as the place where the necessary institutional practices might be found, he was finally unable to advocate such a central role for the church rather than the state.

The question where those practices can be found that will secure space for faithful living plagued Ramsey until the end. In *Speak Up For Just War Or Pacifism*, he considers this dilemma and writes to Stanley Hauerwas:

> So almost thou persuadest me that there are resources in our Wesleyan heritage by which our church could become an alternative society to that of the sword -- if I was finally convinced that the ethos of modern nations has ceased to be amenable to transformation by just war traditions.

He goes on to explain why he was only "almost persuaded." Ramsey understood the radical transformation within the church that would be necessary for the church itself to be able to bear the necessary practices to secure some alternative space.

> If we are to nurture our children in Christian faith, and "fruits" in life, will we not be driven to establish Methodist parochial schools for their education? The world is too much *with* us, *in* our church's life. In a period of "withdrawal" for as long as we can see into the future, in order to find our way to *being* the church again, what ought we to do with the Methodist Building, strategically located in Washington, D.C., when we were a "denomination" in the original sense? The hour cometh and now is, when the practices accepted within Methodist hospitals may require the removal of the name "Methodist" from them -- if we are, with our physicians and health-care professional resolved to *be* the church of Jesus Christ.[84]

Although Ramsey wrestled with the question of where those people were who could be counted upon to preserve his anthropology,[85] he was unable to locate them. Neither the church, nor the state, nor the medical practice alone was sufficient[86] Ramsey's casuistry required a commitment to a specific tradition; that requirement was met by the "western Judeo-Christian tradition." Yet his casuistry also required specific institutional practices. Unfortunately, those practices were not easily found, and something as broad and abstract as the "western Judeo-Christian tradition" was incapable of furnishing specific practices.

Casuistry and Narrative

To be finally persuasive, and capable of creating the alternative social space for the practice of the Christian life, Ramsey needed to give us a more definitive account of specific practices that would carry his anthropological commitments. Such an analysis was present in the work on narrative done by MacIntyre and Stanley Hauerwas, but Ramsey did not think he needed the category "narrative." Ramsey's use of casuistry shares a great deal in common with a "narrative" approach to ethics, but he refused to use the term "narrative." This is not so much due to his rejection of "narrative," as to his claim that he did not need this category to do what he was already doing. That others distinguished a principled-ethic from narrative exacerbated him. In the paper written by David P. Schmidt , Mr. Schmidt writes:

> While Ramsey sometimes speaks as if Scripture's authoritative aspects is its narrative of God's action in history, biblical narrative plays no role in shaping his theology. They simply give him grounds for formulating concepts which he lifts from the text and restates for his ethical system.

Ramsey, as was his custom, responded.

> The foundation of the Christian moral life might have been more Biblically narrative if (but only if?) I had ascribed independent moral authority to the Ten Commandments. Instead, I said somewhere, and still believe, that each shows its validity because it is "reducible" to simple corollaries of covenant-fidelity. Still how you can say that Biblical narratives qua narratives play "no role" for me I do not see. In addition to the history of the covenant (and in that context: fidelity, hesed, agape, righteousness, a saving justice), what I have written about sexual morality and anthropology endorses and uses Barth's "creation is the external basis and condition of the possibility of covenant" (with the parallel to that). . . . I sometimes suspect that greater emphasis today on the narrative form of Christian identity and life is but another instance of giving primacy to a secular perspective: this time, the aesthetic-literary concept of dramatic narrative.

In this response, Ramsey poses three challenges to the use of "narrative". First he asks, in his rather circuitous way, what do you mean by "Biblical narrative"? If you mean the literal word of Scripture then the only way to be more Biblically narratable would be to allow the ten commandments to stand on their own, uninterpreted. If this is not what is meant, then the second challenge is how can covenant be construed as non-narratival, for it is the ongoing history of the covenant which provides intelligibility to the ten commandments. If this second usage of covenant is not what is meant by "narrative," i.e. the specific covenant between God and Israel and God and the Church, then Ramsey poses a third challenge -- is the use of "narrative" giving primacy to a "secular" notion -- the "aesthetic-literary concept of dramatic narrative?"

The result of this challenge is that Ramsey finds an opposition between a principled ethic and a narrative one unwarranted because his principles are "reducible to simple corollaries of covenant fidelity." Thus, central to his work is the story of God's covenant with Israel and God's redeeming work in Jesus.

What is at stake in Ramsey's refuting the principle/narrative distinction? Nothing less than his need for a principled casuistic ethic as an alternative to secular culture. He needs both principles and narrative to stand against the dominant pragmatist discourse with its future-centered sense of agency. A casuistry which utilized principles reducible to the narrative of God's covenanting activity was as viable a rehabilitation of Christian tradition against an encroaching secular hegemony, as was a lived narrative account which claimed that rightly telling the Gospel story entailed specific virtues. The latter is Stanley Hauerwas' position. Ramsey saw similarities with his position and that of Hauerwas'. They shared a common enemy.[87]

Ramsey wrote a forty-five page review of Stanley Hauerwas' *A Community of Character*. The review explained why Ramsey was not as favorable to the narrative approach as was Hauerwas even though they had similar criticisms of Protestant ethics.

Ramsey begins with an admission as to the increasing irrelevance of his own work: "For some time I have known that my life's work in Christian ethics was a part of the 'eclipse of Biblical narrative' -- along with the rest of the neo-orthodox theology that was written in the United States in the middle of the 20th century." He states that Frei's indictment of this type of biblical theology is "properly drawn". Frei's indictment is as follows:

[There was in this biblical theology] an at least partial dependence on the narratives. And yet the progress in the forms that biblical ideas took, from sensuous to spiritual, and the fact that the meaning of the Bible lies in concepts, pointed "biblical theology" in a new direction: the unity of the canon lies in the development of the moral and religious ideas taught in it, the purest of them . . . being the norm for what is accepted of biblical meaning and biblical unity, in which ideas are self-contained entities undergoing self-explanatory progressive development.[88]

That Ramsey even concedes as much as he does here is quite interesting. In *A Community of Character*, taking Ramsey as the "classical example," Hauerwas charged that "biblical ethics" failed to do justice to the complexity of the Gospel narrative. As an example of the problem with "biblical ethics" Hauerwas wrote:

> For example, Paul Ramsey maintains that the conception of justice in the Bible is radically different from all others because it consists in the principle: "To each according to the measure of his real need, not because of anything human reason can discern inherent in the needy, but because his need alone is the measure of God's righteousness toward him," *Basic Christian Ethics* . . . pp. 13-14. Ramsey is a classical example of an ethicist exploiting the assumption that biblical theology is primarily a matter of locating the central "biblical" concepts. Thus, Ramsey stresses the centrality of love and covenant on the assumption that by doing so his ethic is thereby "biblical."[89]

This charge was similar to Frei's accusation against "biblical theology." Ramsey began his review of Hauerwas' book partially conceding both Frei and Hauerwas' claim. While granting this as a proper indictment of past biblical theology, and possibly even of his own work, Ramsey goes on to question if Hauerwas' approach is actually part of the "recovery of biblical narrative" Frei espouses, and he then defends his principled approach.

His defense begins with an insightful passing comment that for Hauerwas Scripture is "community dependent" while the community is "narrative dependent". But, instead of seeing in this an irreconcilable contradiction, he rightly sees it as a "fruitful circularity."[90] Ramsey does not question this circular reasoning, instead he questions Hauerwas' distinction between ethics as decision with an emphasis on principles (Ramsey's approach), and ethics as a politics of "power" requiring the primary role of memory and narrative to negotiate adequately the complexities of our world (Hauerwas' approach). Hauerwas claims an ethics which focuses on principles and decisions can only superficially deal with the power dimension of our political life. Ramsey is not opposed to the importance of narrative and the concomitant emphasis upon the authority of a specifiable community to sustain narrative as a corrective to an ethic of principles, but he questions the either-or distinction. He writes:

... I had supposed that steadfast covenant love (hesed, agapé) least of all biblical perspectives is capable of being "freed from the narratives of scripture". Is this so-called "concept" drawn mainly from non-narrative portions of scripture? Which then might falsely be claimed to be intelligible from "reason" or "nature," or readily translated into some "more general theological medium"? Is it not nourished by the shared memory of a particular community, and firmly anchored precisely in biblical narrative?[91]

This is the central question Ramsey poses to Hauerwas -- how can you so easily distinguish between principles or "concepts" and narrative? Can narrative itself be simply one more form of principle or concept?

Ramsey levies two main criticism. 1. Hauerwas seeks a "more rigorous standard of justification" for those who use "principles" language than he does for his own use of "narrative". 2. Hauerwas uses narrative as a "ritualistic solvent". This prevents an adequate development of an ontology or doctrine of creation, and thus he inadequately expresses human "embodiment". Both of these critiques are meant to further clarify "narrative," and not simply dismantle it.[92]

Too Rigorous Standard Of Justification For Principles?

Hauerwas argues that an ethics of principles develops "general admonitions" drawn from Scripture rather than being attentive to the Gospel story itself. In place of this, he advocates the importance of "rightly telling the story." But, Ramsey asks, how are we to adjudicate between "general admonitions" and "rightly telling the story"? Ramsey asks how these "general admonitions" differ from Hauerwas' own "moral notions" such as: "hope and patience; to be courageous and faithful; to understand and face truthfully the divided character of the world; the unexpected, especially as it comes in the form of strangers, can be welcomed as a gift; to live "out of control" truthfully by a truth never possessed and released from the necessity to "control the world in the name of security;. . . turning "the stranger into a friend," etc.".[93] Ramsey then says, "All the above are, according to Hauerwas, prime characteristics of the kind of community that can "rightly tell the stories of God." All I want to say at the moment is: Indeed they are -- and also covenant love."

Ramsey also questions Hauerwas contention that a "biblical ethic" leads to ascribing a distinctiveness to the biblical view which is really not there.

Ramsey writes:

Up front in that footnote #16 was Hauerwas' reference to my view that
"the conception of justice in the Bible is radically different from the storied reality that a human being's need alone is the measure of God's
righteousness toward him" (BCE, PP. 13-14). I should think that if a
term translatable "justice" is in the Bible, its meaning might also be said
to be constituted by "turning the stranger into a friend" (Hauerwas, p.
26) characteristic of a people who can truthfully tell the story of God.
Indeed something like that -- the "sojourner" or alien resident in the land
of God's promise -- was a chief statement of my theme (along with
"justice" to or "judging" the needy, the widows and orphans). But
mainly I need to say here that I do not know how to respond to the
charge that a claim of "distinctiveness" is a flaw in any biblical theological ethics when this charge is brought by an author who himself affirms
that "the results" of being Christian may well, in society's terms, "seem
less than good" (Hauerwas, p. 1).[94]

In this response Ramsey somewhat misses the main import of Hauerwas'
critique. Hauerwas was not arguing against the importance of the distinctiveness of the biblical outlook. He was only saying that "biblical
ethics" was often trapped in a defense of the distinctiveness of some
"biblical" *concept* because it tried to show how this particular moral *concept* or term was distinct from all other explications of it. Thus, in arguing for the "distinctiveness" of the "concept" it missed the true distinctiveness of Christianity – a *lived* narrative. Yet Ramsey did not miss the
point entirely, for he does respond that the "concept" is not abstracted
from a lived narrative, and that lived narratives do not exist without
concepts and principles capable of defining the moral terrain.

Ramsey acknowledges the advantages of Hauerwas' insistence on an
ecclesial context for ethics. He states that Hauerwas' correction to biblical ethics "requires narrative; and the authority of narrative requires this
community," to which he responds, "So far, so good." Narrative, because it presupposes some community to sustain it, helps elucidate the
central significance of power relationships in Christian ethics. But why,
asks Ramsey, are principles excluded from also assisting in this elucidation?

Because he understands his principled casuistic ethic to stand against
"liberalism" as well as Hauerwas' narrative approach, Ramsey challenges
the superiority of narrative for addressing the politics of power. Any
such address, Ramsey argues, will also have room for principles. In fact,
the elucidation of principles is important, because as Alasdair MacIntyre
noted, Ramsey's work reminds us that supposedly neutral principles
perpetuate communal voices from the past even when we fail to recognize those voices.

This should cause us to pause and consider what is meant by the
term "principle." Principle, as "source or beginning or spring of disposi-

tion and action" has a double meaning.[95] On the one hand, it is a law-like generalization -- "rape is wrong." But on the other hand, it is an internalized action, a habit or disposition, by which one negotiates the moral world wittingly or unwittingly. The two senses of principle cannot be easily disentangled. Thus Ramsey knew that his advocacy of certain principles was also an attempt at moral formation. He also knew that the advocacy of certain principles by the U.S. Judiciary or by the Church's "social action-curia" formed people morally as well. There was no "foundational moral sentiment" nor self-evident natural law that was not inscribed by principles. This recognition resulted from his idealism, and it was a vast improvement over the reigning realism that assumed the self-evidentiary presence of the real. For Ramsey the "real" required *discourse* on being. While realism stressed being without the discourse, Ramsey suggested that narrative emphasized the discourse without the being. Because it need not answer any question of ontology, Ramsey thought narrative could not give an adequate account of *bodily* existence.

While both Ramsey and Hauerwas viewed "liberal culture" as a threat to the Christian life, they located the problem differently. For Ramsey, liberal culture destroys the individual by turning every *body* into a "laboratory animal." This led Ramsey to "ontology" to emphasize the body. Hauerwas thought Ramsey needed to go back one step further. Surrounding the body with protection was insufficient if the claim that "the individual itself is a social creation" is not first realized. This led Hauerwas to emphasize the narrative production of the self.[96] While Ramsey's position had the advantage of taking seriously our materiality, Hauerwas' position seeks more earnestly than did Ramsey for specific practices that counter the dominant modes that produce selves.

Narrative and the Body

Ramsey sees Hauerwas' emphasis on narrative contributing to the neglect of any "ontology" or "doctrine of creation". He suggests that the reason this is so is because narrative has a "dualistic account of the human body" incapable of adequately expressing our "embodiment".

In a discussion of Ramsey's ethics of sexuality under the title "Conservative Accounts of Sexual Ethics" Hauerwas takes issue with Ramsey for grounding the exclusivity of the marriage covenant in creation or ontology. He writes, "it must be conceded that . . . the status of [Ramsey's] 'ontological' account of sexuality is far from clear." Hauerwas does not deny the exclusivity of the marriage covenant, but he provides a different reason for it. "What is required for such an argument [i.e., Ramsey's] to be intelligible is an account why marriage should be understood as exclusive. It is my contention that such an account requires a recovery of the political function of marriage in the Christian community."[97]

Ramsey denies that his "ontological account" is unclear. He quotes from his essay "One Flesh" against which Hauerwas levied this charge.

> . . . human sexuality is neither a physiological nor a psychological faculty. It is ontological in the biblical sense of the word. Among philosophers of course, ontology means "discourse about being," even as sociology means discourse about society. All such words in our language naming the sciences direct our attention to an object to be studied. In contrast, the Bible places the stress on discourse, the logos, the word, on being coming to light only in relationship or in the discourse between God and man and among humankind. This is what I mean by saying that human sexuality is the word of one being to another being, whether in the garden of Paradise or in the wilderness of this world of fallen men and women who also, of course, live to the east of Eden.[98]

Ramsey comments on this passage: "If Hauerwas sees no glimmer of meaning in that, then I suspect that we shall soon discover that his account of the human body is 'dualistic'."[99]

What is Ramsey's point? I take it to be this. His understanding of ontology means that language is indeed constitutive of reality -- "the *discourse between* God and man and among humankind" -- and that reality, in terms of bodily presence, is also constitutive of language. These two claims are mutually interpenetrating. If only the first is emphasized, and narrative is used as a term depicting that all reality elides into language, then we have a disembodied account of narrative. This position is a strong contender in a "post-modern world," but it remains as idealistic as Descartes' view of rationality for it neglects our embodiment.

This provides one more interpretation, and perhaps the most persuasive, of Ramsey's use of Barth's "creation as the external basis of the covenant and the covenant as the internal basis of creation." Ramsey uses creation -- being an embodied creature, our materiality -- simply as one necessary aspect of our capability for covenant.

John Milbank made a similar critique in his review of Hauerwas' *Against the Nations*. Interestingly, it is within the context of the significance of just war argumentation for condemning nuclear weapons on the basis of the principle of proportionality because our human bodies are a necessary pre-condition for any human goods. Milbank writes:

> [Hauerwas] underrates the capacity of just-war argumentation to rule out the use and the possession of nuclear arms on the grounds, not of the conditions involved in waging war, but of the ends sought by war. All Hauerwas can see in the arguments of "survivalists" like Jonathan

Schell is a utilitarian concern: but it is possible to argue (like John Locke) that ecological well-being is, if not an ultimate, at least a basic goal, as the presupposition of other human goods in this life (and this life is co-terminous with our present responsibility). This does justice to our embodiment, and without this Hauerwas's pacifism still has a spiritualist and deontological flavour. He fails to distinguish between concern for the survival of "our nation" and a much more ontologically basic concern for the future of the planet and of the human race. It is in a way strange that Hauerwas does not take the opportunity to argue here that the state-Prometheus can make us forgetful of our natural being. Perhaps he is somehow suspicious of the "universal" appeal of the ecological argument. But it is possible to say that Christian ethics, with its rejection of inevitable nemesis and fatality particularly stresses a positive and nurturing attitude towards our finitude. If part of the secular world stresses this also, then well and good — this is a true "point of contact", though it is traceable to contingency and historically and not founded in any recognized law of nature or transcendental anthropology.[100]

Milbank and Ramsey become allies against Hauerwas in emphasizing the role of the body. Both stress the significance of the body and both find a "point of contact" between this emphasis with the "secular world." The difference between Milbank and Ramsey is that Milbank recognizes the contingency of his claim and Ramsey finds in the point of contact a "natural" connection because he grounds the body in a transcendental anthropology.

Milbank will trace the "point of contact" between liberal political philosophy and Christianity to mere contingency, whereas Ramsey will trace it to a love transformed natural law. Yet what good does the recognition of contingency accomplish? Both positions are narrations that read a "point of contact'" into the story. Insofar as Milbank rules out the possibility of a "recognized law of nature" his narrative is no more generous toward differences than is Ramsey's. Recognizing contingency does not allow for the true acknowledgment of the other any more than does Ramsey's ability to explain otherness in terms of a natural law already inscribed by the Christian narrative. The point to be made is that Ramsey's transcendental anthropology or Milbank's emphasis on contingency do not matter. They are theories which have no consequences.[101] Milbank's recognition of our contingency has no more ability to stand against totalitarian forces than does Ramsey's insistence on a transcendental grounding for anthropology. Still, the importance of "embodiment" stressed by both Ramsey and Milbank is an important addition to Hauerwas' narrative emphasis. Even if the body becomes nothing more than a "nodal point for communication networks,"[102] it will still be a *body* being manipulated, controlled or resisting.

Ramsey's transcendental anthropology makes little difference for his ethics. It is a narration that he tells because of his Christian convictions. It is an effort to persuade people that the human body should not be reduced to manipulation for a technological future. But the anthropology requires strong theological convictions. The anthropology itself actually does little work for him, while his casuistry does.

The role of Ramsey's casuistry as an alternative discourse is further clarified by his two critiques of Hauerwas' narrative approach. Hauerwas said that Ramsey's "casuistry rest on his belief that the notion of the absolutely unique, inviolable, irreplaceable individual human life exists in our civilization because it is Christian . . .". In other words, Ramsey can "extend" Christian love into the making of public policy only because he assumes a basis for the possibility of such an extension because of the imprint of Christianity upon western legal-juridical-political process based on the idea of the sanctity of the individual. Ramsey responded:[103]

> There are, of course, stretches in what we may dignify my "special ethics" where the Christian word to be heard is not resounding in every paragraph. Call this Christian "casuistry" if you will -- but not for the reason you state. Your grounds for my endeavor to do public ethics is partially true, as an appeal to *past* Christian influences perhaps not yet altogether lost. Doubtless I may hope against hope that some among the "hearers" may strengthen their adherence to the best of past culture; or maybe search among their premises and find that they have no breastplate of righteousness with which to gird the irreplaceability and unmeldability of every human soul. But I, the author, have not left Christian premises behind when I go on to do special ethics. You may *disagree* with the way I go about doing special ethics theologically, there where you say that my "dramatic and significant assertions" are only "assertions" for which no adequate theological warrant is supplied. I think everyone of them is adequately warranted, and *directly* by the giftedness of life. I judge that simple warrant to be enough. You may want me at this point to pause and retell the whole Christian story. But then we disagree more in style than in substance, for I never left that behind. . . . My foundational work is not [the humanist's] nor [the humanist's] mine. But I do believe that while Christianity ought always to be willing to be a sect whenever necessary, there is always at work a culture- forming impulse as well.

Ramsey's "casuistry" is not opposed to "narrative," rather it seeks to transform reality so that certain principles can be embodied in the structures of earthly existence. Those principles will then "extend" the Christian story so that as many persons as possible might be "surrounded" by a discriminating love.[104]

By "surrounding" as many persons as possible through casuistical analysis, Ramsey sought to stand against the dominant pragmatist mode of moral rationality. The dominant mode neglected the importance of *bodily* existence by reducing the body to a mere means for political ends.[105] A place for the body needs to be secured because the body was a necessary gift for covenant.

Securing a place for the body was not an end in itself. The body was not sacred apart from the covenant. Thus, important ends exist for which bodies are sacrificed, both one's own and others'. Just war principles and a medical indications policy clarified those conditions where bodies could be killed or no longer sustained without violating the covenant that established both the gift of the body, and also placed limitations upon making bodily existence an end in and of itself. Just war principles were to be skillfully used to "extend" the area of non-combatant immunity as far as possible to secure the importance of the body while at the same time refusing to make the body an end in itself. A medical indications policy was to be skillfully used to "extend" care to the non-dying and dying without forsaking the claims others have on us because of who we are.

Yet an important discrimination needs to be made between Ramsey's casuistry on war and medical practice. In medical practice, tragic situations represent exceptions; it is not an essential part of medical practice. We do not live in a state of triage where tragedy is always unavoidable. At a conference on medical ethics, Allen Verhey suggested that Ramsey's medical ethics presupposed an account of tragedy. Ramsey responded, ". . . an account of finitude as tragic or human beings entrapped by their very natures as creatures in irremediably ambiguous moral decisions cannot be a part of biblical narrative."[106] While the practice of medicine is not based on the presumption of a necessarily tragic world, the necessary practice of war is. Thus we return to a central theme in this book, the ontology of tragedy that undergirds Ramsey's work. Although Ramsey's casuistry does offer some alternative space within modern life for the practice of the Christian moral life, his use of casuistry remained limited due to the underlying tragic nature of political existence.

Just War: Casuistry or Ontology of Tragedy?

In Ramsey's work, two specific practices compete as a context to render intelligible his casuistry. His casuistry is on the one hand a pastoral attempt to clarify and preserve Christian faithfulness in the modern era. Scott Davis suggests the term "pastoral responsibility" to define Ramsey's use of Augustine.

> [Pastoral responsibility] is the position of someone within a tradition who speaks out with the intention of protecting and sustaining the integrity of the tradition and its members. . . . Pastoral responsibility requires a constant awareness of the dangers inherent in balancing the goods of a particular human community against the hard teachings of Christ.[107]

Pastoral responsibility defines one of the specific practices that render intelligible Ramsey's casuistry.

Yet Ramsey's casuistry also presupposes a specific political practice best described as "just war." Just war is not merely an ethic about war for Ramsey; it is also a political practice necessary because of tragedy. Ramsey's use of just war reveals these two practices; just war is a casuistry reflecting pastoral responsibility, and just war is a political practice that makes some use of force and violence necessary for political responsibility. These two practices are in contradiction with each other. The casuistical use of just war for pastoral responsibility is a wonderful help for Christian ethical reflection, but the casuistical use of just war for political responsibility where tragedy defines the political rejects *Christian* ethical reflection.

As a pastoral casuistical tool, just war principles are helpful in defining the moral terrain. In the essay, "The Case For Making 'Just War' Possible," Ramsey demonstrated this. He began by pointing out an improper use of the commandment: "Thou shalt not kill."

> However, it is only when the commandment "Thou shalt not kill" is viewed *legalistically,* and only when the actions that are licit or illicit under it are viewed *externally,* that the Christians who formulated the just war theory can be said to have made, in regard to killing another human being, one, single, clearly defined and limited *exception,* and nothing more.[108]

Just war theory was not an exception-making theory. Instead it was the articulation of an exceptionless principle to describe the moral terrain. It is not a "Stoic" importation nor a bifurcation between public and private morality or between justice and love. It is what Christian conscience allows because it expresses the unique polity of being Christian which Ramsey called agape. "It was an *expression* of the Christian understanding of political responsibility in terms of neighbor-regarding love."

The development of just war norms defines the outer boundary of Christian moral reasoning concerning participation in war. Just war is the quintessential casuistical practice for Ramsey. The language he uses in discussing its development within "Christian conscience" is the same language used to define his methodology in "The Case of the Curious Exception." "By the same stroke definite limits were placed upon the conduct of war by surrounding *non-combatants* with moral immunity from *direct* attack."[109] The key word is "surrounding," a word we have seen before in Ramsey's description of his own ethical method. Other terms are also present such as "clarify," "extend," and "render intelligible." The casuistry is useful in illustrating the complexity of our actions, and delineating what would constitute a faithless practice even in tragic situations.

Nevertheless, "tragedy" too rigidly defines responsible political possibilities. I am not arguing against all uses of "tragedy." Yet Ramsey's work falls short in its delineation of faithless practices because tragedy constrains the possible political transformation Christian ethics brings to the "natural." Given Ramsey's political philosophy, with the central role of tragedy, the exercise of just war, or even an unjust war with deferred repentance, is the best that can be accomplished.

An ontology of tragedy is found throughout Ramsey's work, beginning with his metaphysics of democracy where he suggested that democracy is an expression of the idealistic philosophy of the state because it expresses the duality of the finite-infinite self -- "finite in that the individual needs to be transcended and controlled, infinite in that he can transcend and control himself." The individual is caught in an inescapably tragic situation. On the one hand, individuals need to be controlled to prevent the threatening anarchy. On the other hand, individuals themselves can *and must* keep the anarchy and sin at bay through the use of force and coercion.

Ramsey reminds us of a lesson he himself forgot, namely that this view of tragedy was not a Reformation insight, but the reproduction of "contradiction and negativity" as foundational for politics.[110] This leads Ramsey to accept violence as a necessary structure of being within political society. This view of political society finds expression in the subtitle to his 1968 book, *Just War: Force and Responsibility*. Ramsey imposes a necessary dialectic between the use of force and responsible government to political society.

Intrinsic to the nature of a political society is a law, embodied in just war, which can't be violated without at the same time violating the very essence of political society. Force is one of the ends of responsible political society or the political society itself cannot be maintained. But force must be used within certain limits or the political society cannot be *responsibly* maintained. On the one hand, this is a truism. Destructive force is never justifiable because it is destructive. To resort to it destroys the very thing one wants to secure in resorting to it. In this sense, Ramsey's claim about the nature of political society is beyond critique.

On the other hand, this doesn't tell us much. What is the "thing" political society secures? We don't know the purpose of political society; without that knowledge how can we know when the limit is surpassed?

When a law intrinsic to the nature of political society is invoked, even as a truism, and we can't tell precisely what the purpose of political society is, then how will we know if and when that limit for which responsible force is to be used has been surpassed? Without that knowledge, Ramsey's politics become positively harmful. Actors in the international stage, be they nation states or whatever, are supposedly bound intrinsically by being a "political society" to limited war as the only effective option. Yet we still need to know what the purpose of political society is to make sense of this intrinsic law to political being that constrains the use of responsible force.

Ramsey discussed the purpose of political society in the first chapter, "The Uses of Power" in *The Just War*. He claimed that "the use of power, and possibly the use of armed force, is of the *esse* of politics and inseparably connected with those higher human goods which are the *bene esse* of politics in all the historical ages of mankind."[111] He goes on to explain this:

> ... politics is defined by both its *genus* (community) and its *specific difference* (the use of power). What political community has in common with other communities (friendship, economic associations, professional and cultural groups transcending national boundaries) within the *genus* to which they all belong may comprise the higher human qualities. Every community pursues a common good, or a good in common. But the legitimate use of decisive physical power distinguishes political community from these other communities in the formation of the life of mankind. *Generic* social values are the matter of politics; but so also is the *specific* use of power. You can say that the former comprise the higher values to which the latter is a conditional value; but not that the latter is a merely extrinsic instrument that can be dropped. In fact, in the *definitional* sense of "primary" and "secondary," *generic* community values are the secondary (i.e. the distinctly human) purpose of politics while the use of power comprises the differentiating *species* or the primary (i.e. the distinctive) modality of politics. I mean only to repeat this in the proposition: the use of power, and possibly the use of force, is of the *esse* of politics, and it is inseparable from the *bene esse* of politics. This entails no derogation of the uniquely human ends, the generic values, the *bene esse* of political community. Quite the contrary. This puts power in its place in our understanding of politics by definitely placing it within the pursuit of the political good.[112]

Anyone who desires to understand Ramsey's purpose for political society needs to grapple with this convoluted passage. Central is the distinction between primary and secondary. The "generic" community values, such as the common good, are "secondary" in that they are one step removed from the actual specific usage of political force which is "primary". They are not "secondary" in value, to the contrary they "comprise the higher values." Thus, the use of responsible force is always subordinate to these higher values, but these higher values have as their condition the use of responsible force.

In a letter responding to James Childress's dissertation, Ramsey further explained what he meant in this passage.

> I said that order is always and everywhere a <u>conditional</u> value to justice, etc., just as physical life and health are conditional values to the pursuit of any of the higher human activities by an individual. . . . This would entail that (as in Maritain's infravalent and supravalent ends) order or health are values, ends in themselves, not merely menial (as force is in politics) but that these are *also* instrumental or conditional to higher human values or goals on the part of either society or the individual. The upshot of this exposition is to say that I find nothing in this most 'hierarchical' expression of my position to justify your suggestion from time to time that I neglect or omit the higher values of politics or too greatly emphasize order. . . . I would insist also that, while I define the <u>esse</u> of politics to be the use of power or constraint, I have not failed to say in the same breadth (as you report) that the <u>bene esse</u> of politics (the proper act of politics) includes much more, only *always related* to a possible use of force.[113]

This midrash responds to Childress's claim that Ramsey "reduced politics to the use of power and coercion." Childress's claim is quite similar to my own charge, except that I am not arguing that Ramsey *reduced* politics to coercion, but that any responsible political act was "*always related* to a possible use of force." In other words, politics can never escape force, violence, and coercion. Then pastoral responsibility must be exercised within the contours already defined by this political responsibility. While Ramsey may allow for the purpose of political society to be a just order, it could never be a peaceable one.

This understanding of political society fits within a broader context -- the world community and the international good.

> A nation's responsibilities are indeed to be located within an area of congruence between the national common good and the common good of other peoples; but these are not fixed areas of overlap. They are permeable boundaries, and boundaries that can be construed narrowly or with a deeper sensitivity to the meaning of each. The Christian influence in our nation, it would seem, should be in the direction of including within the scope of national policy as much of the world common

good as is realistically possible, and toward this nation providing itself with usable power, and the use of power, commensurate with these responsibilities so far as this can be done.[114]

The political common good is overlapped by the world common good. The boundaries between these goods are permeable. The use of responsible force should be as coincident as possible within the overlap between the international and political good, but only in an ideal world would there be full coincidence. Thus some strife and violence is written into political being; the usage of power is never fully coincident with the world common good for the use of power is first bound by the national political good.[115]

From this understanding of political society, Ramsey attempts to deconstruct the antinomy of Lutheran realism and a Thomist "organic" approach. In essence he is combining Maritain's integralism with Reinhold Niebuhr's "realism". Maritain's integralism assumed a Thomistic organic harmony between the various levels of political government from the family to the international community. This organic view was also the basis for much of the political philosophy of the Social Gospel.

Ramsey synthesizes this organic view with Niebuhrian realism. Niebuhr's criticisms called the organic view into question. This was why Niebuhr's central thesis was that the "liberal movement, both religious and secular, seemed to be unconscious of the basic difference between the morality of individuals and the morality of collectives -- races, classes, or nations."[116] Niebuhr was challenging a tradition which saw an inevitable coincidence between the good of an individual soul, that of the collective in which the individual lived, and the world common good. It was utopian and misleading because it neglected a proper analysis of power.

Ramsey represents a convergence of these two traditions. The view of political society he offered contained elements of both Niebuhrian realism and the organic model. But it was a fluid view. The boundaries were permeable. One could not say *a priori* that no coincidence existed between the private and public good; but one could say that full coincidence was impossible.

Ramsey reveals his effort to converge the realist and organic models of political society in an important footnote in *The Just War*. He writes:

> It is, of course, possible for natural law teachings so to stress the *bene esse,* the common good, that the component of power is lost from view; and for the Lutheran view to stress restraint and lose sight of justice and the other community values that also belong to the essence of political authority and the action of rulers.[117]

While this is an effort at convergence of the organic and realist traditions, the result resembles the idealistic "metaphysics of democracy." Tragedy follows. Tragically, the area of coincidence *cannot be* complete. The person who understands Ramsey's political philosophy . . .

> . . . will ceaselessly call attention also to the fact that the longing for peace, and cries that we cannot police the world, can lead to an ever more narrow coincidence of Christian impulses within Fortress America. He will lend no credence, not even by silence, to the notion that we can be involved in the world's problems economically, and not politically and militarily (i.e. tragically).[118]

Because the tragedy of human existence is that no complete coincidence is possible, conflict is inevitable. Contradiction and negativity define the political. To be political is to be involved militarily and tragically. No other option is possible.

Notice how intelligible Ramsey's work becomes because of his political philosophy. The role of "tragedy," rather than Christian theological concerns such as sanctification and regeneration, construct a vision for what is possible if we are to be involved in the "world's problems." Economic and political problems cannot be redressed without the tragedy of military means.

Just war as a casuistic exercise, arising from an ecclesial tradition, and delineating possible ways in which Christians can be involved faithfully in the use of force, has been supplanted by just war as the description of a necessarily tragic political order. The Church only represents an "ethos" within this structure of political being. Christians cannot avoid participation in the structures of suffering, sin, guilt, (and tragedy). Within the gray area of coincidence between the political and world good, the Christian thinks "politically in the light of Christ, and he will think politically in the light of the revealing shadow thrown by the cross of Christ over our fallen human existence."[119] What does this mean for how one thinks politically?

> It means that in the time of God's patience, our political offices must serve to preserve the world against the destructiveness to which otherwise we all would be driven. The state is ordained of God as a "garment of skin" (Genesis 3: 21) in which human nakedness may be clothed, and in which men may together find a tolerably secure dwelling place. This, in turn, means that among the collectives and in all collective action, identification and community and love pass not directly from man to man, but *through structures.* There are no "outcomes" and no right pursuit of better "outcomes," in the larger questions of domestic justice, and certainly not in diplomacy and international relations, that do not require us to look inside the existing political structures for cracks or

places where a structural change may be initiated and take root -- over which a greater political identification of man with man may pass.[120]

Political possibilities can only be found in "*existing* political structures" which are defined according to the tragic dialectic of Niebuhrian realism and philosophical idealism. An alternative is not countenanced.

Within Ramsey's political philosophy, just war is understood as regulating the nature of political conflict where that nature is defined by the unavoidability of tragedy. Yet, in contrast to this, just war as an ecclesial practice of penance suggests the possibility of living God's righteousness because of the presence of the Kingdom. For instance, in the Penitential of Theodore, Jesus' words, "Repent for the Kingdom of Heaven is at hand" (Mt. 4: 17) were interpreted not as a threat, nor a restraining force, but as the possibility for a new way of life. "Do penance" is interpreted as "the law of penance which the Lord Jesus, when he was baptized before us all, proclaims as the instrument of his teaching for those who had no means of healing."[121] This possibility is lost when just war is understood as the law regulating the nature of political conflict. Instead of just war as a confessional practice for the possibility of healing -- just war as therapy, it becomes a preservative ordinance requiring as a positive duty the employment of force and violence.

Because the best the Church can do is look for "cracks" in the "existing political structure," the Church as a possible alternative political society where the tragedy of the necessary use of force and coercion are not known is impossible. The world political community is so "structured" that just war as an ecclesial practice, as therapy, standing against this structure providing an alternative vision for a different way of life is lost. Just war is constrained by the nation-state system; the two are even synonymous. Thus, just war as an ecclesial practice cannot be expected to offer a definitive critique of that system.

The usurpation of possible faithful alternatives by the necessary politically tragic misleads Ramsey's casuistry on the Viet Nam war and on nuclear deterrence in three important instances. First he assumes that democracy is necessary for a politically good life, as long as democracy can be secured without violating the test of discrimination that defines the politically good life.

> I would say that no Christian should assist communism of any variety in coming to power; we should prevent or assist in the prevention of this if we can. The obligation disappears, however, if we cannot, or if we cannot without causing greater evils in the process.[122]

Because Ramsey's metaphysics of democracy defines true political being, alternatives such as communism cannot be countenanced.

Second, Ramsey's commitment to democracy and the defeat of communism led him to expand the principle of non-combatant immunity to the point where it became non-combatant non-immunity.

> . . . it is the insurgency and not counter-insurgency that has enlarged the area of civilian death and damage that is legitimately collateral. When war is planned and carried out by an opponent on the principle that the guerilla lives among the people like a fish in water, we may be justified in accepting the destruction of an entire school of fish (and the unavoidable and foreknown destruction of a great many people intermingled with them) incidental to the elimination of the guerrillas, provided only that the elimination of the school of fish is important enough to the whole course of the war the winning of which is judged to be the lesser evil (or greater good).[123]

This argument amounts to saying that we will live by our "principled" ethic unless our enemy does not, and then we will blame him for our failure to be "principled" in our actions. How is this warranted from the best of Ramsey's own casuistical ethic?

As far as I know, Ramsey never changed his mind on the enemies' ability to enlarge the area of non-combatant immunity. In 1981 Ed Santurri wrote Ramsey inquiring about a debate Santurri had with a colleague. Santurri asked Ramsey whether this enlargement meant only that more non-combatants could be legitimately killed indirectly with proportional limitations (Santurri's read) or whether "the enlarging of the target transformed the status of the non-combatants to the status of combatants and thus they could justifiably be killed directly" (the colleague's read). Ramsey responded:

> The thesis of the par. on p. 435 is that the insurgents have enlarged the legitimate target, and the thesis of the par. on p. 435 is that they also have enlarged the area of death and damage that is legitimately collateral. So I think you and your colleague were both correct.[124]

Ramsey went on to explain his position.

> Something more had to be said descriptively than that one does not have to know who or where non-combatants are, but only that they are there, in order to know that a military strike should be limited in its destructiveness as closely as possible to the legitimate objective determined to be important enough in a proportionate defense. In Vietnam one didn't know who or where the combatants were, but only that they were there! So I argued that whole areas could be deemed morally to be "legitimate target" for judgments of discrimination. Whether legitimate by the test of proportion is always the next question.

I'd still defend for a while the language of these two paragraphs until someone gives me better terms to use. If a man who has just committed a murder (say shoot a cop) is running away in the crowd on Times Square, another cop under a supposable circumstance, should not seize (or shoot) him. But if he is continuing to kill randomly, he is responsible for enlarging the area of permissible indirect deaths incidental to the cop's duty to stop that. That's p. 436. If the criminal has seized a hostage to use as a shield while fleeing, the cop ought not to shoot, but again should wait, etc. However, if from behind a hostage-shield the criminal is continuing to kill randomly, he is responsible for enlarging the target to include the hostage, he has rendered the target ambiguous, in contrast to the first case of random continuous killing that the cop's duty is to stop. And he shouldn't limit himself to shooting at the four legs he sees at a distance in front of him!

You do understand, however, that I was trying to see my way clear in the specifics of insurgency/counter-insurgency warfare, up against those who alleged that we were "aiming at whole areas and their populations," who allowed the insurgents to determine that there were no legitimate targets, and who -- to say the least -- allowed the principle of discrimination to be used to win the war in the minds and hearts of Americans at home. Since I'm writing personally, let me go on to say that I was too long in reaching the conclusion that that war became disproportionate. The cause was just, I believe, it was not deliberately fought indiscriminately. . . . In extenuation, I could call attention to the fact that I have always argued that *jus in bello* judgments are clearer than *jus ad* (or *contra*) *bellum* judgments, discrimination more readily applied than proportion (which seeks to trammel up all consequences of to war or not to war), and -- most important of all -- that Christians and moralists reach the point where they should see that they no longer see what's politically and militarily right comes in the latter than in the former sort of verdicts. This means that in the latter sort, one decides as a citizen-magistrate one way or the other, and not as a Christian *as such*, or as a moralist. I do believe that Christians, moralists, et cetera, did the right thing (stopped the war) for the wrong reasons. If I were a consequentialist, I would be happier with the results, but for the fact that precisely the same sort of confusion still afflicts our public discourse in the emerging debate about this nation's military policy. Witness what's said about the neutron battlefield weapon (it's a "bomb" that kills "people" without destroying "property") without at the same time explicitly urging and campaigning for other means of war by conventional forces redressing the imbalance in the European theatre and elsewhere.[125]

In 1981 Ramsey still understood the enemy to define who would be a non-combatant and who would not. Even though he maintains the test of proportionality as a limitation on war's destructiveness, the ability of the enemy to define non-combatancy renders the just war as pastoral responsibility, useless.

I would suggest that the reason Ramsey can allow the recipients of the bombing to enlarge the bombers target is directly due to Ramsey's own expansion of his "principled" ethic in the face of real threats to democracy. Because democracy defines the natural limit for the political good, and because just war expresses that natural limit, the just war criteria serve the purpose of establishing democracy rather than clarifying the church's witness. At this point, Ramsey's casuistry exists not for the purpose of illuminating particulars and surrounding people with steadfast love. Instead it lives in the ambiguity which an abuse of casuistry can always create, and in so creating, it justifies the cultivation of the appearance (if not the reality) of evil.

The third instance where tragedy defines Ramsey's ethical response rather than casuistry is when his casuistry is intentionally used to cultivate deception. Casuistry as creating ambiguity and appearance of evil is never more clear in Ramsey's work than when he briefly flirted with the moral viability of "the bluff." Ramsey's argument for the bluff went through four important stages. The first stage established that "collateral civilian damage" would result from "counter-forces warfare." This was an *indirect* effect of a legitimate act of war. Thus the possession of nuclear weapons for counter-forces purposes is legitimate. The second stage of the argument suggests that the "mere possession" of these weapons has a deterrent effect. Built into this deterrent effect is the "dual use" the weapons have; they can be used either against strategic forces or centers of population. Based on this dual usage Ramsey's third stage distinguishes between the "appearance" and "actuality" of a counter-population deterrent policy. The actuality of such a proposal he rules out on just war grounds, but not so the "appearance." His point is that if such an appearance arises, then "such deception cannot be said to be based on the criminal intention or conditional willingness to murder." The fourth stage of his argument raises the question whether such deception is legitimate. At least this much must be said on Ramsey's behalf, at this point he recognizes danger and treads gingerly. Nevertheless, he still allows for the deception, it "may be necessary to save *their* [the enemies'] lives as well as those of our own civilians." Not being purely a utilitarian, Ramsey understands the weakness of that argument, so he continues,

> it [the deception] may be necessary in order to save them (and ourselves) from a measure of complicity in their government's conditional or actual willingness to save them by doing mass murder, or from the *tragedy* (not the *wickedness*) of actually being saved by murderous intention (if a wrongly willed deterrent worked) and some of them from the tragedy of living on in a world in which their lives have been spared in

the midst of the greatest possible wrong-*doing* by a government which in remote degrees of participation was still their own (if the shared intentional risk does not work). So the question resolves itself into the question whether it is ever right to withhold the truth in order to save life, to save from moral wrong-doing, to save from sheer tragedy.

Ramsey suggests, and only suggests, the need for deception to keep from people the tragedy that defines their lives. In fact, he goes on to say:

> I am so far from believing that one ought readily to justify this deception that it seems to me that the first two types of deterrence must, if at all possible, be made to work. Still if deterrence were based on a *cultivated ambiguity* about our real intentions, and if "deception" in an objectionable moral sense would thus in some measure be perpetrated, it would still be an intent to deceive and not an intent possibly to do murder. Perhaps we should say that we ought to be conditionally willing to strive for this ingredient in deterrence, that is, on the condition that it is necessary to deter and save life.[126]

This is Ramsey's casuistry at its worst. He uses it not to illumine particulars for the purpose of faithfulness, but to "cultivate ambiguity" for the purposes of the nation state. Coupling this hesitant legitimation of deception by political leaders with the enemy combatants' ability to enlarge the combatant target, what could this casuistry not legitimate? We are back to Nietzche where we have gone completely beyond good and evil, this time, by way of casuistry.

Casuistry to cultivate ambiguity directly opposes Ramsey's casuistry as a means to illuminate particulars. While "principles" were supposed to be employed as a way of moral formation directing us toward faithfulness, they now lose all positive pedagogical usefulness and only teach people ambiguity and deceit.

At its best, Ramsey's casuistry serves the purpose of illuminating the Christian life by rendering particulars intelligible to people who have been formed by the Christian vision. At its worst, Ramsey's casuistry serves the purpose of cultivating ambiguity so that particulars become unintelligible to the exercise of someone's practical wisdom. In the latter situation, Ramsey's distinctions serve to further diminish the already diminishing space for the practice of the Christian moral life. This latter usage embodies everything Ramsey worked against. It constrains his casuistry within a proportionalism; for whatever is most useful "to save or defer life" defines the moral terrain. A proportionate moral reasoning cannot avoid a "necessary evil" argument because it cannot discriminate between incommensurate goods.

154

I will conclude this chapter with the best usage of Ramsey's just war casuistry. We already saw Ramsey's critique of the relationship between means and ends within proportionate reason in Protestant social ethics.

> No properly ethical statement has yet been made so long as our moral imperatives are tied to unlimitedly variable ends. Nor has a properly ethical statement yet been made so long as the means are unlimitedly variable that are supposed to lead to fixed, universal ends, even the ends determined by *agape*.[127]

We also saw how the principle of discrimination, proportionality, and a discussion of intentionality by Fr. Ford provided for Ramsey an alternative to proportionate moral reasoning. However, with Fr. Richard McCormick's essay "Ambiguity in Moral Choice," Ramsey sees the principle of double effect confined within the bounds of proportionate reason alone. If double effect is so interpreted, Ramsey fears that no criterion of choice between incommensurable goods will be possible. He voices his concern in a collection of essays he and McCormick edited, *Doing Evil to Achieve Good*.[128]

In *Doing Evil To Achieve Good*, Ramsey's essay, "Incommensurability and Indeterminancy in Moral Choice," critiques McCormick's encompassing the principle of double effect within proportionate reasoning. Ramsey writes:

> My thesis, then, is this: Insofar as proportionate reason refers to choice among commensurable goods, there is, of course, no need for the rule distinguishing between direct and indirect intentionality; one simply directly chooses the measurably greater good and the means thereto even if the latter are evils. But if proportionate reason encompasses also (and we need some term to refer to this sort of decision) choice among ends or goods that are indeterminate or not measurably comparable, then the rule of twofold intentionality has lexical priority in cases of important conflicted values in deciding what manner of action may *morally* be posited which, as a physical action, does evil to achieve good.[129]

Proportionate reason plays a role in determining action among both "commensurate" and incommensurate goods. But conceding doing evil to achieve good only applies to the former.

> The point is for us to understand clearly these two different usages; and to understand why, in the case of indeterminate choice of significant importance morally, a human agent ought not deliberately to intend evil or the impairment or destruction of the good he passes by on the way to his primary goal. If and only if proportionate reason always means

commensurate reasons should we, strictly speaking, ever *do* evil to achieve good.[130]

What is at stake here? The same thing which was at stake in Ramsey's criticism of pragmatism in Protestant social ethics -- "If there are any lessons from the past, surely it is this: that we should not go about revising our moral tradition by pragmatically justifying what we are now preparing to do, but that we should frankly state -- if this is the case that wholly unjustifiable, immoral warfare has now become a necessity." Because of the relativity of our justices, indeterminate goods constitute political existence. Therefore, our reasoning is not "commensurate." We do not have a single continuum by which we reason, but a plexus of overlapping circles. Proportionate reasoning requires the continuum. If the continuum existed, doing evil to achieve good would be possible. But, to entertain the possibility of doing evil to achieve good with respect to indeterminate goods is to discard any Christian approach to the moral life. It requires placing the greatest good -- friendship with God -- on par with other goods.

Ramsey believes that giving primacy to proportionate reason leads to this end. However, this is a belief which has as its presupposition that the "greatest good for persons is friendship with God," and this is "not measurable."[131] This is why double effect must be a matter of discrimination and not proportionality. Because this is the highest good, and it is incommensurate with all other goods, no greater "good" could ever be brought about by its violation. Non-combatant immunity expresses the incommensurability of this good with all other goods. The "inviolability of physical human life" is "the necessary precondition to all other values. . . ."[132] Non-combatants cannot be directly killed because this violates the precondition for the possibility of friendship with God.

What then about combatants? How does their death not violate this precondition? -- through the principle of double effect. The warrior's intention is not to sever a person from the possibility of friendship with God, but only to incapacitate, even if that means kill, a combatant who threatens the life of the neighbor.

The obvious objection to this line of reasoning is that it is casuistical in the pejorative sense. It allows for compromises to be legitimated without cleanly confessing that compromises are being made. In *When War is Unjust: Being Honest in Just-War Thinking*, John Howard Yoder argues that "[double-effect] constitutes a powerful intellectual argument contributing to the downward drift."[133] By "downward drift" he means that as just war reasoning is employed it tends to decrease the "effective restraints" against killing.[134] Yoder argues that double effect especially leads to this lack of restraint.

Yoder's argument seems historically verifiable. Just War most often serves the interests of the ruling class.[135] "Any set of rule," he argues, "will tend to favor the interests of those who wrote the rules."[136] Ramsey, as well as Reinhold Niebuhr, made similar claims. Yet Yoder doesn't use this argument to dispense with rules.

> The normal penchant of the human heart for such excuses is precisely why we need rules. Precisely because there is not much time, decision makers need reminders of the fundamental rights of the other parties in the conflict, which remain even in the midst of unavoidable conflict.[137]

But he does use this argument to dispense with the efficacy of double effect as a rule.

Still Yoder's non-resistant alternative depends upon a type of double effect argument. He states that "if the cross defines *agape* " then "letting evil happen is [not] as blameworthy as committing it."[138] The structure of such an argument is that if evil happens which I could have prevented, but I did not prevent it because to do so would have violated this other highest good defined by the cross, then I am not culpable for allowing evil because my intention was not to allow it, but not to violate the higher good. Such an argument is a species of double effect thinking.

Double effect is difficult to avoid, perhaps impossible. Because it has been, is, and will be abused, it is not thereby discredited. It only means that its use should be carefully considered and cautiously invoked. This was Ramsey's purpose in the essay "Incommensurability and Indeterminancy in Moral Choice." This purpose, Ramsey concedes to Yoder, he failed to convey.

> I have publicly stated that ours [McCormick and Ramsey's] was a failed book; my chapter in particular was insufficiently revised to make clear the meaning (to Yoder, for example) of an "indeterminate" decision. So let me say here that I too, would short-shrift double effect if I took the meaning to be the texture of complex compromises Yoder comprehends it to be.[139]

Ramsey is not so blind as to ignore the abuses of double effect. Remember he himself suggested such abuses in the essay "Destructive Force is Never Justifiable." But rather than discarding double effect, he invokes just war criteria as public means of assessing intentionality.

Public criteria are needed not only to assess one's intentions in war, but in all ethical analysis. Therefore when Yoder claims "that to say that one does not 'intend' the evil results of one's deeds, even though one chooses so to act with full knowledge that those results will follow . . . is a sophistry," Ramsey is quite right to reply:

Nothing, however, could be more revealing of Yoder's failure to comprehend justified-war teaching than that sentence; indeed it would appear to reveal his lack of acquaintance with an entire literature dealing with the centrality of intentionality in ethical analysis (not by double-effect advocates alone). One can drop the whole modern elaboration of double-effect, double intentionality. One need no longer speak of *indirect* effect, *indirect* intention, or the *indirect* voluntary. But without the core notion of *intention* itself (which then encompasses directionality), no ethical analysis at all is possible. A *human* act, a moral (or immoral) act, a human, responsible "doing" *means* an intentional act.[140]

Unless we concede a private account of intention which allows an individual full authority over question such as: "I released the bomb because my intention was . . ." or; "I allowed this evil to happen and did not resist because my intention was . . . ," then some "public" criteria must be invoked.[141]

Casuistry as a public activity to create space for the practice of Christian morality is the best interpretation of Ramsey's work; Casuistry as a political practice constrained by tragedy is the worst interpretation. We need not dismiss casuistry as an exercise of pastoral responsibility because it is mixed with casuistry as "political" responsibility, yet if the former is Ramsey's main intent then the latter must go. The former is the best interpretation of Ramsey's work because the end for which he worked was that same end Jonathan Edward's holds forth in his dissertation on the end of creation. Ramsey's purpose was always to assist us in participating in God's redemption. His work is unintelligible separate from that end. Just as heaven is an infinite state of progression into an "infinitely perfect union of the creature with God,"[142] so the moral theologian's task is to seek infinitely to capture that perfection in this time between the times; a task that is unending. To that end, I offer the following criticisms of Ramsey's work.

Notes

1. Barth, *Church Dogmatics,* III/IV, (Edinburgh: T & T Clark, 1978), p. 7.

2. Brunner, *The Divine Imperative,* (New York: The MacMillan Company, 1942), p. 74.

3. For a wonderful criticism of this idea which seriously addresses the issue of the difference between Jesus and "Hebraic legalism" see E.P. Sanders' *Jesus and Judaism.* The notion that Jesus rejected "Hebraic legalism" fails to take into account Barth's central theological affirmation that when God assumed flesh, God assumed Jewish flesh. Of course, the assumption that Judaism is primarily

concerned with laws and abstract principles is false because it assumes Judaism is about repression and Christianity about freedom. The "law" in Judaism is a short hand way of telling the story of God's redemption.

4. Reinhold Niebuhr, *The Nature and Destiny of Man*, vol. II, (New York: Charles Scribners' Sons, 1941), pp. 39-40.

5. Ramsey papers, box 8, June 29, 1965.

6. *Ethics at the Edges of Life*, (New Haven: Yale University Press, 1978), p. 204.

7. *Basic Christian Ethics*, p. 351.

8. Donald Evan's "Exceptionless Moral Rules" in *Love and Society*, p. 30.

9. Letter to Stephen Rose, Feb. 9, 1970

10. *Christianity and Crisis*, March, 1963, p. 24.

11. *Who Speaks For The Church*, (Nashville: Abingdon Press, 1967), p. 15.

12. Ibid., p. 13.

13. Ibid., p. 31.

14. Ibid., p. 157.

15. Ibid., p. 26.

16. Ibid., p. 55.

17 . Ibid., p. 24.

18. see "The Limits of Nuclear War," particularly pp. 250-258 and "Again, the Justice of Deterrence," in *The Just War*, (New York: University Press of America, 1983).

19. see "A Political Ethics Context for Strategic Thinking," in Morton A. Kaplan, ed.

20. Walzer, *Just and Unjust Wars*, (New York: Basic Books, Inc., Publishers, 1977), pp. 278-283.

21. Ramsey papers, letter to Michael Walzer, June 12, 1979.

22. *Just and Unjust Wars*, p. 279.

23. Of course, there is also the tradition of precisionism and tutiorism, both of which do associate casuistry with exceptionless principles.

24. *Situation Ethics*, (Philadelphia: The Westminister Press, 1966), p. 19.

25. Ibid., p. 29.

26. Ramsey papers, box 35, Niebuhr lecture, p. 1.

27. *Church Dogmatics*, (III/IV), p. 10.

28. *Situation Ethics*, p. 31

29. Schmidt, p. 2, Ramsey papers, box 25.

30. Ibid., p. 3.

31. Ramsey makes the same point in *The Patient as Person*, p. xvi where he writes that Roman Catholic manuals and the moralists who produced them "are not to be criticized for being deductive. They were not; rather they were commendable attempts to deal with concrete cases. These manuals were written with the conviction that moral reasoning can encompass hard cases, that ethical

deliberation need not remain highfalutin but can "subsume" concrete situations under the illuminating power of human moral reason. However, the manuals can be criticized for seeking finally to "resolve" innumerable cases and to give the once and for all "solution" to them."

32. Ian Ramsey, ed. *Christian Ethics and Contemporary Philosophy*, (London: SCM Press, 1966), pp. 234-262.

33. Ibid., p. 241.

34. Ramsey, "The Case of the Curious Exception," in Outka, Ramsey, ed. *Norm and Context in Christian Ethics.*, p. 103. Notice how in contrast to Crombie's "definite action-rule," Ramsey uses "definite-action rule."

35. Ibid., p. 75

36. *Church Dogmatics*, III/IV, p. 6.

37. Ibid., p. 7. Barth states that even though Protestantism rebelled against Jesuit casuistry, it fell into such a legalism itself: "While the ethics of the Jesuit order brought Catholic casuistry to a certain completeness, the Reformation with its return to the exclusively normative Word of God and the *libertas christiana* at first heralded a change. But even if a good deal of ballast was thrown overboard as regards tradition, there was no agreement or clarity at two points: first, in the question of the validity and function of the traditional propositions of natural law; and second and supremely in the question of the sense in which the newly recognized witness of the divine Word, and therefore the newly recognized basis of a freedom to be called Christian namely, the Holy Scriptures of the Old and New Testaments, are or are not to be regarded and treated as a general law for concrete human action. And in the second half of the 16th century there was more and more clearly repeated what had already happened in the 2nd century. There was so little assurance of the divine Word and of Christian freedom under its lordship that ethical instruction had again to be sought in the legal sense, the need being felt for a kind of handy *Codex iuris* for the *civitas dei*. The ethical sections of the *Syntagma* of Polanus (1609) and the *Compendium* of Wolleb (1626) are examples of the way in which a legal text was again being strangely compiled from the Ten Commandments of the Old Testament and from all sorts of definitions of virtue from Greek and Roman antiquity" (p. 8). Barth's desire to restore the freedom of the Word requires his criticism of casuistry. Yet Barth, while supposedly avoiding constraints on the freedom of the Word, bases his "special ethics" on a "formed reference" which is supposedly different from casuistry in the legal sense, yet maintains a great deal in common with this "legal sense" of casuistry as Ramsey notes.

38. It is on this point that Fletcher lost Barth's nuance.

39. Ramsey, "The Case of the Curious Exception," p. 76.

40. Ibid., p. 104.

41. Ibid., p. 105.

42. Ibid., p. 76.

43. Ibid.

44. Part of the difficulty in the debate over "principles" centers on any lack of discussion as to what a "principle" is. Usually "principles" are given such as never tell a lie, do not commit adultery, etc, but a definition of "principle" is simply assumed. In his work on Jonathan Edwards, Ramsey has a telling comment which is fruitful for his own understanding of "principle," and which, I believe, fits well with my interpretation of Ramsey's casuistry. Ramsey writes, "Edwards used the word "principle" in the sense of the Latin *principium* or the Greek *arché*. The word "principle" means a source or beginning or spring of disposition and action. But it also means the direction, shape or contours of human hearts and lives, as in the root of our word "archetype," or the *arché* or formative power of Plato's ideas, such as justice or beauty, or triangularity. So when the first verse of St. John's Gospel reads "In the beginning was the Word," that in Greek is *en arché* and in Latin *in principio*. The verse not only points to the source and beginning of all things, without whom "was not anything made that was made." These verses also tell us something about the channel in which the whole creation runs, its shape, meaning, and direction." *Works of Jonathan Edwards*, vol 8, (New Haven: Yale University Press, 1989), p. 16.

45. Oliver O'Donovan, "Obituary: Paul Ramsey (1913-88), "Studies in Christian Ethics," 1988, p. 85.

46. See Toulmin & Jonsen, *The Abuse of Casuistry*, (Berkeley: University of California Press, 1988), pp. 2-36.

47. One of the problems with Ramsey's methodology is that he finds more coherence to the "western tradition" than I believe is descriptively possible. His promethean use of tradition will be examined in the next chapter.

48. *Ethics at the Edges of Life*, (New Haven: Yale University Press, 1978), p. 235.

49. Ibid., p. 236.

50. Ibid., p. 69.

51. *Patient as Person*, (New Haven: Yale University Press, 1970), p. xii.

52. *Fabricated Man*. p. 18.

53. The independence of Christianity from scientific "facts" represents a distinctive separation between the work of Ramsey and that of the other most important ethicist of our time trained by H. Richard Niebuhr, James Gustafson.

54. Ramsey papers, box 12.

55. Ramsey's criticisms here are similar to his criticisms of "Niebuhrian pragmatists" in *War and the Christian Conscience*.

56. *The Patient as Person*, pp. 5-6.

57. Ibid., p. 1.

58. Ibid., p. 41.

59. Ibid., p. 22.

60. Ibid., p. 42

61. Ibid., p. 37.

62. *Basic Christian Ethics*, p. 278.

63. Patient as Person, p. xvi. See also *Ethics at the Edges of Life*, p. xv where Ramsey also accepts "pluralism" as descriptive of contemporary life.

64. Ken Surin, "A Certain 'Politics of Speech': 'Religious Pluralism' in the Age of the McDonald's Hamburger," pp. 78-9, *Modern Theology* 7:1 October 1990.

65. *Fabricated Man*, pp. 90-1.

66. Ibid. Ramsey never connects this premise with Kantianism, but this modern premise is obviously indebted to Kant's revolution.

67. Ibid., p. 93.

68. "Human Nature," Sept. 1978.

69. Ibid., p. 25.

70. Ibid., p. 28.

71. Toulmin's 1988 work is much more nuanced on "casuistry" than this 1978 review. Still, one finds there the same problem. Where do these "fundamental moral sentiments" come from which provide the basis for the "soundness of particular judgments" when they are not based on "ethical principles?" Toulmin stated that his 1988 book developed out of work of the National Commission for the Protection of Human Subjects of Biomedical and Behavioral Research because he found that, despite the differences of the underlying commitments of the people on this commission "particular judgments" were more "sound" than the ethical principles from which they supposedly began (see pp. 18-19). However in a footnote he does add, "On a *completely* general level, it is true, the members of the commission were able to share certain agreements -- for example, as to the principles of autonomy, justice and beneficence. But these shared notions were too comprehensive and general to underwrite specific moral positions" (p. 356, n. 14). Clearly on Toulmin's own grounds it is more amazing that agreement could be found concerning these principles rather than on practical matters.

72. "The New Republic," May 6, 1978, pp. 28-30.

73. in *Knowledge, Value and Belief*, 1977. ed. H. Tristam Engelhardt, Jr., pp. 24 - 93.

74. MacIntyre, "Can Medicine Dispense With A Theological View On Human Nature," p. 77.

75. Ibid., p. 43, n. 10.

76. Ibid., p. 45.

77. Ibid., p. 76.

78. Whether Ramsey gives a coherent account of "tradition" is a different matter. All that is at stake at present is to demonstrate that Ramsey, the Protestant natural law theologian, explicitly required a "traditioned" ethic. Only when this is established will his casuistical approach be properly understood.

79. *Ethics at the Edges of Life*, p. 207.

80. Ibid., p. 191.

81. See the appendix, #95-105.

82. *Ethics at the Edges of Life,* pp. 12, 26, p, 71, p. 317

83. Dec. 20, 1976 in Ramsey Papers.

84. *Speak Up For Just War Or Pacifism,* (University Park: The Pennsylvania State University Press, 1988), p. 145.

85. See also *War and the Christian Conscience,* p. xxii-xxiii.

86. In *Ethics at the Edges of Life,* Ramsey suggests that the medical profession might even need to be sectarian if it is to practice medicine honorably, see p. 210.

87. See Appendix, particularly 1- 20 and 30-50.

88. Hans Frei, *Eclipse of Biblical Narrative,* (New Haven and London: Yale University Press, 1974), p. 172, Ramsey, p. 2.

89. Hauerwas, *A Community of Character,* p. 241, n. 16.

90. Ramsey, "A Question Or Two For Stanley Hauerwas," p. 5.

91. Ibid., pp. 6-7.

92. Hauerwas himself has become somewhat critical of the use of narrative. See his "How My Mind Has Changed" in *The Christian Century.*

93. Ibid., pp. 9-11.

94. Ibid., pp. 12-13.

95. See Ramsey's introduction to *Works of Jonathan Edwards,* Vol 8, p. 16.

96. See Appendix, # 36.

97. Hauerwas, *A Community of Character,* p. 186.

98. Ramsey, "One Flesh," p. 6.

99. Ramsey, "A Question Or Two For Stanley Hauerwas," p. 18.

100. John Milbank, "Critical Study," *Modern Theology* 4:2, 1988. p. 214.

101. See Stanley Fish's "Consequences," March 1985, *Critical Inquiry.*

102. See Lyotard's *The Postmodern Condition.*

103. Ramsey's complete response is found in the Appendix to this volume, #71-137.. Hauerwas' response to Ramsey is also included as well as a condensed account of two years of correspondence which is insightful midrash into both of their work.

104. Hauerwas himself concedes a similar claim in an earlier work, *Vision and Virtue* in an essay entitled "The Nonresistant Church: The Theological Ethics of John Howard Yoder." Hauerwas critiqued Yoder for refusing to use the language of "justice". "Yoder seems to assume that the language of justice is completely determined by sin and thus from the perspective of faith can only be negatively understood. . . . Yet it must be questioned if any discriminating social judgments by the Christian can be made without buying in at some point to the language of justice. But this does not necessarily mean that the Christian's use of the language of justice is limited to the form as he receives it from the world. Rather the Christian must realize that it is exactly his task to transform the language of justice by refusing to accept it as given and by insisting that justice is only properly understood under the norm of Christ. This suggestion contradicts

Yoder's insistence that Christian ethics can only be based on revelation, but it is consistent with his refusal to accept as normative language that is independent from revelation. Christian ethical reflection cannot completely divorce itself from the world's categories of justice, but this does nor mean, as Yoder seems to suggest, that it must necessarily be limited by them." Christian ethics requires the use of "the world's *categories* " even though it need not be limited by such categories. Hauerwas, *A Community of Character*, (Notre Dame: University of Notre Dame Press, 1981), p. 183, n. 15.

105. I prefer the term "body" to "individual" even though the latter was the term most frequently used by Ramsey. "Individual" conjures up too many Enlightenment presuppositions, whereas the term "body" reminds us of the necessary materiality of our existence.

106. Vaux, ed., p. 292.

107. Scott Davis, op. cit., p. 32.

108. *The Just War*, p. 150.

109. Ramsey's casuistry as pastoral responsibility challenges those who argue a pacifist position against a just war one on the grounds that a just war position is inherently Constantinian. The Constantinian critique argues that Christians give up their distinct identity and polity for the power to control the empire and attempt to control history. Notice for Ramsey this is not at all what just war does. Instead it is the expression of the distinct polity of Christians negotiating the nation-state system. It does not seek to control anything but the employment of violence for the sake of a faithful witness.

110. see Ramsey's dissertation, p. 226.

111. *The Just War*, p. 7.

112. Ibid., pp. 7-8.

113. emphasis mine.

114. Ibid., p. 459.

115. see also *The Just War*, p. 499 where Ramsey argues that "the nation-state system is in a state of war." Thus, warfare is never an exception for Ramsey; it is the normal course of politics with differing manifestations.

116. *Moral Man and Immoral Society*, (New York: Charles Scibners' Sons, 1932), p. xi.

117. *The Just War*, p. 7. Ramsey was also suspicious of his own Methodist heritage with its doctrine of sanctification because of its neglect of the "component of power." He thought this rivaled natural law teachings for an optimistic utopianism to the neglect of the Two Cities doctrine. In *Speak Up For Just War Or Pacifism*, he writes,"Among Wesleyan distinctives none can be more fundamental than our teaching concerning Christian perfection. It sometimes seems that this emphasis in our understanding of the common Christian doctrines of *regeneration* and *sanctification* has begotten more optimism

concerning *natural* "man and his communities" than that afforded (until lately) by the more inherently optimistic teaching based on "natural law"."

118. Ibid., p. 486. Also on p. 510, in reference to counter-insurgency warfare, Ramsey writes, "Tragically, or in God's inscrutable providence, neither villages nor nations are impervious to one another in our fated and fateful togetherness." This is a very odd claim for a Christian theologian to make, and it makes a great deal of difference whether we define our togetherness as a fated tragedy or as God's providence! The *Just War* is the work where Ramsey uses tragedy as a subject to justify intolerable practices. See also pp. 11, 15, 23, 27, 29, 43, 154, 159, 213, 256, 305, 319, 326, 414 and 435.

119. *The Just War*, p. 529.

120. Ibid., p. 530.

121. ed. John T. McNeill and Helena M. Gamer, *Medieval Handbooks of Penance* (New York: Columbia University Press, 1938) p. 183.

122. *The Just War*, p. 508.

123. Ibid., p. 435.

124. Ramsey papers, letter to Santurri, Oct. 20, 1981.

125. Ibid.

126. *The Just War*, pp. 252-7, my emphasis.

127. *War and the Christian Conscience*, p. 7.

128. I will not attempt to discuss whether Ramsey got McCormick "right" or not. As far as I can tell, they never had a fruitful debate on this issue because each believed the other to have misread him. This may be. Perhaps this is another reason why Ramsey called this "a failed book" (see *Speak Up For Just War Or Pacifism*, p. 103). To try to sort out the differences between Ramsey and McCormick would take us too far afield. Thus, the reader should know that the interpretation of McCormick presented here is done for the sake of elucidating Ramsey's position alone.

129. Ramsey and McCormick, eds., *Doing Evil to Achieve Good: Moral Choice in Conflict Situations* (Chicago: Loyola University Press, 1978), p. 74.

130. Ibid.

131. Ibid., p. 70.

132. Ibid., p. 83.

133. John Howard Yoder, *When War Is Unjust, Being Honest in Just-War Thinking* (Minneapolis: Augsburg Publishing House, 1984), p. 63.

134. Ibid., p. 56.

135. Could not the same argument be made against pacifism? It was precisely pacifism's contribution to the "total war" of World War II which led Ramsey to posit just war norms. Yoder wants to distance himself from those pacifists. Ramsey wants to distance himself from the abuses of just war.

136. Ibid., p. 57.

137. Ibid., p. 62. Also in Ramsey *Speak Up For Just War Or Pacifism*, p. 100.

138. Yoder, *The Original Revolution* (Scottsdale, Pennsylvania: Herald Press, 1977) p. 81.

139. *Speak Up For Just War Or Pacifism,* p. 103.

140. Ibid., p. 104.

141. Much needs filling in with the invocation of "public". For Ramsey just war is a "public" criterion for a variety of "publics". This variety of publics, not his account of intention, creates problems.

142. *The Works of Jonathan Edwards,* vol 8, Yale edition, p. 536.

4

Tragedy, Tradition, Transformism

Two different agendas characterize Paul Ramsey's work. The first is the employment of casuistry as a pastoral activity to discriminate between faithful and faithless responses to complex moral predicaments. The second is the preservation of a "metaphysics of democracy" for a politically "responsible" social order. The metaphysics of democracy he defends becomes more fundamental to his casuistry than the pastoral responsibility. Because this metaphysics establishes tragedy as a fabric that undergirds all possible politics, Ramsey's political philosophy seals off the space his casuistry as a pastoral activity opened for living the Christian moral life. Once "tragedy" describes the structural base for political possibilities, "tragedy" then functions as a hermeneutic by which Ramsey reads the "tradition." The "western tradition" becomes too coherent and complete, always resulting in the metaphysics of democracy. Ramsey then employs "tradition" with a promethean power to further guarantee his practice of political responsibility.

Tragedy as a structural basis limits the possibilities for a true transformation of political existence. This is not to say that tragedy as a category should always be avoided in pastoral casuistry. Tragedy names a reality many experience. The criticisms that follow do not seek to avoid tragedy, but to make discriminations between uses of tragedy, tradition, and transformism that will result in a grounding of casuistry in the end I believe Ramsey desired it to serve -- a pastoral activity participating in God's redemptive purposes.

Tragedy

No one should deny the aptness of "tragedy" as a description for much of political existence in the twentieth century. While tragedy became a basis for political existence in Ramsey's work, he was one of the last liberal hold-outs for the Christian century; for a full decade after Reinhold Niebuhr's *Moral Man and Immoral Society*, Ramsey adhered to an unqualified optimism of the State's possibility to transform existence. He was tardy in adopting Niebuhr's critique of liberal Christian ethics, but he too came to see the place of tragedy in the Christian life.

Reinhold Niebuhr introduced "tragedy" into Christian ethics for good reasons. The liberal, ideological utopianism of the Social Gospel movement assumed too easily society's transformation into the Kingdom of God. Walter Rauschenbusch had stated, "Progress is more than natural. It is divine," and claimed that the only thing standing in the way of progress was the "conservative stupidity and stolidity of human nature." Only recalcitrant individuals, unwilling to let progress run its course, prevented the complete transformation of society. Assuming too much of society was already converted, and that the rest would be too easily converted, liberal theologians were insufficiently suspicious of their powerful patron's abilities to use Christianity for ulterior motives. Niebuhr invoked tragedy as an antidote to this lack of any analysis concerning the problem of power.[1]

Still, "tragedy" does not represent a single, univocal tradition or ethos. How tragedy is defined makes a great deal of difference for the type of ethical responses one can even countenance. Tragedy can be invoked as a critique of ideological utopianism without thereby constraining ethical discourse by necessary evils, as Niebuhr did, or reading it into the base of existing political structures, as Ramsey did.

While philosophical idealism planted the seed for Ramsey's political philosophy, Reinhold Niebuhr's tragic dictum -- "man's capacity for justice makes democracy possible, but man's inclination to injustice makes democracy necessary" and his monumental *Moral Man and Immoral Society* brought that seed to fruition. Although this political philosophy supposedly centers on humanity's sinful nature, it is actually not based on an account of sinful human existence. Niebuhr's *Moral Man and Immoral Society* is not an exploration of human sin based on Christian reflection; it is an explication of Greek tragedy. "Individual men may be moral in the sense that they are able to consider interests other than their own in determining problems of conduct, and are capable, on occasion, of preferring the advantages of others to their own," writes Niebuhr, "But all these achievements are more difficult if not impossible, for human societies and social groups."[2] Where is the theological warrant for such a claim? Is it not more a result of Sophocles' *Antigone* than Scripture and Christian tradition?

For Niebuhr tragedy functions as conflict between the individual and society. Yet it is a mistake to place Niebuhr's view of the tragic in society rather than in the individual. Instead, tragedy manifests a character defect within the human soul.

> The cross does not reveal life at cross purposes with itself. On the contrary, it declares that what seems to be an inherent defect in life itself is really a contingent defect in the soul of each man, the defect of the sin which he commits in his freedom. If he can realise that fact, if he can weep for himself, if he can repent, he can also be saved. He can be saved by hope and faith. His hope and faith will separate the character of life in its essential reality from life as it is revealed in sinful history.
> This man on the cross who can say "Weep not for me" is also able to save us from our tears of self-pity. What he reveals about life transmutes tears of self-pity into tears of remorse and repentance. Repentance does not accuse life or God but accuses self. In that self-accusation lies the beginning of hope and salvation. If the defect lies in us and not in the character of life, life is not hopeless. If we can only weep for ourselves as men we need not weep for ourselves as man.[3]

For Niebuhr Christianity overcomes tragedy by locating the defect not finally in the character of life itself, but in the individual soul. Thus, grace and new life are possible as overcoming the contradiction in the soul. But new life is also limited to the individual soul.[4] It is not a "social" reality.

Niebuhr's position is typical of "liberal tragedy."[5] As Raymond Williams suggests, "liberal tragedy" resulted when "the stage was at last reached when there was skepticism about the possibility of any social order, and then resolution was seen as altogether outside the terms of civil society." Thus, he argues, the "point of reference" for tragedy shifted from a "general order" to the "individual." Niebuhr's view of tragedy seems to exemplify Williams' analysis.

However, Ramsey's view of tragedy is different. Indeed he inherited the concept from Niebuhr, and there are residual effects in Ramsey's work from Niebuhr's liberal view of "Greek" tragedy, such as the notion that salvation is individual: "salvation . . . is that in the self . . . ."[6] Still, Ramsey shifted tragedy's location. It was much more fully a part of the fabric which *undergirded* political society. At the base of political society is a contradiction; that which makes political society possible, also makes it necessary. This contradiction is not merely descriptive, it is normative. It defines what is necessary for an endurable political order that prevents the onslaught of anarchy. Democracy is just war; the nation-state system is a system of war.

There are benefits to Ramsey's location of tragedy. Unlike Reinhold Niebuhr, Ramsey's view of tragedy does not reflect a liberal interpretation. The problem of tragedy is not resolved in the individual. Ramsey's view is much more similar to Nietzche's . There is a contradiction at the very core of human existence which cannot be eradicated. Whereas for Nietzche, all that could happen is that through the power of music and myth the contradiction becomes beautiful, for Ramsey, through just war categories the contradiction becomes barely endurable.

Although he locates tragedy at a different level than does Reinhold Niebuhr, it would be wrong to say Ramsey locates it socially rather than individually. Tragedy is not located socially, it is not the fabric of political society; rather it is a fabric which undergirds political society. If it was within the fabric of political society, then something more constructive could be done about it. But because it is the basis of political society, nothing can be done. Thus arises the need for war as a now Christianized and obligatory duty to preserve a barely endurable order. Pacifism then can only be considered immoral or a temporary sectarian option necessary during anarchic times while we wait until just war principles can be used to restore order.

Ramsey's view of tragedy does have this advantage over Niebuhr's -- response to tragedy requires the social categories of just war and not merely an individualized grace which heals the contradiction in the soul. Here is where Ramsey assists us in creating some moral space for the practice of the Christian life, albeit always within the context of the existing political structure. Just war categories are Christian principles that are to structure Christian political responses, and we should not be surprised that these principles will also be found in the natural order. If these principles cannot be practiced, then Christians have no choice but to be sectarian until they can be. By searching out this small space for the practice of the Christian moral life, Ramsey's tragic political philosophy does not simply serve the powers of the nation-state but stands as a limited critique against them.

As a *critique* tragedy is an important and indispensable category. Nevertheless, the ontology of tragedy that gives rise to the critique too thoroughly defines the possible responses, and the limitations of those responses. Then tragedy functions as a *hermeneutic* and as *legitimation* for a particular political configuration.

The function of tragedy as *critique* is important if we are not to assume political society can be transformed without conflict and loss. Most of our political configurations abandon someone. The question that the "tragedy" of our political structures poses to us is who is abandoned? The invocation of tragedy reminds us to be vigilant in seeking new configurations where those who exist at the edges can be incorporated. Yet tragedy is not only "critique," it is also a *hermeneutic* by which Ramsey reads the tradition, particularly the Augustinian tradition. And it is Augustine who, for Ramsey, legitimates tragedy which in turn necessitates and justifies war and the metaphysics of democracy.

When Ramsey constructs a genealogy of Just War according to Augustine, Augustine is read as advancing the tragic and inescapable connection between the earthly and heavenly cities. Ramsey quotes from book XIX of *The City Of God*. But a great deal is left out of this quote, and what is left out is of crucial importance. Let me place the full quote next to Ramsey's version, highlighting the relevant differences.

Ramsey's version	*Augustine's version*
The "heavenly city, while it sojourns on earth . . . , not scrupling about diversities in the manners, laws, and institutions whereby earthly peace is secured and maintained, but recognizing that, however various these are, they all tend to one and the same end of earthly peace . . . [is] so far from rescinding and abolishing these diversities, that it even preserves and adopts them . . . . Even the heavenly city, therefore, while in its state of pilgrimage avails itself of the peace of earth, and . . . . desires and maintains a common agreement among men regarding the acquisition of the necessities of life. . . . "	The "heavenly city while it sojourns on earth . . . , not scrupling about diversities in the manners, laws, and institutions whereby earthly peace is secured and maintained, but recognizing that, however various these are, they all tend to one and the same end of earthly peace . . . [is] so far from rescinding and abolishing these diversities, that it even preserves and adopts them *so long only as no hindrance to the worship of the one supreme and true God is thus introduced.* Even the heavenly city, therefore, while in its state of pilgrimage avails itself of the peace of earth and *so far as it can without injuring faith and godliness,* desires and maintains a common agreement among men regarding the acquisition of the necessities of life . . . ."

At both points where Augustine qualifies the relationship between the two Cities, highlighting worship, faith and godliness as central categories

for a critical relationship between the two cities, Ramsey omits the qualification. Then he draws this conclusion:

> Thus, a Christian in this life finds his own life and will bound up *inextri-
> cably* with such a *common agreement* among men as to the objects of
> their political purposes, and he is bound to foster the *combination* of
> men's wills to attain the things which are helpful to this life. Doubtless
> he seeks not only to preserve but also *to enlarge such agreements of will*
> and the scope of peaceful *orders* on this earth.[7]

Ramsey omits Augustine's qualification of the relationship between the
two cities and instead moves to emphasize their "inextricable" relatedness. Once that happens, Ramsey then finds the two cities so "bound" to
each other that the heavenly city cannot exist apart from the earthly. The
"inextricable" relatedness of the two cities connects them such that their
lives are tragically bound together. A Christian cannot be political without the "common agreement" of those of the earthly city.[8]

Ramsey reads into Augustine one overarching political structure
marked by a "common agreement" arising from the "combination" of
people's wills which defines the "orders of this earth." The Christian according to Ramsey is *inextricably* bound up with this overarching structure. One cannot escape it. The best one can do is "enlarge" or "extend"
the area of coincidence.

But for Augustine there are two important qualifications to the relatedness of the two cities -- "so long only as . . . " and "so far as it can . . . ".
Thus a different interpretation of Augustine would emphasize that the
heavenly city can and does use the earthly city in its pilgrimage, but only
to a point. No overarching political structure exists, but several politics
which can make contingent alliances. The two cities mutually interact,
but never to the point where the heavenly city is hindered in its worship
or faith and godliness are injured. This creates more space for the practice of the Christian moral life as well as more of a possibility for the
transformation of the earthly city than Ramsey's "inextricable binding"
allows.

But for Ramsey such space is always already limited and qualified.
The ambiguous and paradoxical disturbs all possible true political transformations.

> An unrectified *nisus* toward the eternal disturbs every people's pur-
> pose: that is why they see in their good *the* Good, in the laws of their
> peace the conditions of universal peace, and are resolved that this too
> shall not pass away.[9]

This is the condition of "Babylon" -- ". . . the world in which we live and all its urgent problems is an objectification of all our Babylonian hearts" and this "won't cease." It is a mark of always standing under God's judgment.[10] True to the heritage of H. Richard Niebuhr, we must always be "humble" about the possibility of goodness or peace, but never humble about "humility" itself.

War's necessity and justification results from this overarching structure. It is why Ramsey writes, "We need to attend first of all not to the business of getting moral facts but to the business of Christian reflection upon all sorts and structures of human activity." If this were done, according to Ramsey, ethicists would inevitably realize this overarching structure and would not have such simplistic solutions about political events. They would realize that an analysis of this "structure" shows war is "necessary and justifiable."[11] They would realize that the "relationship properly called political which bind men together requires always and everywhere that they be controlled also by force."[12]

Tragedy requires accepting "responsibility."[13] Political *responsibility* is exercised only within the single structure of the nation-state system. Responsibility requires upholding the "order" of the necessary structures even when "order warrants the tragic permission of injustice" as in refusing support to the Hungarian freedom fighters.[14] Tragedy legitimates a certain level of "deterrence," thereby making deterrence a tragic necessity but not "wicked."[15] Tragedy requires "double effect." Counter-force warfare is "tragic," counter-people warfare is "murder." But the scope of "counter-force warfare" enlarges with "counter-insurgency warfare." Tragedy legitimates deterrence, injustice -- even upholding order over justice, and an extension of non-combatant non-immunity. The accountability on behalf of the state or the Church for these affairs is eclipsed by the all pervasive character of "tragedy." "Tragedy" becomes an agent, an active subject which warrants these activities.

"Tragedy" defines all possible responses to situations of conflict. "Absolutely related to the Absolute, we should be content to be relatively involved in the relative."[16] Any possible response is only a "relativized" one. The best one can do is find a "crack in the structure" and "transform" it -- "There is no solution but to look inside the existing structures for cracks where a change might take place." Finally then any political response is constrained by the view of political society tragedy legitimates. The view is that of the "ethos" of a society created by a combination of the will of a people who exist within an international structure "surrounded by arbitrariness on all sides; [where] the other is always a potential enemy, etc., where there are no dependable structures through which identification may pass." This is the "nation-state system." It is necessary and it "is in a *state* of war."[17]

Any ability to respond politically within this system requires some form of warfare. Given these constraints, Ramsey developed the most appropriate Christian response by seeking to limit war through just war norms. For Ramsey, tragedy is an *ontology* which exists at the basis of any and every political society. No social or political configuration can escape from "Tragedy's" all pervasive hand .

If Ramsey's ontology of tragedy is correct, then his justification of order is unavoidable. The best any political society can attain is an endurable order with as little force and injustice as is possible. But if there is an alternative, then his claim that "Just War's presumption favors the defense of an ordered justice"[18] must be called into question. "Order", "responsibility", "double effect", and the category of "tragedy" itself will take a different shape if the terrain is not constrained by an ontology of tragedy. Here lies the first point which must be made in a critique of Paul Ramsey's reasoning -- *Pastoral responsibility is eclipsed by a political practice where an ontology of tragedy undergirds the fabric of the social order, legitimating a single, hegemonic order. All possible responses are defined by that order. The different responses are marked by either an acquiescence to the order, and thus accepting moral evil, or struggling against it, as best one can, and thus only accepting non-moral evil which is "tragedy."*

Tradition

We have already seen in Ramsey's selective appropriation of Augustine how tragedy functioned as a hermeneutic by which he viewed the "tradition." It was as constrained by Ramsey's ontology of tragedy as were any possible responses to political conflict. Political conflict was unavoidable. Three responses were possible. The Church could accept a consequentialist ethic and sacrifice its integrity; it could become a sect and maintain its integrity but sacrifice political responsibility; or it could cling to its "ancient traditions" and maintain both its integrity and its political responsibility. While these three responses were possible, only the latter two could be justified as a "Christian" ethic. However, only the last one represented a "responsible, Christian" ethic.

These three possible responses involved Ramsey in different discussions. He spent a great deal of time challenging ethicists who advocated the first position. It represented a pragmatic acquiescence to the ontology of tragedy. Ramsey invoked the possibility of the second and third responses against this first one. Thus, he often conceded the possibility of the "sectarian temptation."[19] For instance, if the political order were in such a state that a traditional just war teaching was impossible, then the only appropriate response was not to develop a new ethic which would be possible in such a political order, but for Christians to prescind from such a political order. Likewise, if Christian physicians and nurses were required by law or hospital administrators to assist with abortions, then an interim alternative medical order should be established. Still, even though Ramsey realized Constantinianism was dead, he was unwilling to concede finally the "sectarian" option. So he initiated a second discussion against a "realist" pacifist position, represented by John Howard Yoder and Stanley Hauerwas.

The third possible response was for Ramsey the only valid one. After his move away from liberal pacifism, and the further move away from a consequentialist war ethic, Ramsey consistently held that any realist analysis of political existence, and exploration of the Christian tradition revealed the same result -- just war teaching was the only way the Church and the State could live in harmony and each maintain its integrity.

> The Protestant Churches between World Wars I and II spent their thought and energy expelling a utopian pacifism from their bosom. That was a proper work, but in doing this, and in creating a religiously motivated political realism in its stead, we have neglected to keep alive the teachings that should be constantly addressed to the churches, to political realists, and to the nations. Before policy making becomes such that in relation thereto Christian teaching can only be that of a sect apart from the central political policies of our nation, the churches must learn their ancient teaching about war and trumpet them in high places. . . . Whether Christianity is a sect in a world gone mad and gone apolitical, or whether its teaching may still be regarded as a relevant context for high policy-making, the churches need to know *where* are the principles by which the nations may be guided in this critical hour. To insure that *somewhere* these principles *are* in the allegiances of men is our most essential task.[20]

The ontology of tragedy was too pervasive to think Christians could avoid complicity in the tragic nature of *political* existence. Because of this, for Ramsey, the sectarian option was not really possible. The "sectarian" option was always an a-political one. It might be necessary for a time, but only until Christians could be more successful in transforming the single, overarching political order.

In fact, the ability to use the term "sectarian" often betrays a commitment to a single overarching order. The charge "sectarian" implies a neutral politic where all differences can be successfully managed. The term preempts the discussion from the beginning by assuming a unified "public" independent of Christian particularity. More important questions such as the relationship between the Church and GM, or the Church and Republicans, Democrats, Anarchists, etc. are neglected for questions of the Church and "culture" or the "society at large," or "political government." The latter become abstractions that only serve to legitimate some mystified political order.

Because at the base of political existence was one, single, all encompassing order based on contradiction and negativity, only two options were available -- confronting that single, hegemonic order, or removing one's self from it and thereby becoming "apolitical." If the Church had to accept this temptation, and Ramsey considered that possibility quite seriously, then it meant creating a utopia which would be necessary for the preservation of the integrity of the Church during dark ages until the just war tradition was once again possible. Thus, for Ramsey, even the "sectarian temptation" was only an interim ethic which served the purposes of just war. The pacifist, sectarian option was possible and perhaps necessary only until political existence could once again be made amenable to the ethos of the just war tradition.

The only viable option for a Christian ethic within political existence based on an ontology of tragedy was just war. Just War represents the non-utopian, Christian alternative to a simple acceptance of life's tragic nature. Just War functions as an alternative tradition to that of a complete acquiescence to life's tragic nature. This involves Ramsey in constant appeals to the "ancient tradition" that assume the tradition of "western thought" or "western tradition" or "the Christian west" was so complete and uniform, and on Ramsey's side, that we stood at a cataclysmic brink where this unity and completeness were now being jeopardized.

> [Just war represents] the working politico-military doctrine that was governing in Western thought until just lately. Plainly it is necessary for most people to come to terms again with the terms of the ancient limits of civilized warfare.[21]

> As in the past -- when wars were somewhat more reasonable -- it is still the case today that the threat of war can be used to deter war only if by "war" something is meant that can be done, done politically as well as militarily.[22]

> ... western political thought did not until recently stand clothed only in an "aggressor-defender" concept of warfare, nor did it justify any sort of reply believed to be technically required to stop an aggressor. Warlike action was not justified, until recently, merely by a calculation of the future consequences and choice of the lesser evil in aiming at hypothetical results. . . . Certainly Christian ethics did not first concern itself with estimating the consequences. Instead, out of responsibility *to* God *for* all men before God, Christians sought to discover the meaning of just and

loving *present* action toward them. . . . This states *why* the theory of justifiable warfare was developed in the Christian West.[23]

Similar totalizing claims, based on "discrimination," were also utilized for medical practice.

> . . . the medical ethics developed in western Christendom set its face resolutely against the direct killing of terminal patients which it judged to be murder, whatever warrants may be alleged in favor of the practice.[24]

> . . . the Judeo-Christian tradition decisively influenced the origin and shape of medical ethics down to our own times . . . . the notion that an individual human life is absolutely unique, inviolable, irreplaceable, noninterchangeable, not substitutable, and not meldable with other lives is a notion that exists in our civilization because it is Christian; and that idea is so fundamental to the edifice of Western law and morals that it cannot be removed without bringing the whole house down.[25]

In these quotes, Ramsey finds the "ancient tradition" to be a seamless whole that directly resulted in western civilization. The practice of medicine has a moral grounding in Judeo-Christian tradition that overlooks the differences even with respect to the point of life within and between those two traditions. And wars of the past were fought with meticulous care for non-combatant immunity that was abandoned only in the 20th century. Such reasoning does not stand up to scrutiny. Trébuchet artillery, as well as the common siege form of warfare used throughout the Middle Ages were no more, and perhaps much less, discriminatory, than modern weapons. The practice of projecting diseased animals to induce epidemics certainly did not reflect a "somewhat more reasonable form of warfare."[26] Nor did a single unified, coherent theory of just war exist which could be called "the working politico-military doctrine" of the "ancient limits of civilized warfare." In fact, Frederick H. Russell argues that just war, rather than a theory developed "in the *Christian* west," was a "potent instrument of rule" whereby "*secular* rulers were able to oppose the violence of justice to the violence of private warfare, for to control justice was to limit internal warfare." Thus:

> What with Augustine had started out as a problem of morality and scriptural exegesis ended up as a tool of statecraft in the hands of secular monarchs. . . . In spite of themselves, the medieval theorists of the just war assisted at the birth of the Leviathan.[27]

Russel's argument suggests that the just war theory did not preserve Christian tradition, but gave rise to a secularization in opposition to Christian tradition.

As a historical claim, Ramsey's appeal to the ancient just war tradition is deeply suspect. Still, the primary purpose of appealing to the "ancient tradition" is not so much to assert a descriptive historical claim about the past as to critique present practices. In this respect, appeals to just war "tradition" function as a critique against a complete acquiescence of present practices to the underlying ontology of tragedy. Ramsey's appeal to the tradition attempts to secure some space for an alternative to these present practices. He does not argue that tragedy can be avoided; rather he argues that because of tragedy, some form of social principles are necessary to prevent tragedy reducing us to barbarians. His use of tradition should be appreciated for the critique that it is.

Tradition as critique challenges existing practices. It challenges, primarily, a consequentialist ethic which always seeks to develop a new ethic to face the supposed new moral problems. This Ramsey envisioned as the central problem facing Christian ethics.

> I rather think that the effort to translate Biblical and Christian ethical terms into another universe of discourse to be, necessarily, reductive and misleading -- and finally no more effective than had the translation not been made. The main peril, however, is that one will soon deceive oneself, and the Christian community into thinking that this was what was meant to bear witness to. The final result is that 'preach the Gospel' comes to mean that the Gospel is the preachable, and so Christian substance is evacuated.

> I say to my students that in all I do I am trying to explore what Christian being-in-the world *means* so that if one day I wish to depart from it I will know *which way to go*. Most liberal churches today seem to me to have been led by the nose of relevance so much that one could not learn how decisively to cease to be a Christian.[28]

The purpose of Ramsey's invocation of the "ancient tradition" is first to critique this supposed need for relevance. It functions as a way of reminding the present generation of ethicists that they, in the name of relevance, too easily dismiss the Church's tradition on moral reflection. This is what Ramsey termed "casuistry without principles." For instance, the reason congress refuses to allow selective conscientious objection is due to . . .

> . . . the steady erosion, for at least the last three or four decades, of shared basic convictions concerning normative structures in social ethics having for religious people final theological warrant. . . . The shared so-

cial and ethical convictions in and among the religious communities
have suffered the relativization of the times. . . . The name of the game
is casuistry without principles, decision-making that is believed to be
more responsible because situations are so unique that there are no relevant, *specific*, norms.[29]

Ramsey uses tradition to critique present responses which appear more
"relevant" than the just war tradition because they jettison any principles
based on past Christian teaching.

Still, Ramsey was not so blind as to impose the "ancient tradition"
without qualification. On several occasions he admits the "ancient theory" was not so coherent and unified. For instance, in response to the
"contention" that Victoria and Suarez did not allow aggressive wars but
only defensive ones, Ramsey wrote:

What then must a Christian moralist say to this? Surely that this
would only show that the just-war theory itself, as this existed
in the past, is greatly in need of revision.[30]

And we have already seen that Ramsey rejected the view that just war
norms were a simple system of moral rules for the classification of cases,

subject to no significant historical development, freighted with few ambiguities, there to be accepted or rejected as a single, if ancient or
"classical," formulation of one possible position in Christian ethics, with
no significant decisions to be taken *within* this tradition itself.[31]

Thus, he calls for the "recreation" of the just war "tradition."

While one should appreciate Ramsey's use of tradition as critique,
his use of tradition creates substantial problems. He could both use just
war as "the ancient tradition," as a unified landmark against which to critique present practices, and at the same time proclaim the necessity of
historical development within the tradition, even a "recreation" of it, to
suit present purposes. This provides him with a Promethean power
through appeal to "tradition" when it serves his purpose as critique, and
at the same time, the power to pick, choose, and alter the "ancient tradition."

A keyword by which Ramsey acquires such Promethean power is
"civilization." Just War represents the "western tradition of *civilized* warfare." It does this by preventing the person from becoming a "mere
means of achieving political and military goals."

At stake in preserving this distinction [principle of discrimination] is not
only whether warfare can be kept barely civilized, but whether civilization can be kept from barbarism. Can civilization survive in the

> sense that we can continue in political and military affairs to *act civilized,* or must we accept total war on grounds that clearly indicate that we have already become *totalitarian* -- by reducing everyone without discrimination and everyone to the whole extent of his being to a mere means of achieving political and military goals? Even if an enemy government says that is all its people are, a Christian or any truly just man cannot agree to this.[32]

With the loss of just war reasoning, "civilization" itself is at stake. That is to say, the individual has no recourse to stand against the encroaching hegemony of the State. For Ramsey, "civilization" and "just war" are synonymous terms. Both represent the freedom of the individual to be more than a political pawn.

Ramsey claims the reason for the threatening barbarism is due to a shift in the "ethos," the informing spirit of modern times. "War first became total in the minds of men."[33] Because it is within the "minds of men" that war first became total, the appropriate response is to provide an alternative informing spirit or ethos. And this is done primarily through public policy. "Policy formation gives new shape to the world."[34] Public policy transforms existing structures by issuing forth a new "ethos." Through the theoretical explication of a public policy the "western civilized tradition" of just war extends itself, transforming the present, neo-barbaric ethos.

Ramsey appeals so easily to the "western civilized tradition" because "tradition" represents nothing but a very general theory based on the "ethos" or informing spirit, of past times to critique the "ethos" or "informing spirit" of the present. For Ramsey, just war is a "theory of statecraft." It is only a "criterion" addressed to government officials. Because this is all that it is, he can too easily call for the recreation of an "ethos" he already admits is lost, with little social analysis as to what practices might be necessary to sustain this ethos.

Ramsey suggests that the way to change current practices, which he rightly critiques, is to offer government officials a better criterion for understanding the ethos of the western civilized tradition. He doesn't seriously consider that, as Russell suggested, the "ethos" could legitimate political configurations contrary to its intended articulation. He doesn't pursue the possibility that the consolidation of Christian thinking about war into a single, purposeful theory -- whenever such a single theory was advocated, i.e. Gratian with the consolidation of the Penitentials in his *Decretum,* or Grotius with his *Rights of War and Peace* -- could be used more as a "form of surveillance" constructing individuals, and thereby furthering the hegemonic power against which Ramsey rightly set his pen.

For instance, Michel Foucault suggested that the move from the public "spectacle" of violence against persons, to a more "civilized" form of private control through "disciplines,"[35] results in less, rather than more, capacity to stand against a hegemonic order.

> Our society is one not of spectacle, but of surveillance; under the surface of images, one invests bodies in depth; behind the great abstraction of exchange, there continues the meticulous, concrete training of useful forces; the circuits of communication are the supports of an accumulation and a centralization of knowledge; the play of signs defines the anchorages of power; it is not that the beautiful totality of the individual is amputated, repressed, altered by our social order, it is rather that the individual is carefully fabricated in it, according to a whole technique of forces and bodies. We are much less Greeks than we believe. We are neither in the amphitheatre, nor on the stage, but in the panoptic machine, invested by its effects of power, which we bring to ourselves since we are part of its mechanism.[36]

Just War could be one more technique by which "individuals" are merely "fabricated" into the present society.

Perhaps Just War has nothing to do with faithfulness to Scripture or Christian moral reflection? Perhaps just war is a discipline whereby the nation-state coopts sons and daughters of the Church to be part of the fabric of a hegemonic order? If this is so, then Ramsey's appeal to "just war tradition" as a critique of the present, existing order, does not serve the purpose he intends. In fact, it only further entrenches those powers.[37]

Foucault's analysis, much like Nietzsche's view of tragedy, should be used for Christian theology only with the utmost circumspection. The thoroughness of his panoptic vision cannot *completely* include the redemption wrought by Christ constituting an alternative vision located in the Church.[38] If it does, then there is no Christian redemption, and Christian ethics is no longer possible. Yet this theological theme does not allow us to dismiss critiques such as Foucault's, but to receive them with a great diligence of effort. They cause us to be wary of advocating an "ethos" based only on a general "theory," and instead force us to ask where those practices might be located which do allow for an alternative vision.

Ramsey offers little guidance in locating such practices. This is because the Just War tradition poses just war norms only as a "criterion" addressed to whomever is in temporal control. It is not positive ecclesiastical law, or primarily a confessional discipline in the life of the Church. It is a "criterion". Ramsey makes this explicit in comments on Lynne H. Miller's "The Contemporary Significance of the Doctrine of Just

War."[39] Ramsey was asked to referee Miller's essay by the editor of *World Politics*. His seven-page response to Miller's essay suggests how Ramsey interpreted the just war "tradition" more than his published work reveals.[40]

Miller begins his article with a five page summary of the "historical development" of the Just War tradition. He begins with the claim, "The *bellum justum* doctrine first took shape in Christian moral theology at a time when the church was attempting to become the universal religion of a universal political order."[41] He concludes his essay with a section, "Appraisals of Relevance," where he suggests:

> The traditional Western theory of the *bellum justum* originated as an ethical and a moral doctrine of the Christian church which for centuries -- because of the closeness of the ties between church and state -- sought expression in positive law. With the greater cleavage between political and religious authority that followed in the West, the attempt to incorporate the doctrine into the secular law of nations never met with real success, and an international system arose which was forced to regard war as a natural, uncontrollable phenomenon in order that war or the threat of war could be used as a catalyst that gave the system stability. Just war doctrine survived, if at all, as an ethical and not a juridical force. In the twentieth century, when that balance-of-power international system broke down, the attempt was made once again to incorporate some sort of just war doctrine into the international legal framework. The traditional theory, still an important moral guide, did not seem to lend itself any better than it had formerly to being somehow translated into the law of nations; or if it did, such an attempt was not made seriously. Instead, that doctrine was examined once again in the attempt to apply it as a moral formula, urged on the consciences of men, to the potential situations of war which were regarded as likely in the mid-twentieth century.[42]

Miller poses five challenges to Ramsey's development of the "ancient tradition." First, he suggests that just war was not, nor never has been, the "working politico-military doctrine" within the past two centuries. Second, he challenges the much heralded claim that just war became embodied in international law, and thus created the "western tradition of civilized warfare." Third, he originally stated that Ramsey's own just war position "may be suggestive of that type of *Weltanschaung* giving rise to a just war doctrine in the twentieth century which has altered rather radically the traditional *bellum justum* theory."[43] In other words, Ramsey's development of the just war doctrine fits more within twentieth century American politics, than it does within any ecclesial tradition. Fourth, Miller suggests that with Grotius, a decisive shift occurred in the just war tradition. Grotius "sought to rescue the *bellum justum* doctrine from a then-outmoded theological framework which had little connection with the legal requirements, the attempt to incorporate the doctrine into the secularized positive law of emergent nation-states had only a fleeting triumph . . . . Grotius regarded just war as a legal procedure for the assertion of positive rights."[44] And finally, Miller suggests that just war, rather than a theory which mitigated against war, only further entrenched it -- "as in other historical situations when moralists have attempted to provide a guide for political behavior, the mere presence of a formula often worked to inhibit considerations of morality in individual cases of warfare, and the garment of the just war was stretched to cover the naked unjustness of many medieval conflicts."[45]

Ramsey responds to these criticisms stating that Miller has misunderstood the historical tradition. Miller's argument that just war was never the working politico-military doctrine of the West is a result of his neglecting the distinction between the temporal and spiritual powers. Miller asks the just war tradition to do something it did not intend -- to offer positive legal concepts. Ramsey writes,

> I believe that it is wrong to stress so much the just war as a positive legal concept during the pre-modern period. This emphasis arises from vagueness and error in the paper about the church's attempt "to become the universal religion of a universal political order," "the universal political order," and "expression in positive law" "because of the virtual union of church and state." This pictures the church as some sort of world-court determining the justice of wars. It takes at face value the church's maximum claims in the bull *Unam Sanctum*, issued after its decline had set in. It ignores that both *in theory* and especially *in fact*, the early and medieval Christian centuries rested upon two powers, the temporal and the spiritual -- variously related, but rarely in theory and never in fact by the spiritual legislating for the temporal or the temporal made a mere means to the spiritual.[46]

Because Miller fails to understand the distinction between the spiritual and temporal, he attributes failure to the just war theory for its lack of *legal* proscription. Ramsey suggests that this is not a failure, and the just war theory cannot be indicted on this basis. The just war theory was not intended as a "positive legal concept," therefore it can not be dismissed because it is not "embodied in international law" (Miller's second critique).

Rather than a "positive legal concept," the just war theory was a "criterion."

> Certainly, the just war theory was of a "useful guide" to priests in the pastoring of souls, and to laymen in guiding judgments as to war (cf. p. [254]). But that did not make it a positive legal concept, as Miller recog-

nizes at the top of p. [255]. That meant rather that the just war theory was mainly a criterion during the centuries of its first evolution, as it is to date in the history of mankind. The requirement of "declaration by legitimate authority" was, of course, of *practical* importance because of vendettas (p. [255]). But this indicates the source of the highest judgment on earth about the application of natural justice to the rule of war: the top-most prince in the temporal order, not positive ecclesiastical rules of law descending from the church. He, the prince, had the responsibility, not his confessor or the Pope.[47]

Once Ramsey makes just war a "criterion" addressed primarily to the "top-most prince," then he can find a continuity and totality to the just war tradition. For instance, as to Miller's claim that Grotius represents a decisive shift in the just war tradition, Ramsey writes:

Grotius may have rescued the [just war] doctrine from the "then- outmoded theological framework": but this was *not* because the latter had "become divorced from the *legal* requirements" with which, if I am not seriously mistaken, it had never been connected, except as the Empire may have been or pretended to be a "universal" legal order. Grotius is therefore continuing the doctrine as it always was -- a criterion, not a positive law, addressed to the temporal authority — and on the basis of natural justice prescinding from its theological foundation in previous ages. The growth of nation-states had multiplied the problem of attaining justice in war: it had not changed its essential character as a matter of political decision.[48]

Ramsey's description of just war theory as a "criterion" answers Miller's third critique. Even though, with Grotius, just war theory exists within a new social configuration, this does not change its "essential character." The reason it does not is because what just war is remains constant -- a criterion addressed to the "temporal authority." Not even the development of nation-states alters this basic identity.

Just war theory as a "criterion" also allows Ramsey to answer Miller's fourth critique. Contrary to Miller's claims, Ramsey himself has not altered the essential character of just war, and is not simply part of new post-war American developments.

The statement following the quotation from my book leaves me entirely non-plussed over the author's failure to understand not me but the earlier period, when he can think it right to say, with no attempt to prove, that my remark "may be suggestive of that type of *Weltanschauung* giving rise to a just war doctrine in the twentieth century which has altered rather radically the traditional *bellum justum* theory." Now, that statement of mine, and my entire book, may be the sheerest eye-wash; but the statement and the book are through and through *Augustinian*. I and

185

the traditional theory (except for my greater emphasis on just conduct) stand *or* fall together. I can only seek to *explain* the author's failure to comprehend the theory in its first and theological stage. He allows (a) natural justice as a criterion and legal rules, when the former are put forward by the church, to merge together in his mind and (b) the determination of justice which was sought to be made and urged upon the prince to become equated with absolutes and ultimates and infinite goals and the consequent fury of war born out of too-loftily aspiring expectations and objectives to which only a non-religious age is susceptible. Anyway, the age that knew to distinguish between the temporal and the spiritual power, knew also the limited and qualified justice attainable by war or any other political instrumentality in the "terrestrial city." That is the *Weltanschaung* of my remark (against a Calvinistic reformism gone to seed in utopian goals), and it is Augustine pure and simple.

This is a revealing paragraph. Because just war is a criterion addressed to the temporal authority, Ramsey can find a continuity to the tradition which allows even himself and Augustine to stand or fall together.

Just war is a "criterion" primarily addressed to temporal leaders. Thus, the political or social configurations in which it exists are not of primary importance. The "essential character," the "ethos," remains constant.

While for Ramsey just war is the reappropriation of the Church's heritage, it is primarily appropriated through theoretical explication. One can ignore any practices within which it exists because it is primarily a criterion for public policy the Church suggests to temporal authorities. Even when Ramsey finds a place for ecclesial practices such as penance and confession, these practices only make sense within the context of just war as a "doctrine primarily addressed to the leaders of nations."

It may be that a searching examination of the problems which would be raised by the just-war doctrine, if it became operative at all as a matter of private judgment, would cause us to draw back on the ground that this would seriously impair the government's power and right to repel injury (also the heart of the just war theory); and that instead we would be forced to see the wisdom of the ancient tradition, and still largely the emphasis in the Roman Catholic interpretation of it, which held this doctrine to be primarily addressed to the leaders of nations, and which still today requires the private citizen to serve in a war in which unjust means are used, provided that just means are also used. This, then, raises the question of a Christian's action as a soldier during wartime in refusing to participate in the use of immoral means. I say only that such questions as these have to be faced, and frankly and openly debated in the churches, at the same time that any discipline as to warfare is under-

> taken; and in these deliberations may the Holy Spirit be more than the odd man! If the decision is reached that the church's doctrine of just or limited war is *not* addressed to private citizens and soldiers, then, if also penance is good for anything, consideration should be given to reviving the requirement of forty day's penance following participation in war.[49]

In this quote, Ramsey is clear that the "ancient tradition" was first and foremost a matter of policy directed to "the leaders of nations." Now, because of Protestantism's stress on "vocation," every citizen is a "lesser magistrate," and therefore the possibility of selective conscientious objection should be available to all. Still, this could make it difficult for the "nation" to repel its injuries. Thus, the possibility exists that just war should not be the domain of all citizens, but only of the leaders as the "ancient tradition" suggested. And then penance is invoked as a way of maintaining some form of "discipline" concerning soldier's participation in war because they themselves must follow the advice of the "leaders of the nation."

Only because just war marks a general theory whereby the Church addressed its criterion to the temporal authority can Ramsey suggest that the "ancient tradition" was a public policy primarily directed to "leaders of *nations*." Ramsey's critique of "the need for relevance" overthrowing Church tradition leads him to a too thorough continuity which he himself, in his better moments, knows is not present. For the sake of the continuity of the tradition, these different practices within which just war exists must be part of any discussion of the tradition. Otherwise no social and political analysis is necessary. The general rubric by which continuity is found, becomes so broad that any writer on Just War, even the pagan Cicero, is coopted for the continuity of the tradition. Thus, Augustine's critique of "earthly justice" is finally turned back on itself and used as an "Augustinian" legitimation for war.

Augustine did an immanent critique upon the idea of the Roman justice based on Cicero's view of the commonwealth. He does this to suggest that there never was a Roman republic!

> For I mean in its own place to show that -- according to the definitions in which Cicero himself, using Scipio as his mouthpiece, briefly propounded what a republic is, and what a people is, and according to many testimonies, both of his own lips and of those who never took part in that same debate -- Rome never was a republic because true justice had never a place in it.

Augustine uses Rome's own definition of "The People" to critique Rome. "The People" . . . [is] an assemblage associated by a common acknowledgment of law, and by a community of interests." This, he argues, is not what the "commonwealth" was, therefore, on these grounds, it did not exist. Instead, he grants only that "there was a republic of a certain kind." And he argues that true justice is found only in that "republic" which has as its unifying feature that "Glorious things are said of thee, O city of God" -- "true justice has no existence save in that republic whose founder and ruler is Christ, if at least any choose to call this a republic; and indeed we cannot deny that it is the people's weal."[50] Augustine uses Rome's definition of *temporal* power to suggest that the Church, rather than Rome itself, embodies this definition.

Whereas Augustine uses Rome's definition to critique Rome, Grotius uses Rome's definition to legitimate the "existence of the Law of Nature" and prove that "war is not repugnant to the law of nature."[51]

Augustine used Cicero to challenge Rome; Grotius used Cicero to legitimate the law of nature, then to base war on the law of nature, and finally to show that while the Gospel "imposes duties beyond the law of nature" it does not abrogate it. "But the rights, which any one derives from the law of nature, are no less his own than if God had given them: nor are those rights abolished by the law of the Gospel."[52]

A fundamental and decisive shift has taken place between Augustine and Grotius. Perhaps one could say that they both pose just war as a criterion addressed to the temporal authority, but the nature of that authority has so radically changed that such a statement is not helpful. Grotius, through the term "civilization" appropriates Cicero to legitimate just war, whereas Augustine uses Cicero to call Rome's warring into question.

Neither Augustine, Aquinas, Victoria, or Grotius developed a just war theory based on any idea of the current nation-state system. Just war as a policy for the present nation-state system cannot be a continuous traditional development incorporating these four figures. Simply because they all used the term *justum bellum* does not a tradition make! For the sake of a viable just war tradition, a discriminating principle should be used to delimit the various just war traditions each represent. All should not be lumped into a single overarching tradition called "western civilization." Once this is done, Foucault's critique is valid. Through a single hegemonic play of signs, "just war theory," bodies are invested in depth such that Augustine's critique is no longer possible. Instead, just war fabricates individuals into a monolithic community -- western civilization -- from which there is no escape.

Grotius alone fits easily within Ramsey's "ancient tradition." He understands just war as an ethos primarily addressed to (and therefore for) temporal leaders, continuous throughout history because of natural law. His development of just war deprives individuals of recourse to war against that order. This was certainly not Victoria's understanding. Thus, Grotius writes,

> Franciscus Victoria allows the inhabitants of a town to take up arms, even without such a case of necessity, to redress their own wrongs, which the Prince neglects to avenge, but such an opinion is justly rejected by others.[53]

Obviously, from this statement, Grotius and Victoria's view of "temporal authority" differed. Victoria certainly did not develop a doctrine of just war primarily addressed to the "leaders of nations." "Nations" were only beginning to develop when Victoria wrote his "Lessons on the Indians and on the Right of War." In fact, Victoria states that the opinion of the Prince is not sufficient, in and of itself, to declare a war just. If a subject knows a war to be unjust, and the enemy innocent, then the subject is bound not to participate. And the reason has nothing to do with the preservation of order, or creating the best possible justice in earthly political existence; the reason has to do with Scripture. Victoria quotes Romans 14: 23 -- "For whatever does not proceed from good faith is sin." His reasoning is based primarily on the need to avoid sin; thus it is based on the importance of confession and penance, and not primarily on the "Law of Nature."[54]

Victoria did not write international law, nor did he simply give a "criterion" addressed to the topmost political authority. He even states that "one must not undertake war on the sole advice of the King, nor on the advice of a few people, but only on the advice of a number of wise and honest citizens."[55] Victoria primarily refuted the argument for the subjugation of the peoples of South America, and the loss of all their political and civil rights, based on the universal power of the pope.[56] He was not developing public policy, as a criterion, to then be used as international law within the nation-state system; Victoria was not even understood as the "father of international law" until 1926 when the Institute of International Law met at the University of Salamanque. In fact, he was providing a theological "*relecciones* " to be used by pastors in the theological education of priests and missionaries, as well as a confessional help concerning "certainty of conscience," and a liturgical help challenging the forced baptism of Indians. These are the practices within which Victoria's work was born. Nowhere will one find his primary audience being that of "leaders of nations."

Even to translate *jus gentium* as the "law of nations" rather than the "law of peoples" is highly misleading. The native peoples of South America were certainly a people, that I take to be Victoria's point, even if they weren't a "nation." Perhaps, and only perhaps Spain could be called a "nation" at that time. Thus, to assume *jus gentium* is the "law of nations" can suggest that native peoples of South America were indebted to the law of "civilized" nations for their political and legal rights. Through translation, the reverse of Victoria's point is made, and his critique is turned inside out to further entrench the "civilized *jus gentium* " rather than calling the "civility" of "nations" into question.

Victoria and Grotius do not represent a continuity of tradition. They have different views of temporal authority and how that authority is to be addressed. These views of authority are not based primarily on just war criterion. All do have some version of non-combatant immunity, but it is based on differing practices within which just war exists. For the first two, ecclesial practices, such as theological education, catechism, confession, penance and baptism, are necessary for sustaining just war. For Grotius, an international system of civilized nations is primarily necessary. Because Ramsey only sees the continuity of the just war tradition in its *criterion* addressed to temporal leaders, he fails to discriminate between these practices. In the end, his just war theory loses its critical edge, and rather than challenging temporal authority, as with Augustine and Victoria, he legitimates it, as with Grotius.

Only because Ramsey can find the word *justum bellum* embedded within a variety of discourses can he find anything called a "tradition." But that is not sufficient to define a tradition. An epistemological rupture occurs in moving from just war as an ecclesial practice to just war as international law. Of course, "tradition" could certainly be used with such generality and flexibility that a continuity could be seen in the move from church to nation-state system. But doesn't assuming the continuity to reside completely in the "theory" of just war, or in the "ethos" of it, overlook some central questions as to what just war is concretely? Is just war only a theory with certain principles expressed under the category *jus in bello* and *jus ad bellum*? Or is it a practical activity by which the Church involved lay and clergy in the meaning of the Christian life within political society through the practice of confession and penance? Certainly it is both. But what happens when the former is divorced from the practices of the latter and made into public policy or international law? Here is the second point of my critique of Ramsey's reasoning -- *because the continuity of "tradition" resides primarily in just war theory as a criterion, the critical edge of just war theory as a critique of temporal authority is evacuated, and in its place, temporal authority is only further legitimated.*

Transformism

"Transformation," as well as "tradition" and "tragedy," functioned both as critique and as a constructive position for Ramsey. H. Richard

Niebuhr's transformationist motif provided Ramsey's primary impulse in Christian ethics. All of his work was an extension of Niebuhr's "Christ transforming culture." Ramsey constantly sought to transform the discourse of Christian ethics in its self-incurred tutelage to a secular, sectarian culture. But, and this is the third critique which needs to be highlighted, "transformation" had a limit. *Transformation was only partial and relative. True community, true solidarity was impossible. The best one could hope for in a transformed political existence is one which was just endurable.*

Ramsey sought to limit the legitimating capacity of "transformation" because of the "Calvinism gone to seed" in America. As he argues, "transformation" became a utopian ideology embodied in "an inarticulate pacifism that has in mind at every point the final and complete prevention of war." He challenged this usage of transformation stemming from H. Richard Niebuhr's work much like Reinhold Niebuhr challenged the utopianism of the Social Gospel. The keyword by which both posed this challenge is "tragedy." Yet Ramsey went one step further than R. Niebuhr. Tragedy was not located solely in the individual's life experience, there to be eradicated through an individualized grace; Ramsey located it beneath the social fabric. This had two effects, the first positive, the second negative. First, it led to social criteria, in the form of traditioned-principles, socially established and embodied, by which to challenge, as best one could, the underlying tragic nature of existence. The best one could hope for was not to be morally complicitous in it. Second, because tragedy was *beneath* the social fabric, "transformation" was only partial and limited to existing political structures that were defined by the unavoidable need for coercion and violence. One could not expect a social life sufficiently transformed such that the need for war, or some form of resistance against others, was eradicated. Transformation was constrained by this fact.

Because "tragedy" constrained all possible political transformations, and provided the hermeneutic by which "tradition" was read, Ramsey constantly reiterated that in the time between the times "war is necessary." When "war is necessary," Ramsey's pastoral casuistry is lost. He can develop an ethic which struggles courageously against the hegemonic practices of a secular culture, but he has no recourse to a genuine alternative. Too much is conceded to the Leviathan. It remains too powerful.

Theological Prescriptions

Let me conclude with some theological prescriptions that I hope maintain Ramsey's pastoral casuistry without the "political responsibility." These prescriptions do not necessitate pacifism; by challenging Ramsey's tragic ontology, I do not think I have marshalled an argument that results in the superiority of pacifism. Nor have I ruled out the importance of any discussion of order, double effect, discrimination, etc. What I do hope I have shown is that Ramsey's theology is constrained by a politics of tragedy. Once that is removed, pacifism does not logically follow, but the presumption for peaceableness (and not order) is at the center of the Christian life, and the practice of just war takes its rightful place at the margins.

If Ramsey is correct, if "war is necessary," then the practice of just war is the best the Church can offer. But, if he is correct, then his theology seems suspect. If at the base of human nature is an inescapable tragic nature, then as Grotius said, "Now the Law of Nature is so unalterable, that it cannot be changed even by God himself. For although the power of God is infinite, yet there are some things to which it does not extend."[57] Tragedy as ontology deprives God of God's redeeming activity. The Leviathan appears to triumph over God. This idea Ramsey does not want to endorse. His Barthian theology could not allow it. Thus, he appears caught in a palpable contradiction. If he is to remain theologically (neo)orthodox, then he cannot claim that tragedy is a fabric which undergirds all political existence legitimating evil, even if it be non-moral evil. On the other side, nor can he simply dismiss "tragedy" and adhere to the liberal, ideological utopianism of the Social Gospel, or the "Calvinist "transformation" gone to seed." Is there an alternative?

Any viable alternative must avoid a liberal, ideological utopianism which sees the possibility of transformation in all-encompassing global categories. This position views the primary task of Christians to transform the world at large. It assumes that political responsibility requires public policies capable of complete and universal transformation, or otherwise we are politically irresponsible. Such an ideological utopianism is readily seen in the United Methodist Bishop's pastoral, "In Defense of Creation:"

> We write in defense of creation. We do so because the creation itself is under attack. Air and water, trees and fruits and flowers, birds and fish and cattle, all children and youth, women and men live under the darkening shadows of a threatening nuclear winter.

The term "Global Village" is often used to support this paternalistic view. Certainly many places exist in the world where life would not be affected at all by a limited nuclear exchange among "first" world countries. The language of "world transformation," and the "Global Village" can be one more way those countries maintain their "benevolent" position of power over others.

As Ramsey rightly envisioned, such statements also deny God's purposeful redeeming activity. They were theologically flawed. As he said,

> I can understand the dread of secular humanists over the alleged possible destruction of all human life on "planet earth," since for them that would be the end of all known *purpose* in the universe. We who believe in God, however, should not suggest by thought, word, or deed that the end of planet earth would be the end of *the world*, the end of God's *purpose* for his creatures, the end of his *creation*. The Prologue of St. John's Gospel is the Christian story of creation, our chief creation story, primary over Genesis as John 1:3 states.[58]

Utopian transformation must be avoided not only because it often legitimates hegemonic power, but also because of what it says about God. It usurps God's place over creation and claims that we must ourselves secure the existence of creation. This was the problem with the Social Gospel and its heir, "Calvinism gone to seed," in the United States.

But with his underlying ontology of tragedy Ramsey does not finally free himself from his own critique. Tragedy also usurps God's place over creation, and this constrains how Christians can and should act in the world. Thus, rather than responding to God's call, Christians are required first to respond to tragedy. It defines how the tradition is read, and it limits the transformation possible in human communities. This is why for Ramsey, *war is necessary*. This is his first "deep truth." If war is necessary, then just war is unavoidable. If war is unnecessary, then just war is, at most, permissible. It is only the outer limit of permissible activity for Christians, given shape and substance by the practice of penance and confession, and not a general claim about the structure of political existence. That it is only a sometime, permissible, outer limit, I take, to be Augustine's point. Only the "earthly city" *must* fight. The difference between it and the heavenly city is the possibility that the latter need not war.

> The quarrel, then, between Romulus and Remus shows how the earthly city is divided against itself; that which fell out between Cain and Abel illustrated the hatred that subsists between the two cities, that of God and that of men. The wicked war with the wicked; the good also war with the wicked. But with the good, good men, or at least perfectly good men, cannot war: though, while only going on towards perfection, they war to this extent, that every good man resists others in those points in which he resists himself.[59]

And in book XIX, chapter 13, Augustine explicitly claims that peace, not tragedy, exists at the base of all political existence -- " . . . there may be peace without war, but there cannot be war without some kind of peace."

This is Augustinian realism. Niebuhrian realism, perpetuated by Ramsey, reverses Augstinian realism for it claims that there may be war without peace, but there cannot be peace without war.

Transformed political existence, for Ramsey, is too limited because of "tragedy." Tragedy need not be dismissed therefore. It needs to be more accurately located so that appropriate statements can be made about God. If tragedy is made a general ontological structure undergirding political existence, then a general theory of war is warranted. A general theory of war cannot avoid Miller's fifth criticism -- "as in other historical situations when moralists have attempted to provide a guide for political behavior, the mere presence of a formula often worked to inhibit considerations of morality in individual cases of warfare, and the garment of the just war was stretched to cover the naked unjustness of many medieval conflicts."

Ramsey's answer to this charge was *Abusus non tollit usum* -- the abuse of a thing doesn't take away its usefulness. Certainly that is an appropriate response, but it is inadequate. More must be said. How can the use of just war theory not be so stretched that it extends solely to further entrench unjust secular powers? No certain usage of just war can be asserted which will not run the risk of cooptation by the principalities and powers. Of course, this is no less true of pacifism than it is of just war. After all, Ramsey converted from pacifism to just war for precisely this reason. The pacifism he early espoused only further entrenched the warring power of the nation-state. Just War was a critique of that power.

Simply because just war can be coopted does not mean that it must thereby be discarded. But nor should it be a general theory of statecraft. Christians must hold to a more possible transformed social and political existence than those have who stand with the "Niebuhrian Realists." For Christians, this possible transformed existence is necessary because of who God is. As Jacques Maritain wrote:

> . . . a decorative Christianity is not enough, even for our existence in this world. The faith must be an actual faith, practical and living. To believe in God must mean to live in such a manner that life could not possibly be lived if God did not exist. Then the earthly hope in the Gospel can become the quickening force of temporal history.[60]

The purpose of just war theory is not to make our existence in this world easier, but to make our living in tragic conflicts intelligible only because of God's compelling presence in our lives.

My critiques of Ramsey are not for the purpose of overthrowing the place of just war reasoning in moral theology, but only resituating it. Just war reminds us that tragic conflicts do appear to be part of our earthly pilgrimage, but that as Christians we are not to be constrained by

194

such appearances. Those theologians who have kept the just war doctrine alive in theory and practice pay homage to God's redemptive activity. Such a witness is a means of grace making it possible for us "to believe in God." How else are we to explain the potential sacrifices people
are willing to make? But for just war to be such a witness it must be constantly and vigilantly preserved from its potential legitimating power as
a discipline of the state over the Church.

The possibility of a transformed social and political existence freed
from an underlying ontology of tragedy requires the following theological adjustments. First, maintaining this possibility is necessary as a
statement about God. Second, it is, therefore, an existence which is primarily found in the Church's political existence. Third, it also can extend
to other socio-political communities. It is not solely the domain of the
Church. Fourth, this transformed existence does not rule out all tragedy,
nor does it discard just war theory. But it does place just war theory, not
as a separate position distinct from pacifism, but in continuity with it, as
the outer limit to which Christians can go in their participation in violent
resistance to the principalities and powers. Fifth, this requires that just
war be primarily viewed not as international law, nor as grounded in the
law of nature or political existence, but within the ecclesial practices of
confession and penance. For it is within these practices that sons and
daughters of the Church can have their lives fabricated within the transformed social existence of the Church. These points are important if
Ramsey's casuistry is to be a pastoral activity.

Just War must be freed from an underlying ontology of tragedy to witness more faithfully to who God is.

In Paul Ramsey's own United Methodist tradition, before probation-
ary members are ordained as elders they are asked this question, "Are
you going on to perfection?" If they are to be ordained they must answer
yes. Then they are asked not only if they are going on to perfection, but
also "Do you expect to be made perfect in love in this life?" Once again
they are required to answer yes. The reason these questions are asked is
not because United Methodist Christians are hopelessly utopian; rather it
is a necessary part of their theology. For Wesley and the Methodists,
righteousness is not an alien work in human existence, it is "inherent." It
is a fruit of sanctification. Wesley notes this in his sermon "The Lord Our
Righteousness."[61] First he asks the question, "But do not you believe in
inherent righteousness?" Then he answers:

> Yes, in its proper place; not as the *ground* of our acceptance with God,
> but as the *fruit* of it; not in the place of *imputed* righteousness, but as

consequent upon it. That is, I believe God *implants* righteousness in every one to whom he has *imputed* it.[62]

What is at stake in this 18th century theological argument? Wesley explains it as necessary to prevent the phrase, "The Lord Our Righteousness," from being nothing but a cover for our unrighteousness.

> In the meantime what we are afraid of is this: lest any should use the phrase, 'the righteousness of Christ', or 'the righteousness of Christ is "imputed to me",' as a cover for his unrighteousness. We have known this done a thousand times. A man has been reproved, suppose, for drunkenness. 'Oh, said he, I pretend to no righteousness of *my own* : Christ is *my righteousness*.' Another has been told that 'the extortioner, the unjust, shall not inherit the kingdom of God.' He replies with all assurance, 'I am unjust in myself, but I have a spotless righteousness in Christ.' And thus though a man be as far from the practice as from the tempers of a Christian, though he neither has the mind which was in Christ nor in any respect walks as he walked, yet he has armour of proof against all conviction in what he calls the 'righteousness of Christ'. It is the seeing so many deplorable instances of this kind which makes us sparing in the use of these expressions. And I cannot but call upon all of you who use them frequently, and beseech you in the name of God our Saviour, whose you are and whom you serve, earnestly to guard all that hear you against this accursed abuse of it. . . . O warn them that if they remain unrighteous, the righteousness of Christ will profit them nothing![63]

Has not Ramsey's Niebuhrian realism mitigated against this insight from his own ecclesial tradition? Unfortunately he viewed the use of the United Methodist doctrine of perfection as another form of that optimistic utopianism symptomatic of Calvinism gone to seed.[64] He writes:

> Of course, among Methodist distinctives is our teaching concerning Christian perfection. But does this mean that *nations* -- interrelated collectives -- are to be urged always to be going on to perfection? That nations are the brand to be plucked from the burning? That statesmen and citizens in their political vocations should expect political holiness and perfect love to descend upon the system of collectives in which they live and work -- any moment, any hour, any day now? Or for that matter any *time*? It is God's redeemed people, individually and collectively, who are going on to perfection and to a World of Love. That is the "progressive" element stressed in the Wesleyan heritage; that is the meaning of our legacy joining knowledge with vital piety, and of yearning for holiness. Whenever this is directed (without differentiation between church and world) toward secular problems (however urgent), we swap our birthright for a "pot of message."[65]

Ramsey is correct that Christian perfection is a practice primarily rooted in the Church. But notice in this quote the correlation with "political" to nations. Only statesmen and citizens are those who represent the "political." These people are concerned with "secular" matters. The Church is the redeemed community going on to perfection, but this is not a "secular" matter? What then could it mean to claim that the Church is going on to perfection? Because Ramsey assumes only one political configuration, the nation-state system, he loses Augustine and Wesley's insight that the Church is to be a holy republic (and therefore a politic) in the temporal realm.

Constrained by an ontology of tragedy, buttressed by double effect and non-moral evil, the "*justum*" in the just war too easily becomes a cover for our own injustice. The Wesleyan, et. al., doctrine of perfection is a critique against all such uses. It is a statement about who God is in God's righteousness and justice, and what that means for God's people. This rules out tragedy as the basis of human existence, and it rules out Ramsey's sharp demarcation between the political and the ecclesial. True righteousness, and not only a relativized justice, is possible in earthly, political existence. If not, how has God redeemed?

This transformed life is to be found primarily in the political life of the Church.

Remember that Augustine claimed it was not wrong to use the term "republic" to refer to the heavenly city. This suggests that the "earthly" and "heavenly" cities cannot adequately be termed the temporal and the atemporal. They are two different temporal societies which sojourn together for a time. Ramsey's ontology of tragedy underwrote one single "political" order -- only the "temporal." To be political was to live in this world where war was necessary. Alternative "political" orders such as the republic of the Church were not possible within his single, hegemonic, "temporal" order. Freed from the constraints of Ramsey's ontology of tragedy, we can search for alternative political orders. The Church is such a political alternative.

Of course, the Church as a political alternative is Stanley Hauerwas' position. And Ramsey did in fact consider it. "To be the church in your [Hauerwas] sense would require mutual discipline. We would need to search for agreement concerning the fruits of our life in Christ as specific as were the "rules" John Wesley drew up for the nurture of his "societies" in class meetings."[66] As I noted earlier, Ramsey countenanced this possibility but rejected it for two reasons. 1. He remained convinced that "the ethos of modern nations" was "amenable to transformation by just-war traditions." 2. He argued that "the world is too much *with* us, *in* our Church's life."[67] His first reason uses "transformation" only in the relative and partial sense constrained by his view of tragedy. He could offer such a reason only because "just-war traditions" were criteria addressed to temporal authorities. His first reason offers little hope. His second reason challenges the view that the church is, or can be, a political alternative. In a strange way, his first reason only furthers the truth of the second. Because one "political" order undergirds society, the church must respond on its terms. Thus, just-war traditions speak the language of the nation-state. But then, if we must speak that language why should we be surprised that "the world is too much with us?" Are not theologians of Ramsey's ilk partly responsible for the world being with us when they make us speak a single language even if our speech is intended to be oppositional?

Perhaps Ramsey's second reason is correct, but even he cannot give up hope that he is wrong. What he didn't see was that his view of the "political" constrained the possibility of any alternative and worked against his own best hope. Still, he offers this vision.

> I have a dream, for example, that the people called Methodist become a church that never unnecessarily aborts unborn life, and at the same time a people that refuses technological "cures" of infertility that use *donor* sperm or eggs. This means, positively, that I have a dream that we become a church in which couples feel abortion to be a far graver violation of their "parenting" than to give a child, even only for serious reasons of domestic economy, to another couple that desperately wants one. We would no longer be content simply to favour adoption agencies to do that job for us. Instead, the dream is that we *as a church* become an extended family of God's people in quite realistic ways that would *separate* us from the world of free-choice abortion and the world that "cures" infertility by putting utterly asunder the communicative and procreative goods of marriage. We would develop "adoption liturgies" by which couples who cannot provide for the upbringing of another baby would publicly, "in the presence of God and this congregation," give their infant to a couple needing and wanting a child of their own.[68]

Just as "tragedy" was a keyword in Ramsey's own view of war, it is also a keyword in ethical debates on abortion within the United States. Abortion is "tragic." The irresponsibility of fathers, mothers, the Church, the federal government, the national government, the medical institutions, etc. is all eclipsed by the word "tragic." Abortion is a tragedy, therefore we are caught up in the midst of forces that are in some sense beyond our control and this legitimates an abortifacent society. Ramsey did not accept this argument. And he offered a vision which suggested an alternative based on the ecclesial practices of the Church.

The vision he offers us concerning the abortifacent society of the Church's pilgrimage, needs also extended to a warring society. Where are those practices, those alternative societies which can sustain a just war vision as the outer limit to which they can go? If we are to discuss a just-war tradition, then the discussion must not focus only on the criteria of *jus ad bellum* and *jus in bello* , but it needs to focus on the practices within which those criteria were embedded so that we might be able to locate such an alternative society.

Ramsey's casuistry, if it is to be pastoral, must primarily be viewed as an ecclesial practice, not as positive law, international law, nor mere criteria abstracted from any specific practice. This means that it will be contextual and historical. We will need to point to specific practices that allow us to show where and how just war is something more than an abstract theory. This will also mean that we cannot simply ground the possibility of the practice of morality in transcendence. Simply because we can reflect on ourselves as historical and finite beings does not mean that we somehow can transcend those particularities anymore than the fact that when someone can reflect on her or himself in pain they somehow transcend pain. Ramsey's claim, "The fact that we know we are God's special creature raises us above physical nature and above bondage to the social group . . . . Man is a theonomous animal," misleads him. Better the remembrance of Ash Wednesday, "dust you are and to dust you shall return." As material, historical beings, we need to give an account of those practices that render intelligible our ethics and not assume that a transcendent grounding of morality actually accomplishes anything.

Just war as an ecclesial practice requires the practice of confession and penance. Until these practices are present in the life of the church today, we should refrain from using the language of "just war," because without these practices, just war is, for us, a foreign and alien language.

This transformed socio-political life is not solely the domain of the Church, it can be extended to other socio-political communities; and we can expect them to live in this state.

In Wesley's words, while "God hath tied us" to the means of grace found only in the Church, "God hath not tied himself." To ask any society in which the Church pilgrimages to live to the best its own vision, as Augustine did with the so-called "Roman republic" is also a part of the Church's witness. Therefore, even among warring nations, the Church uses its just war theory to challenge the practices of those nations. Even though an epistemological rupture occurs when these norms are translated from ecclesial practices with their language of sin, redemption, and holiness to the language of "law," and "rights," Christian ethicists should hold the nation to the fire and require them to live faithfully to their own language -- and expect them to do so.

The Possibility of Transformed Political Existence does not discard "tragedy," but resituates it. This makes just war and pacifism not two distinct positions, but a continuum in which just war defines the outer limit.

Liberal tragedy, as with Reinhold Niebuhr, makes the individual the center of the tragic drama. The "moral hero" plays the key role. Ramsey's ontology of tragedy does not center on the "moral hero." Tragedy is much more complex. It is the substrate of political existence. The advantage to Ramsey's position is that tragedy is challenged only by social categories. The disadvantage is that those social categories are too fully defined by the substratum. The tragic substratum defines the necessity of war, and a transformed political existence which is not partial and relativized is ruled out *a priori*.

One response to Ramsey's ontology of tragedy would be to deny the validity of the term for Christian ethics. The problem with denying a role for "tragedy" is the ideological utopianism against which Ramsey and others wrote. Some form of tragedy does occur in our lives, this is unquestionable. We live it. Simply avoiding the term won't avoid the lived experience. The question is how we locate the term. We must not locate it either in the "moral hero" or in the substratum of a general order. Both of these locations neglect a sufficient analysis of the causes of "tragedy." Tragedy is not a subject, it has no sense of agency in and of itself. It is situated within, not beneath, our social and political existence. If transformed political life is possible, then tragedy must primarily be located within human agency. Tragedy is inflicted by someone or something on someone. This does not rule out completely the category of non-moral evil or the principle of double effect, but it greatly minimizes their usage. War does not simply "break out" as a natural result of political life. The Christian life requires that every avenue of naming our complicity in sinful agency, resulting in tragedy for ourselves and others, be named so that it might be confessed. Only once this avenue has been exhausted can the categories of non-moral evil, and double effect be introduced. And even then, some form of restitution for the sake of the holiness of the community, such as forty days penance after war, needs to be made. This is the true power of the just war theory.

If tragedy is re-situated within the life of political existence, then one can not say *a priori* that war is necessary. Therefore, Just War cannot begin with Ramsey's presumption -- "Just war's presumption favors the defense of an ordered *justice* (which sometimes may not consist with peace)."[69] Ramsey argues that one crucial difference between just war and pacifism resides in different presumptions. Pacifism's presumption "is in favor of *peace*," while just war favors an ordered justice. These differing presumptions appear to make pacifism and just war discontinuous. Thus, the debate between them is framed in the language of "Speak Up For Just War *Or* Pacifism." But, if tragedy exists within socio-political existence rather than beneath it, one need not assume the priority of "ordered justice." Ordered justice resulted from the inescapability of life's tragic nature. If that tragic nature is escapable, then the assumption is invalidated.

But neither does just war share with pacifism a presumption which always favors peace. Tragedy does exist within political existence. Sometimes, no alternative exists but the use of force and violence, whether one calls it down upon one's self, or whether one inflicts it upon the other. Justifiable cases of abortion, police actions, and possibly some war-making possibilities can be exercised on the basis of an inescapable tragedy within a particular socio-political configuration. Here double effect, and non-moral evil are important categories. Their importance is emphasized by re-situating tragedy. They are not "common" categories of Christian existence, they are only boundary concepts. Here you can go and no further.

Resituating tragedy means that one cannot assume war. But still, "tragedy" has been re-situated, not done away with. Thus, it is not possible to cry "peace" when there is no peace. Any Christian response to participation in war favors the righteousness of the Church's corporate life. It is not only a matter of peace or justice, or peace with justice. It is a matter of the integrity of the corporate Christian life. Just war and pacifism are not two different positions. They are related parts of a broader Christian ethic which cannot be fully displayed *a priori*. Otherwise we would once again be asking for the production of the particular from a general theory. We have a general shape whose outer lines are drawn by the just war theory. Pacifist responses fall both within that general shape and also without it. Simply because we favor peace does not mean we maintain the integrity of the Christian life, any more than favoring justice. Which peace, and which justice must be set forth. Only those accounts of peace and justice which fall within the corporate Christian life are allowable. Those accounts are only known through participation in the corporate Christian life.

Thus, just war should be primarily viewed not as international law, nor as grounded in the law of nature or political existence, but within the ecclesial practices of confession and penance. For it is within these practices that sons and daughters of the Church can have their lives fabricated within the transformed social existence of the Church.

This is the final point. Just war is not primarily a theory of statecraft. Instead it is an ecclesial practice which requires practices, such as the confessional that embody, produce, and sustain these norms. To expect the government to sustain these norms through theory alone is to live an illusion. Only a Church which requires in its corporate life something like the *Penitentials* is capable of living just war as an outer limit of faithful response to God. Is there a voice in the Church asking for the practice of just war based on the need for a righteous and holy life fitting to those redeemed by Christ? If not, then it is not Ramsey's fault that he spoke only to those who would listen, even if they took his theory placed it in different practices, and used it as a garment to cover their own nakedness.

Notes

1. See *Moral Man and Immoral Society*, (New York: Charles Scribners' Sons, 1932), particularly pp. 2-3.

2. Ibid., p. xi.

3. "Christianity and Tragedy," in *Beyond Tragedy*, (New York: Charles Scribners' Sons, 1937), p. 168-9.

4. See "Why the Christian Church Is Not Pacifist" in *The Essential Reinhold Niebuhr*, ed. Robert McAfee Brown, (New Haven: Yale University Press, 1986), p. 102.

5. See Raymond Williams, *Modern Tragedy*, (Stanford: Stanford University Press, 1966), p. 68.

6. *Basic Christian Ethics*, (Chicago: The University of Chicago Press, 1977), p. 151.

7. *War and the Christian Conscience*, (Durham, North Carolina: Duke University Press, 1961), p. 29, my emphasis.

8. James Turner Johnson uses this exact same quote, leaving out the same passages as Ramsey in his *The Quest for Peace*, (Princeton: Princeton University Press, 1987) see p. 64. He then concludes that "the immediate significance of this concept, in the context of Augustine's own time, was dual: it provided a theological justification of the goods of order, justice, and peace in civic society (the "city of earth"), and it related the peace of this society to the ultimate goal of

man, the enjoyment of everlasting peace in God." This last sentence does not seem warranted by the full quote. Only when the relevant parts are omitted can Augustine be read as suggesting such a close relationship between the two Cities. Johnson, like Ramsey, coopts Augustine's critique of Roman society, and completely reverses the thrust of the City of God by using it as a theological justification for the inevitability of Christian participation in a certain political structure.

9. Ibid., p. 31.

10. *Who Speaks For The Church?*, (Nashville: Abingdon Press, 1967), p. 55.

11. Ibid., p. 109.

12. *The Just War*, (New York: University Press of America, 1983), p. 71.

13. Ibid., p. 27.

14. Ibid., p. 11.

15. Ibid., p. 319 and 326.

16. Ibid., p. 180.

17. *Who Speaks For The Church*, p. 116.

18. *Speak Up For Just War Or Pacifism*, (University Park: The Pennsylvania State University Press, 1988), p. 54.

19. See Appendix, # 85-98.

20. *War and the Christian Conscience*, p. 272.

21. *The Just War*, p. 156.

22. *War and the Christian Conscience*, p. 158.

23. Ibid., pp. 151-2.

24. *Patient as Person*, p. 119.

25. *Ethics at the Edges of Life*, p. xiv.

26. See Philippe Contamine, *War in the Middle Ages* (Basil Blackwell: 1984), esp. pp. 100 -106.

27. Frederick H. Russell, *The Just War In The Middle Ages* (Cambridge: Cambridge University Press, 1979) pp. 302-3.

28. Letter to John Kilner, Feb. 16, 1979, Ramsey Papers, box # 13.

29. *The Just War*, pp. 104-5.

30. Ibid., p. 205.

31. *War and the Christian Conscience*, pp. 15-6,

32. *The Just War*, p. 146.

33. Ibid., p. 145.

34. *Just War*, p. 526.

35. I would suggest that the "just war theory" could be understood as such a discipline, although Foucault nowhere suggests this.

36. Michel Foucault, *Discipline and Punish* (New York: Vintage Books, 1979), p. 217.

37. For a discussion on this see the Appendix, #63-80. It is insufficient merely to attack "autonomy" and think one has challenged present society.

38. For a different sort of critique of Foucault's monolithic view of power, not by any means drawing upon Christian theology, but still challenging the "monolithic emphasis upon the ubiquity of power" by "new philosophers" such as Foucault, see Anthony Giddens *The Nation State and Violence* (Berkley: University of California Press, 1987), especially pp. 22-31; and Giddens' *The Constitution of Society* (Berkeley: Univ. of California Press, 1984) pp. 145-162.

39. *World Politics*, 1963, pp. 254-286.

40. The only other place where Ramsey actually develops and discusses the historical development of just war is in Chapter Two and Three of *War and the Christian Conscience* and pp. 205-7 in *The Just War*. Ramsey's commentary on Miller's essay provide a much more thorough account of Ramsey's view than these spotty, references. Ramsey's comments on Miller's essay can be found in the Ramsey Papers, Perkins Library, Box 16, correspondence with Jean MacLachlan.

41. Miller, p. 254. I should say that Ramsey endorsed Miller's essay but suggested some revisions in his section on historical development. Evidently, Miller took Ramsey's advice for some of the quotes he critiques from an earlier draft of Miller's essay are not present in the final, published draft.

42. Ibid., p. 282.

43. Quoted in Ramsey's letter to MacLachan, p. 4.

44. Miller, p. 256.

45. Ibid., p. 258.

46. Letter to MacLachan, pp. 1-2.

47. Ibid., p. 2.

48. Ibid., p. 3.

49. *War and the Christian Conscience*, p. 132-3.

50. *City of God*, (Grand Rapids, Michigan: William B. Eerdmans Publishing Co., 1979), bk. II, Chap. 21.

51. Grotius, *The Rights of War and Peace*, Book I, Chapter II, II, see allso Chapter I, and XII.

52. Ibid., Bk. I ,Chapter II, VI -VII.

53. Ibid., Bk. I , Chapter III, IV.

54. See Victoria's "Lesson on the Right of War," para. 60-68. In Maurice Barbier's translation, in *Les Clasiques De La Penseé Politique*, (*Libraire Droz Geneve, 1966)*, see, pp. 128-9, and his commentary on this passage on p. LXVI.

55. Ibid, para. 68, p. 130.

56. See *Leçons sur Les Indiens et sur le droit de guerre*, in *Les Classiques De La Penseé Politique* (*Libraire Droz Geneve, 1966)* translated by Maurice Barbier, o.p. Barbier's introduction is particularly helpful.

57. Grotius, *The Rights of War and Peace*, Ibid. Bk. I, chap. I, X.

58. *Speak Up For Just War Or Pacifism*, p. 21.

59. *City of God*, Book XV, chap. V.

60. *The Social and Political Philosophy of Jacques Maritain*, ed. Joseph W. Evans and Leo R. Ward, (New York: Charles Scribners' Sons, 1955), p. 186.

61. Wesley's sermons are a source of temporal authority for United Methodists. "The Lord Our Righteousness." ed. Albert Outler, *The Works of John Wesley*, vol. I, (Nashville: Abingdon Press, 1984), pp. 449 - 465.

62. Ibid., p. 458.

63. Ibid., pp. 462-3, for a fuller discussion of this sermon and Wesleyan theology see my "A Wesleyan Social Gospel," in *Living the Discipline*, William B. Eerdmans Publishing Co., 1992.

64. See *Speak Up For Just War Or Pacifism*, p. 48.

65. Ibid., p. 36.

66. Ibid., p. 143.

67. Ibid., p. 145.

68. Ibid., p. 146.

69. Ibid., p. 54.

Appendix

This first round of correspondence developed out of Hauerwas' claim that Ramsey was an "individualist," and a "Kantian," especially because he used the term "person" in his book *Patient as Person*.[1]

*Ramsey to Hauerwas (Sept. 27, 1977):*_ Concerning the ms. of mine entitled "Ethical Dimensions of Experimental Research on Children" I hope that you will pay special attention to: 1. Footnote 31, about the *title* of my book [*Patient as Person*] which ought not to be allowed to outweigh the convenantal-concept and Biblical norms governing the substance of all my writings -- as I think you sometimes do. (2) My explicit use of "roles and relations" language here, to the point of saying throughout that it is the meaning of parenthood and of guardianship that I'm after. (3) Join with this my footnote 19 to my article in *Hastings*
10 *Center Report*, August 1977, in my exchange with McCormick; and you shoud see that my use of *Kantian language* is just that, and that his meaning does not supplant the grounds for care that I espouse -- and within that my search for the nature and limits of parental and physician responsibility. (4) This should add up to your not joining in spreading the canard that I am an "individualist" except only in contrast with McCormick's solidaristic notions. "Individualism" is not the only alternative to the latter. It really is strange to have that charge lodged, since I think that liberalism in all its forms is precisely that kind of fragmentation and is the deadly disease of modern societies. Whatever
20 I finally may think of your final appeal to a narrative in which to set and explicate the ultimate issues (or what I finally can learn from you and from Harned: his latest book is great!), you in turn ought not to diminish in that cause the Biblical themes and imagery that are central in all that I do. It's too easy a victory -- first of all -- to make me an individualist. That certainly cannot be established by reference to a title, or by the use of the word "person" or by Kantian "end also, never means only" language.

Hauerwas to Ramsey Oct. 3, 1977: I did find footnote 31 of "Ethical Dimensions of Experimental Research on Children" extremely

interesting. I also apologize for the reference on page 209 [in *Truthfulness and Tragedy*] that was context-less as well as suggesting that your heart ultimately lays with the Kantians. . . . That said, however, I would encourage you to write something where it is clear that you only "use" Kantian language. Because I think that is indeed a tricky business of how one can use one position without buying into its deepest commitments. . . . I think your suggestion that "individualism" is not the only alternative to "solidaristic" notions is the heart of the issue. Indeed it is liberalism that teaches us that the problem should be phrased in
40   that way at all -- i.e. that the political issue is the relation between the individual and the social order. What that fails to account for is that the "individual" is a social creation. However I think that neither you or those of us that oppose liberalism on this point have sufficiently indicated what the other "alternative" may be. Indeed it is my view that until we recover a richer notion of "ecclesia" we will not have the means to do that -- conceptual claims finally depend on the social experience of people. I fear that the church has taken on the "voluntaristic" characteristics of liberalism so deeply that it cannot even call on its own experience for what might offer an alternative to
50   liberalism sense of the individual. That is exactly why I am trying in my work to direct attention to the family as it seems to me that it is the last non-liberal institution we have left though it is quickly fading. . . . Of course it is not my aim to make you buy into the appeal to narrative but rather I hope that some of the analysis I have provided might help give the conceptual means for you to better articulate your sense of the moral significance of "covenant." For it seems to me that exactly part of the reason you have been misunderstood in a Kantian direction is that the conceptual status of your appeals to covenant have been unclear. It seems to me that covenant works for you exactly like a narrative context
60   to delimit the normative status of certain notions. Anyway that is the way I would prefer to interpret you. I would be interested in what you think about the suggestion, as "care" also needs to be storied.

The next correspondence results from Hauerwas' review of Ramsey's *Ethics at the Edges of Life* (Hastings Center Report, Oct. 1978) as well as from their previous discussion. In this review, Hauerwas argues that it is wrong "to accuse [Ramsey] of providing a theological warrant for the destructive individualism of our society." But, he argues, Ramsey's "use" of Kantian language does suggest a "kind of individualism other than he now appears to hold." And "Ramsey's commitment to speak to the wider society has tended to blunt the full display of the theological convictions that inform his work". This prevents him from showing how ". . . 'righteousness, faithfulness, canons of loyalty [etc.]' function conceptually and religiously for ethical reflection."

Ramsey to Hauerwas, Aug. 4, 1978: A minor point, and then a major one, about what you say about *Ethics at the Edges of Life*. You seem more grudging than you were in your letter to me in admitting that I am not an individualist, and more defensive than you were of that interpretation because of my Kantian language. You wrote, as I recall, that "covenant" functions for me as "story" does for you -- with the wealth and depth entailed by each term in their supportive context. I 70 think also that I had written you that, on specific issues (e.g. vs. McCormick on research using children), I intend to be developing a "role and relations" ethics in my search for the meaning and outer limits of parental protection. I was a little surprised by this (minor) point, since *Edges* mounts an attack upon individualism, and not only in the first chapter, in search of the meaning of both parental and physicians' caring roles, and of the state's *parens patriae* power and obligation. My attack on "autonomy" shows, moreoever, that I do *not* believe that our present and coming culture is anything like Christian.

80 This brings me to the major point. Concerning this Jeff Stout remarked that you seem to want me to write longer prefaces! Or like Kierkegaard's "author" who wrote a book of prefaces -- because his wife wouldn't let him write whole books -- you seem to fobid me to go on to the terrain of specific public problems. . . .

I certainly do *not* believe that "it is still possible to do Christian ethics for those who do not share Christian convictions" (was it ever?); or that "there is no difference between the best in our culture and Christianity". It is true that I do not *herald* the end of "Christendom," or believe that we 90 and our children's children will at last be free to be truly Christian when the fading imprint of Christian ethics upon our law or traditional medical ethics -- upon the structures -- has been finally obliterated. Still from the preface to BCE to the preface of *Edges* I think I have in mind the proper audience (of this, more anon). Readers who are not Christian are invited to read as if overhearing an ongoing conversation from which they may *learn* something (not be convicted).

There are, of course, stretches in what we may dignify by calling my "special ethics" where the Christian word to be heard is not resounding 100 in every paragraph. Call this Christian "casuistry" if you will -- but not for the reason you state.[2] Your grounds for my endeavor to do public ethics is partially true, as an appeal to *past* Christian influences perhaps not yet altogether lost. Doubtless I may hope against hope that some among the "hearers" may strengthen their adherence to the best of past culture; or maybe search among their premises and find that they have no breastplate of righteousness with which to gird the irreplaceability and unmeldability of every human soul.

But I, the author, have not left Christian premises behind when I go on to do special ethics. You may *disagree* with the way I go about doing
110 special ethics theologically, there where you say that my "dramatic and significant assertions" are only "assertions" for which no adequate theological warrant is supplied. I think everyone of them is adequately warranted, and *directly* by the "giftedness" of life. I judge that simple warrant to be enough. You may want me at this point to pause and retell the whole Christian story. But then we disagree more in style than in substance, for I never left that behind. . . . My foundational work is not [the humanist's] nor [the humanist's] mine. But I do believe that while Christianity ought always to be willing to be a sect whenever necessay, there is always at work a culture-forming impulse as well.
120

When, therefore, I say I am disinterested in finding out whether the King is clothed, naked or wears a simple jock strap, I mean to say that Christian special ethics would still come to the conclusions I do. Just as in *Deeds and Rules* I showed that *agape* leads to ruled behavior, without or with natural justice (as in *Nine Modern Moralists*).

You may properly respond to all this that I have never made up [my] mind whether there is a sense of natural justice to which when Christ came he came to his own, although his own received him not.
130 Nevertheless, you know that for me the *agape* of Christ has the primacy and overridingness, and would structure a world even if natural justice is a mirage of Catholic imagination.

You remark that I do not "help us understand how appeals to the 'righteousness, faithfulness, canons of loyalty, the awesome sanctity of human life, humankind in the image of God, etc.' function conceptually and religiously for ethical reflection." I have already responded to this contention by what I said above about the "giftedness" of life. You may believe that I have not succeeded, but that is all I have been trying to do:
140 to extend those outlooks and onlooks into actual life cases. O.K. for a book review; but *yours* is only an *assertion*.

I said I would return to whether I have discriminated the audience for whom I write. I'll tell you candidly; you will find this also, I believe in a footnote to "Liturgy and Ethics." I have never consciously chosen any audience or readership for whom I write. Or to say the same thing: every word I have ever written has been written *to myself.* I have always been exploring the meaning in practice of the Christian faith -- for myself. I have wanted to know *which way* to go if I ever wanted to
150 depart from it. The great benefit of teaching unbelieving or nondescript undergraduates is that they only ask what you think Christianity means, however outrageous. In seminaries, the question is whether it is believable or important or relevant; and the temptation yielded to is to cut corners or bowlderize to prove it so. So in a funny sort of way, by

taking myself to be the person always addressed, I turned out to be something of a church theologian addressing the people of God who were, and are now (this, surely, *has* to be believed) and are to be to the end of time.

160 *Hauerwas to Ramsey, August 8, 1978:* . . . As far as the minor point about individualism I guess I was more grudging in the review because I think you really do not make the covenant language work as fully as you want or should. In particular I think that even though you "intend" to develop a "role and relations" ethics in terms of the limits of parental protection it does not come through that way. I suspect it does not because you want to say that the role of the parents is formed by how God regards their child, therefore the worth of the child is not or should not be dependent on the parents understanding of the worth of the child. But the latter point does not come through strongly and as a
170 result it almost appears that the worth of the child is an end in itself – i.e. as an individual. . . . .

I suspect the claim that you think that it is possible to do Christian ethics for those that do not share Christian convictions was too strong. I should have said you think it is possible to do Christian public policy ethics for those that do not share Christian convictions since they may be able to agree with the conclusions as they either continue to assume Christian convictions or have other convictions that support our point of view. However, I think the claim that there is no difference between
180 the best in our culture and Christianity remains true if you are going to stand by your claim that general medical ethics is simply Christian "casuistry". I think that claim by the way needs much more support than you provide for it. It is a historical claim but you never show that it is historically true and even if you could then you would need to show that the "ethics" really had to be that which formed actual medical practice.

Like you, I do not think that the end of Christendom is anything to herald nor do I think it will make us free to be "real" Christians again -- I
190 always assume the business of "being" a Christian is more ambiguous than that, but I do think that you might bend a little more toward us "sectarians" in as much as you have, as you well know, powerful sectarian claims embedded in your own work.

As a sectarian I often write trying to show that our culture cannot make its presuppositions work consistently. After all we sectarians have a responsibility to try to make and help our social order live up to its best impulses. But if you have not made up your mind about whether there is a "justice" that love "transforms" but that love is overriding then I
200 think you still have not shown how love works adequately. I think the interest to get on to the cases is the problem (and maybe Stout is right I

want you to write longer prefaces), as love tends to become a norm that is separable from the story. As I am sure you are aware, my use and emphasis on the narrative is a way to resist the constant temptation of ethicists to find a "moral essence" to the gospel. The story of God is the "essence" and there is no clear ethical upshot to be abstracted from it. So I guess I do think there is a problem with the casuistry in so far as it lets us assume that love, and I am sure you do not mean it to have this effect, is a norm that is intelligible apart from how Jesus taught us to love by learning to be his disciples.

210

Notes

1. For the exact issue which sparked this correspondence see Hauerwas *Truthfulness and Tragedy*, pp. 128-131, and n. 32 on p. 209. Hauerwas writes, "Thus, the notion of 'person' functions for Ramsey as a Kantian or deontological check on what he suspects is the utilitarian bias of modern medicine".

2. Hauerwas said that Ramsey's "casuistry rests on his belief that the notion of the absolutely unique, inviolable, irreplaceable individual human life exists in our civilization because it is Christian . . . ." In other words, Ramsey can "extend" Christian love into the making of public policy only because he assumes a basis for the possibility of such an extension because of the imprint of Christianity upon western legal-juridical-political process based on the idea of the sanctity of the individual.

References

Works by Paul Ramsey

Ramsey, Paul, "The Futility of War," *Christian Advocate*, Feb. 15, 1935
____ . "The Current Christian Anti-Pacifism," unpublished, 1940? Duke
University Library, Ramsey Papers, box 35
____ . "The Manger, The Cross, and the Resurrection," *Christianity and Crisis*,
April, 1943
____ . "A Social Policy For Liberal Religion," *Religion in Life*, 13/4 Autumn, 1944
____ . "Natural Law and the Nature of Man, " *Christendom*, 9/3, 1944
____ . "A Theology of Social Action," *Social Action*, 23/2, October, 1946
____ . "The Theory of Democracy: Idealistic or Christian?," *Ethics*, 56/4, 1946
____ . "Protestant Casuistry," *Christianity and Crisis*, March 1963
____ . "Professor N. H. Søe on Natural Law and Christian Ethics," Ramsey
Papers, Box 16
____ . "A Question Or Two For Stanley Hauerwas," unpublished, Duke
University Library, 1981
____ . "A Letter To James Gustafson," *Journal of Religious Ethics*, 1984
____ . *The Nature of Man In The Philosophy Of Josiah Royce and Bernard Bosanquet*,
unpublished dissertation, Ramsey Papers, Duke University Library
____ . *Basic Christian Ethics* (Chicago: The University of Chicago Press, 1977)
____ . *Faith and Ethics: The Theology of H. Richard Niebuhr*, ed. vol. 1 (New Haven:
Yale University Press, 1957)
____ . *Freedom of the Will*, ed. in *The Works of Jonathan Edwards*, vol. I (New
Haven: Yale University Press, 1957)
____ . *Christian Ethics and the Sit-In* (New York: Association Press, 1961)
____ . *War and the Christian Conscience: How Shall Modern War Be Conducted Justly*
(Durham, N. C.: Duke University Press, 1961)
____ . *Nine Modern Moralists* (New York: University Press of America, 1983)
____ . *Deeds and Rules in Christian Ethics* (New York: University Press of
America, 1983)
____ . *Who Speaks for the Church?* (Nashville: Abingdon Press, 1967)
____ . *The Just War: Force and Political Responsibility* (New York: University
Press of America, 1983)
____ . *Norm and Context in Christian Ethics* ed. with Gene Outka (New York:
Charles Scribners' Sons, 1968)
____ . *The Patient as Person: Explorations in Medical Ethics* (New Haven: Yale
University Press, 1970)
____ . *Doing Evil To Achieve Good: Moral Choice in Conflict Situations* ed. with
Richard A. McCormick (Chicago: Loyola University Press, 1978)
____ . *Ethics at the Edges of Life* (New Haven: Yale University Press, 1978)
____ . *Speak Up For Just War Or Pacifism* (University Park: The Pennsylvania
State University Press, 1989)

_____ . *Ethical Writings* ed. in *The Works of Jonathan Edwards* vol, 8 (New Haven: Yale University Press, 1989)

Other Works Cited

Anscombe, G.E.M., *Intention* 2nd ed. (Ithaca, New York: Cornell University Press, 1963)

Aquinas, Thomas, *Summa Theologica* vol. II and III in *Christian Classics* trans. by Fathers of the English Dominicans, Westminster, Maryland

Augustine, *City of God* in *A Select Library of the Nicene and Post-Nicene Fathers of the Christian Church* vol. 11 (Grand Rapids, Michigan: Wm. B. Eerdmans Publishing Company, 1979)

_____ . *The Enchiridion on Faith, Hope and Love* (Regney Gateway: A Gateway Edition, 1987)

_____ . *Treatises on Marriage and Other Subjects* in *The Fathers of the Church* (Washington, D.C.: The Catholic University of America Press, 1955)

Bainton, Roland H., *Christian Attitudes Toward War and Peace: A Historical Survey and Critical Re-evaluation* (Nashville: Abingdon Press, 1988)

Barth, Karl, *Church Dogmatics* III/I, III/IV, IV/I (Edinburgh: T & T Clark, 1958, 1978, 1956)

Book of Discipline, United Methodist Church (Nashville: Abingdon Press, 1988)

Brown, Robert McAfee, ed., *The Essential Reinhold Niebuhr* (New Haven: Yale University Press, 1986)

Brunner, Emil, *Man in Revolt: A Christian Anthropology* (Philadelphia: The Westminster Press, 1939)

_____ . *The Divine Imperative* (New York: The MacMillan Company, 1942)

Cadoux, C. John, *The Early Christian Attitude to War* (New York: The Seabury Press, 1982)

Contamine, Phillipe, *War in the Middle Ages* (Basil Blackwell, 1984)

Curran, Charles, *Politics, Medicine and Christian Ethics: A Dialogue with Paul Ramsey* (Philadelphia: Fortress Press, 1973)

Ellul, Jacques, *Anarchy and Christianity*, trans. by Geoffrey W. Bromley (Grand Rapids, Michigan: Wm. B. Eerdmans Publishing Co., 1991)

Englehardt, H. Tristam, Jr., ed. *Knowledge, Value and Belief* 1977

Fletcher, Joseph, *Situation Ethics: The New Morality* (Philadelphia: The Westminster Press, 1966)

Ford, John C., S.J., "The Morality of Obliteration Bombing," *Theological Studies*, September, 1944

Frei, Hans, *The Eclipse of Biblical Narrative: A Study in 18th and 19th Century Hermeneutics* (New Haven and London: Yale University Press, 1974)

Foucault, Michel, *Discipline and Punish* (New York: Vintage Books, 1979)

Giddens, Anthony, *The Constitution of Society* (Berkeley: University of California Press, 1984)

_____ . *The Nation State and Violence* (Berkeley: University of California Press, 1987)

Grotius, Hugo, *The Rights of War and Peace* (Westport, Connecticut: Hyperion Press, Inc., 1979)

Gustafson, James, "Context Versus Principle: A Misplaced Debate," *Harvard Theological Review* April, 1965

____. *Ethics from a Theocentric Perspective*, vol. II (Chicago: University of Chicago Press, 1984)

____. *James M. Gustafson's Theocentric Ethics: Interpretations and Assessments*, ed. Beckley/Swezey (Mercer Press, 1988)

Hauerwas, Stanley, *Vision and Virtue* (Notre Dame: University of Notre Dame Press, 1974)

____. *Truthfulness and Tragedy* (Notre Dame: University of Notre Dame Press, 1977)

____. *A Community of Character* (Notre Dame: University of Notre Dame Press, 1981)

____. *Against the Nations* (Minneapolis: Winston Press, 1985)

James, William, *Pragmatism* (Cambridge, Massachusetts: Harvard University Press, 1978)

Johnson, James Turner, ed. with David Smith, *Love and Society, Essays in the Ethics of Paul Ramsey, JRE Studies in Religious Ethics/I* (Missoula, Montana: American Academy of Religion and Scholars Press, 1974)

____. *Can Modern War Be Just?* (New Haven: Yale University Press, 1984)

____. *Just War Tradition and the Restraint of War* (Princeton, New Jersey: Princeton University Press, 1981)

____. *The Quest for Peace: Three Moral Traditions in Western Cultural History* (Princeton: Princeton University Press, 1987)

Kant, Immanuel, *Critique of Pure Reason*, trans. Norman Kemp Smith (New York: St. Martin's Press, 1965)

Kegley, Charles, ed. *Reinhold Niebuhr, his religious, social and political thought* (New York: The Pilgrim Press, 1984)

Knudsen, Albert C., *The Philosophy of Personalism* (Boston: Boston University Press, 1927)

____. *The Principles of Christian Ethics* (New York: Abingdon-Cokesbury Press, 1943)

MacIntosh, D.C., *The Pilgrimage of Faith in the World of Modern Thought* (University of Calcutta Press, 1931)

MacIntyre, Alasdair, *After Virtue*, 2nd ed. (Notre Dame: University of Notre Dame Press, 1984)

____. *Whose Justice? Which Rationality?* (Notre Dame: University of Notre Dame Press, 1988)

MacKinnon, Catherine A., *Feminisim Unmodified Discourses on Life and Law* (Cambridge, Massachusetts: Harvard University Press, 1987)

McNeill, John T., and Helena Gamer, ed's., *Medieval Handbooks of Penance* (New York: Columbia University Press, 1983)

Maritain, Jacques, *Man and the State* (The University of Chicago Press, 1951)

____. *The Person and the Common Good*, trans. by John J. Fitzgerald (University of Notre Dame Press, 1966)

____. *The Social and Political Philosophy of Jacques Maritain*, ed's. Joseph W. Evans and Leo R. Ward (New York: Charles Scribners' Sons, 1955)

Mayer, Hans Eberhard, *The Crusades*, 2nd ed. (Oxford University Press, 1988)

Milbank, John "Critical Study," *Modern Theology* 4/2 1988

____ . *Theology and Social Theory* (Basil Blackwell, 1990)

Miller, Lynne H., "The Contemporary Significance of the Doctrine of Just War," *World Politics*, 1963

Niebuhr, Reinhold, *Moral Man and Immoral Society* (New York: Charles Scribners' Sons, 1932)

____ . *Beyond Tragedy* (New York: Charles Scribners' Sons, 1937)

____ . *The Nature and Destiny of Man*, vols. I & II (New York: Charles Scribners' Sons, 1934, 1941)

____ . *The Children of Light and the Children of Darkness* (New York: Charles Scribners' Sons, 1944)

____ . *Christian Realism and Political Problems* (Fairfield: Augustus M. Keller Publishers, 1977)

Nietzche, Friedrich, *The Philosophy of Nietzche* (New York: The Modern Library, 1927)

O'Donovan, Oliver, "Obituary: Paul Ramsey (1913-88)" *Studies in Christian Ethics*, 1988

Outka, Gene, *Agape: An Ethical Analysis* (New Haven: Yale University Press, 1972)

Potter, Ralph, B., *War and Moral Discourse* (Richmond, Virgina: John Knox Press, 1973)

Ramsey, Ian, ed. *Christian Ethics and Contemporary Philosophy* (London: SCM Press, 1966)

Rauschenbusch, Walter, *Christianity and the Social Order* (New York: Harper Torchbooks, 1964)

____ . *Christianizing the Social Order* (New York: The MacMillan Co., 1912)

____ . *A Theology for the Social Gospel* (Nashville: Abingdon Press, 1987)

Russell, Frederick H., *The Just War in the Middle Ages* (Cambridge: Cambridge University Press, 1979)

Schmidt, David P., "Methodological Alternatives for Religious Ethics and Public Policy" Ramsey Papers, box 25

Toulmin, Stephen and Albert R. Jonsen, *The Abuse of Casuistry: A History of Moral Reasoning* (Berkeley: University of California Press, 1988)

Troeltsch, Ernst, *The Social Teaching of the Christian Churches* (Chicago: The University of Chicago Press, 1981)

Vahanian, Gabriel, *The Death of God: The Culture of a Post Christian Era* (New York: George Braziller, 1961)

Vitoria, Francisco de, *Leçons sur Les Indiens et sur le droit de guerre* in *Les Classiques de la Penseé Politique* (*Libraire Droz Geneve*, 1966)

Walzer, Michael, *Just and Unjust Wars: A Moral Argument with Historical Illustrations* (New York: Basic Books, Inc., Publishers, 1977)

Wesley, John, "The Lord our Righteousness," in *TheWorks of John Wesley*, ed. Albert Outler (Nashville: Abingdon Press, 1984)

West, Cornell, *The American Evasion of Philosophy* (The University of Wisconsin Press, 1989)

Williams, Raymond, *Modern Tragedy* (Stanford: Stanford University Press, 1966)

Yoder, John Howard, *The Original Revolution* (Scottdale, Pennsylvania: Herald Press, 1971)

____. *Christian Attitudes to War Peace and Revolution: A Companion to Bainton* (Co-op Bookstore, 3003 Benham, Elkhart, IN 46517)

____. *The Politics of Jesus* (Grand Rapids, Michigan: Wm. B Eerdmans Publishing Co., 1972)

____. *When War is Unjust: Being Honest in Just-War Thinking* (Minneapolis: Augsburg Publishing House, 1984)

Index

About the Book
and Author

In this original interpretation and critique of Paul Ramsey's ethical thought, D. Stephen Long traces the development of one of the mid-twentieth century's most important and controversial religious social thinkers. Long examines Ramsey's early liberal idealism as well as later influences on his work, including the just war doctrine, Reinhold Niebuhr's realism, H. Richard Niebuhr's historical relativism, Karl Barth's neo-orthodoxy, and Jacques Maritain's integralism. Long overcomes obstacles confronting any Ramsey scholar — such as a theology that cannot be systematized and the complexities of Ramsey's own writing—and lends sharp insight to the philosophical, theological, and moral issues we face in the twentieth century. Scholars of religious ethics and intellectual thought will find this work essential reading.

D. Stephen Long is Director of Continuing Education at the Duke Divinity School, Duke University.